Vernacular Palaver

LANGUAGES FOR INTERCULTURAL COMMUNICATION AND EDUCATION
Editors: Michael Byram, *University of Durham, UK*
Alison Phipps, *University of Glasgow, UK*

The overall aim of this series is to publish books which will ultimately inform learning and teaching, but whose primary focus is on the analysis of intercultural relationships, whether in textual form or in people's experience. There will also be books which deal directly with pedagogy, with the relationships between language learning and cultural learning, between processes inside the classroom and beyond. They will all have in common a concern with the relationship between language and culture, and the development of intercultural communicative competence.

Other Books in the Series
Developing Intercultural Competence in Practice
   Michael Byram, Adam Nichols and David Stevens (eds)
Intercultural Experience and Education
   Geof Alred, Michael Byram and Mike Fleming (eds)
Critical Citizens for an Intercultural World: Foreign Language Education as Cultural Politics
   Manuela Guilherme
How Different Are We? Spoken Discourse in Intercultural Communication
   Helen Fitzgerald
Audible Difference: ESL and Social Identity in Schools
   Jennifer Miller
Context and Culture in Language Teaching and Learning
   Michael Byram and Peter Grundy (eds)
An Intercultural Approach to English language Teaching
   John Corbett
Critical Pedagogy: Political Approaches to Language and Intercultural Communication
   Alison Phipps and Manuela Guilherme (eds)

Other Books of Interest
Age, Accent and Experience in Second Language Acquisition
   Alene Moyer
Effects of Second Language on the First
   Vivian Cook (ed.)
The Good Language Learner
   N. Naiman, M. Fröhlich, H.H. Stern and A. Todesco
Language, Culture and Communication in Contemporary Europe
   Charlotte Hoffman (ed.)
Language Learners as Ethnographers
   Celia Roberts, Michael Byram, Ana Barro, Shirley Jordan and Brian Street
Language Teachers, Politics and Cultures
   Michael Byram and Karen Risager
New Perspectives on Teaching and Learning Modern Languages
   Simon Green (ed.)
Teaching and Assessing Intercultural Communicative Competence
   Michael Byram

For more details of these or any other of our publications, please contact:
**Multilingual Matters, Frankfurt Lodge, Clevedon Hall,
Victoria Road, Clevedon, BS21 7HH, England
http://www.multilingual-matters.com**

LANGUAGES FOR INTERCULTURAL COMMUNICATION AND EDUCATION 9
Series Editors: Michael Byram and Alison Phipps

Vernacular Palaver
Imaginations of the Local and Non-native Languages in West Africa

Moradewun Adejunmobi

MULTILINGUAL MATTERS LTD
Clevedon • Buffalo • Toronto

For Tinuke, Ayodapo, Moradeyo,
Adedoyin, and Adegboye

Library of Congress Cataloging in Publication Data
Adejunmobi, Moradewun
Vernacular Palaver: Imaginations of the Local and Non-native Languages in West Africa/Moradewun Adejunmobi.
Languages for Intercultural Communication and Education: 9
Includes bibliographical references and index.
1. Africa, West–Languages. 2. Sociolinguistics–Africa, West. I. Title. II. Series.
P381.A36A33 2004
306.44'0966–dc22   2004013752

British Library Cataloguing in Publication Data
A catalogue entry for this book is available from the British Library.

ISBN 1-85359-772-2 (hbk)
ISBN 1-85359-772-4 (pbk)

Multilingual Matters Ltd
UK: Frankfurt Lodge, Clevedon Hall, Victoria Road, Clevedon BS21 7HH.
USA: UTP, 2250 Military Road, Tonawanda, NY 14150, USA.
Canada: UTP, 5201 Dufferin Street, North York, Ontario M3H 5T8, Canada.

Copyright © 2004 Moradewun Adejunmobi.

All rights reserved. No part of this work may be reproduced in any form or by any means without permission in writing from the publisher.

Typeset by Archetype-IT Ltd (http://www.archetype-it.com).
Printed and bound in Great Britain by the Cromwell Press Ltd.

Contents

Introduction vii
Acknowledgements. xi

1 Colonial Encounters and Discourses of the Vernacular 1
     Vernacular Literacy and Colonial Education 4
     African Responses to Colonial Discourses of the Vernacular . . 10
     Major and Minor Discourses of the Vernacular. 15
     Modernity, Contestation, and the Colonizer's Language 23

2 African Literature, European Languages, and Imaginations of the
   Local 52
     African Languages and African Literatures 56
     African Literature as a Pan-Africanist Practice 61
     Imaginations of the Local in Critical and Creative Writing . . . 70
     Debating Language 79

3 Foreign Languages, Local Audiences: The Case of Nigerian Video
   Film in English 101
     Video Film in Nigeria. 103
     English in Nigerian Popular Culture 107
     Defining the Audience 109
     'Foreign' Languages and African Audiences 115

4 Romance Without Borders: Narrating Love, Femininity,
   and the Local in Contemporary Ivory Coast 131
     Visions of Femininity in the Romance Narratives of Ivory Coast. 135
     Biton Koulibaly and Ivorian Popular Writing 141
     Cultural Outsiders and the Politics of the Local 152

5 Languages of Wider Communication and Alternative Sites of
   Belonging 164
     Language, the State, and the Nation 166

    Language and the Charismatic Church. 171
    Languages of Wider Communication and the Community . . 179
    Interactions with the West 189

Conclusion. 203

Bibliography. 206
Index 222

Introduction

The word 'palaver' enjoys a long history in certain regions of the African continent. *Webster's Third International Dictionary* traces its etymology to the Portuguese word *palavra*, meaning 'word,' or 'speech,' and ultimately to the Latin *parabola*, referring to story or word. *Webster's Third International Dictionary* further elaborates: 'An often prolonged parley usu. Between persons of different levels of culture and sophistication (as between 19th century European traders and traders of the African west coast).' The term was probably introduced to the West African coast by Portuguese sailors who visited that part of Africa from the 15th century onwards. Related terms still exist in other Romance languages today, with the French *parole* being perhaps its most celebrated cognate in literature and language studies.

The word *palabre* continues to appear in the vocabulary of French-speaking West Africa where it refers to discussion. Indeed, the *arbre à palabres* used to be a popular authentifying fixture and location in early African literature in French. In Anglophone West Africa notably, *palavra* has entered into the varieties of Pidgin and Creole spoken in Cameroon, Nigeria, Sierra Leone and Ghana. As in French, palaver or *palava* in the West African Pidgin and Creole languages likewise denotes discussion, although frequently and metonymically, it connotes dispute and even trouble, argument, or calamity. Several factors account for the links between the word palaver and contentious discussion in contemporary West Africa. Among these factors, one might consider the fact that in the restored slave forts of the city of Cape Coast Ghana, tour guides will often describe the rooms where European and African traders met to discuss their business as the 'Palaver Room.'

This book then is a contribution to an often contentious discussion about vernaculars in the postcolonial world. It is a palaver about vernaculars. And since I have started by tracing the etymology of key terms in my title, I might as well also point out that many of the early palavers on the West African coast were truly about vernaculars; that is, they were about the traffic in slaves, since the word vernacular derives from the Latin, *verna*, indicating the native-born slave. In African studies, the palaver about vernaculars has engaged the attention of scholars in linguistics, education, literary and cultural studies among others. This book addresses the debate over language specifically from the angle of those working in literary and cultural studies. It therefore does not provide the kind of statistical data that scholars working in sociolinguistics and education might be accustomed to examining. While I have found the work carried out on this subject in the disciplines of education and sociolinguistics extremely helpful, I feel there is a need to consider what the implications of such research might be for the way those of us working in literary and cultural studies approach questions of language and identity in a postcolonial setting. My book then, focuses, specifically, on arguments over language and identity as they have been presented in literary and cultural studies, and particularly in discussions of postcolonial literatures and cultures.

Scholarly conversations about language and identity in the postcolonial world often take as their premise the prior existence of an ideal monolingual order, centered around mother tongues and disrupted by the violent processes of colonization. Those who start from this position also suggest that a return if possible to an emphasis on the mother tongue and to this ideal order would constitute a suitable remedy for a situation where people now carry out much of their significant educational, cultural, political and economic activities in foreign languages imposed upon them during the colonial period. From this angle, instances of recourse to the colonizer's language in particular, are interpreted as signs of cultural subordination, and of a desire for identification with the colonizer's culture and nation.

I begin in this book from a somewhat different premise. Supposing in fact, people in postcolonial contexts had come to terms with life as polyglots in a multilingual world. Supposing in fact their resistance to colonialism, and later still, globalization entailed using different languages for different purposes. Supposing in fact, they did not systematically interpret their own willingness to use non-native languages as indications of a desire to identify with foreign cultures. My aim, in this book, is to try to explain why people continue to produce texts in languages that are not their mother tongues, why they join organizations using languages that are not their mother tongues, why they have not initiated the kind of response to non-native languages that several literary and cultural critics seemed to anticipate. One of the main questions I will be addressing in the book is the following: Does the increased prominence of so-called global languages like English signal a decreased attachment to more localized cultures among non-native speakers? My response to this question is mostly in the negative as I caution readers against systematically interpreting a willingness to use non-native languages as evidence of a desire for identification with cultures previously thought of as foreign.

My first chapter considers the circumstances in which resistance to colonialism or for that matter, support for the colonial enterprise will involve an agenda specifically designed to promote the use of a vernacular or mother tongue. The objective of this chapter is to prove that support for vernaculars can be an integral part of the colonial enterprise, just as support for selective use of non-native languages can play a role in resistance to colonialism. In my second chapter, I argue that the emergence of a literature envisaged as 'African' involved a re-configuration of the concept of the local among those Africans who participated in the creation of this literature. This in turn necessitated the recourse to languages understood by all those committed to this new vision of the local. My conclusion indicates that in cases where the colonized intelligentsia did not at the same time invest in the promotion of an indigenous lingua franca, literatures embodying such visions of the local could not but be expressed in the colonizer's language.

In the third chapter, I consider Nigerian video film as one instance among others where contemporary urban West African audiences have been willing to engage with a cultural practice in a language that is not a mother tongue. I make the case that advanced proficiency may not be the only and main factor at work in determining whether an audience will convene in response to an activity in a foreign language. I also attempt to show that these West African cases do not fit the model of the elite audience often associated with African cultural products in European languages. Looking at recent Ivorian romance fiction, the fourth chapter examines evidence of the continuing preoccupation with questions of local identity in West African texts produced in non-native languages. In fact, I suggest that such concerns over local identity may be even more overtly articulated in cultural texts and styles bearing a close resemblance to cultural trends identified as foreign than in those cultural forms with a longer presence in a given society, and whose affiliations with the local may be less subject to question. The point of departure for my argument in the fifth and final chapter is the assumption that foreign societies are viewed as territorially separate and alternative locations for cultures which are as localized as one's own culture. Where people engage in activities using non-native languages that are also languages of wider communication, the desire may be not so much for identification with a specific foreign culture and society as to transcend the limitations imposed by more localized attachments. My discussion in this chapter is based on a study of the relationship between language use and questions of identity among members of Charismatic churches in contemporary West Africa.

In sum, it is my intention to suggest that recourse to non-native languages does not necessarily reference identification with the foreign. Just as the word palaver has undergone assimilation into the contemporary West African vernacular notwithstanding its foreign antecedents, so also non-native languages have become deeply implicated in contemporary West African productions and imaginations of the local. As to be expected, some readers will take exception to my approach to the issues of language and identity in this book. I too recognize that there is no intrinsic merit in stirring up further palaver on this particular subject. If however this and further discussions do something to advance our understanding of how people actually respond to non-native languages, I will have accomplished at least some of my goals for the book.

Acknowledgements

The research for this book was carried out with funds provided by the Faculty Research Grants of the University of California, Davis. A fellowship with the Davis Humanities Institute and a Faculty Development Award enabled me to take time off to complete writing of the manuscript.

Several friends and acquaintances were most helpful while I carried out research in West Africa. In particular, I wish to thank Anna and Ernest Lartey, as well as Naadu and NiiLarte for their assistance and hospitality while I was in Accra. I would also like to extend my thanks to the Canacoo family in Accra, and to Godfrey Maison, my able research assistant in Ghana. For help in getting round Abidjan and making so many useful contacts, I am much indebted to Chouk and Rafi Amoussa and their brothers. I am also deeply appreciative of the practical assistance provided by Lamide Adesina in Nigeria. Members of my family were an additional and constant source of support, enthusiasm, and ideas. While writing this book, I was unable to spend as much time as I would have liked with Tinuke, Ayodapo, Moradeyo, Doyin and Gboye and to them, this book is dedicated.

Earlier versions of some sections of this book appeared in a number of publications. The permission granted by the University of Minnesota Press, Cambridge University Press, and St. Jerome Publishing, respectively, to quote from these earlier publications is gratefully acknowledged. The publications are as follows: English and the audience in African popular culture: The case of Nigerian video film. *Cultural Critique* 50 (2002); 'Routes: Language and the identity of African literature. *Journal of Modern African Literature* 37, 4 (1999); Translation and postcolonial identity: African writing and European languages. *The Translator, Studies in Intercultural Communication* 4, 2 (1998).

Chapter 1
Colonial Encounters and Discourses of the Vernacular

In his first novel, *Climbié*, published in 1956, the Ivorian author, Bernard Dadié, recalls in the following manner the climate surrounding the use of vernacular languages on school grounds during his early years of schooling in the French West African colonies:

> The decision was therefore made, and circulars were distributed to all corners of the bush and even to the smallest village schools. 'The speaking of dialects on school property is hereby forbidden.' It was precise. The zones were clearly demarcated. On that day was born the token – a piece of wood, a box of matches, anything. It was entrusted to the top student in the class, whose duty it was to give it immediately to anyone caught speaking his own dialect. From the day the token first appeared, a coldness settled over the school. The students sang as well at the beginning of classes as they did at the end, but without the same abandon, the same gusto, the same fire. And the breaks, once so happy and loud . . . they too felt the effects of the new rule . . . Because of the token the students liked to get as far away as possible from the schoolyard as soon as the final bell rang. They waited anxiously for the time to leave and watched the shadows grow smaller . . . (Dadié, 1971: 15–16)

Images of the schoolroom, of the token, and of other humiliations continue to hover over memories of initial encounters with the dominant tongue, with the standard language, with Received Pronunciation in fiction and non-fiction around the world. Certainly, experiences similar to Dadié's have been recounted by a number of other African authors, including Dadié's compatriot, Jean-Marie Adiaffi (1980), but also by the Congolese, Sony Labou Tansi,[1] and most notably by the Kenyan, Ngugi wa Thiong'o (1981).[2] Nonetheless, and despite the inauspicious beginnings, Dadié's protagonist in the novel *Climbié*, does manage to complete his education and to become as an adult increasingly sensitive to the injustices of colonialism. Even more significantly for the argument that I will be developing in this chapter, Dadié wrote this largely autobiographical work with its many criticisms of French colonial rule, manifested inter alia in its language policies, in the very language that had been imposed upon him as a child at school.

Language has been and remains one of the most potent symbols of ethnicity and group identity in human society. In the words of Fishman (1989: 32), language is the 'quintessential symbol' of ethnicity.[3] To wit, there have been an increasing number of mobilizations around questions of language and identity around the world. From the language-based nationalisms of Eastern Europe in the 19th century to the more recent language movements of the post-Soviet Union, from the struggles over Afrikaans in Apartheid South Africa to the conflicts over bilingual education and the English-Only movement in the United States,[4] language seems poised to become even more than in previous centuries, a convenient flashpoint and battleground for resolving disagreements over identity, nation, migrancy and territory.

My interest in this chapter is in what I will describe henceforth as discourses of the vernacular. And because there is a tendency to speak of dissimilar mobilizations around language in terms which obfuscate different types of responses to dominant cultures on the part of subordinated communities, I find it useful to start by explaining what exactly I mean by a discourse of the vernacular. I will use the term 'vernacular' to describe language in its specific function as a mother tongue while I define a discourse of the vernacular as the organized activity undertaken by concerned individuals with a view to making such mother tongues the officially recognized means of communication in the major institutions of a territorially circumscribed community.

I should point out that my concern with issues of language and identity in this chapter derives mainly from a desire to explain the emergence of African literatures in European languages and their continued resiliency in comparison to African literatures in indigenous languages. Scholars of African and postcolonial literatures are generally familiar with narratives recounting the imposition of European languages in the educational systems of colonial Africa. While such narratives provide invaluable insight into the intellectual climate of an age from the viewpoint of those who actually suffered through such experiences of imposition, it is worth noting that the majority of these narratives have nonetheless been recorded in texts produced in European languages. In other words, to the extent that these authors continue to use the imposed languages and have not become involved in movements to change the language policies of the communities to which they belong, their condemnation of colonial educational policy cannot yet be considered a discourse of the vernacular. It is the failure of many African writers to transform concerns about language into active discourses of the vernacular that I find particularly intriguing, and which leads me to some of the following reflections on major and minor discourses of the vernacular in the contemporary world.

In response to a tradition of criticism that largely overlooked writing in indigenous languages, there has been considerable effort in recent years to prove that African literature written in indigenous languages was as significant as writing in European languages. Accounts of this neglect of indigenous language literatures in the canon of African literature generally deploy a vocabulary replete with the well-known oppositions between colonizer and colonized, foreign and native, center and periphery. While the fact of colonialism is absolutely central to any discussion of the marginalization of indigenous-language literatures in Africa, discussions of the language situation that move rapidly from the fact of colonialism to the colonized mentality of the educated elite in explaining the continued dominance of European languages in literary writing, confuse the historical setting with the response to the setting. Like Zachernuk (2000: 183), I suspect that 'colonial intellectuals are [not] predictable simply by virtue of being colonial', and as such, responses to the colonial encounter are preferably studied as distinct from, and not as extensions of a particular administrative system. For even where colonized elites gave assent to colonial policy, their assent represents a distinct phenomenon often motivated and sustained by considerations of a rather different order. To overlook such considerations is to construct colonized elites as being always and totally devoid of agency.[5]

In order to come to a more precise understanding of the response of educated Africans to questions of language choice in the colonial period, I have chosen to concentrate on instances where the colonizing authorities did in fact support the idea of vernacular literacy for the colonized, as happened with the British authorities in several of their West African colonies. Where the colonizers systematically imposed their own language, it is easy to conclude that the colonized elite had little choice but to acquiesce to the policy of imposition. But where colonizing officials embraced a discourse of vernacular literacy, we may have to consider other possibilities in explaining the reluctance of a colonized elite to take advantage of the opportunity that was, as it were, freely offered. Against this background, I intend in this chapter to examine the failure of colonial discourses on vernacular literacy to generate widespread enthusiasm among colonized elites in Africa and to prevent the emergence of vibrant literatures in the former colonial languages, particularly in the West African and southern Nigerian contexts. All colonizers no doubt considered their culture superior to the cultures of the colonized, but all colonizers did not develop a discourse around the vernacular. Most colonized groups sought to defend and safeguard their culture in some way, but all such groups did not develop a discourse of the vernacular as part of their resistance to colonialism. And perhaps for these reasons, the ambivalence of African nationalist figures and writers towards discourses of the vernacular ought to be considered not so much as an aberration to be deplored, but as a fruitful illustration of the circumstances in which discourses of the vernacular become unattractive to those who have been designated as its intended beneficiaries.

Vernacular Literacy and Colonial Education

To start with, in advancing our understanding of these circumstances, I propose to consider 'major' discourses of the vernacular, or discourses developed by those in a position of power, and the kinds of reactions that such major discourses engender on the part of designated beneficiaries who are usually excluded from positions of power. The activity of British authorities in the colony of Nigeria in the late 19th and early 20th century is instructive in this regard, as are the responses of the local educated elite.[6] Here, as was the case in Dadié's narrative, the question of vernacular literacy in the colonies most frequently surfaced in relation to educational policy. In British West Africa, the first policy statements on educational matters by the British authorities were made public in 1882. The fact that the 1882 Ordinance, as it was called, made no provision for the teaching of the local languages, or instruction in the vernacular within the formal school system provoked an immediate outcry from missionaries in southern Nigeria who prepared a memorandum of protest, and from many educated Africans whose reactions were recorded in the lively Lagos press.[7] The vigorous protests addressed to the British authorities on this matter are often identified with the onset of a larger wave of cultural nationalism among educated Africans in Lagos, which lasted from the 1880s roughly until the second decade of the 20th century. But for a host of reasons, which have been adequately discussed elsewhere,[8] and which included the expanding institutionalization of racism, disagreements with the British authorities were increasingly played out on the political rather than cultural arena after the 1920s.

The 1882 Ordinance was apparently the foremost occasion when the colonial authorities disregarded the role of indigenous languages in educational policy in colonial Nigeria. The 1882 incident was also the main instance when politically active educated Africans made a discourse of the vernacular a significant part of their 'political' agenda. However, subsequent Ordinances passed into law as from 1887 reversed the provisions of the 1882 Ordinance regarding the place of indigenous languages in native education. In fact, the 1926 Education Ordinance stated that 'Among infants and younger children, all instruction should as far as possible be given in the vernacular . . .' and it was responsible for such a turnabout in the language policies of the state that Awoniyi (1975: 99, 127) credits it with generating renewed interest in the work done on at least one of the indigenous languages, Yoruba, as from the 1920s onwards. Special memoranda were also issued in 1927 and 1943 by the British authorities stating preference for the use of vernacular, i.e. the mother tongue, at least in the early years of schooling in the colonies.

Support for vernacular literacy in southern Nigeria started long before the 1882 Ordinance. Earlier in the 19th century, Protestant missionaries had begun expressing reservations about the use of English in schools. Reverend Buhler, the German director of the Training Institution established in 1859 by the Christian Missionary Society, complained about the confusion caused by instruction in English, and recommended instruction in Yoruba (Awoniyi, 1975: 50–1). Among the missionaries, the initial impetus for supporting vernacular literacy arose from the desire to provide scriptures to African converts in their own language (Ajayi, 1965: 131). For the same reasons, they also felt that non-native missionaries ought to become proficient in the language of the community where they worked (Smith, 1926: 45–6). But with time, evangelization took a back seat, and the discourse on vernacular literacy was increasingly realized within the context of concerns related directly or indirectly to the form of the education to be provided for colonized Africans. Those who spoke most frequently on the need for vernacular literacy often spoke in the same breath of these other issues, so that they gradually became integral components of the discourse on vernacular literacy.

The European advocates of vernacular literacy in Africa during the colonial period made their views known in books, journal articles, and at international conferences linked to specific interest groups, namely missionaries, education officials, linguists and anthropologists. The international conference on Christian Missions in Africa, which took place at Le Zoute, Belgium in 1926, was one such forum which brought together missionaries and therefore those largely responsible for educational instruction in colonial Africa. The participants at this conference specifically debated on issues of language and in particular on vernacular literacy at several sessions. Opinions on language and education were also to be found in journals dealing with educational questions in the colonies, such as the journal *Oversea Education* published by the British Colonial Government.[9] Articles on the subject appeared regularly in publications belonging either to individual missionary groups or linked to several Protestant missionary organizations such as the *International Review of Missions*, or *The Bible Translator*.

In my opinion, some of the most interesting articles on vernacular literacy and literature were featured in anthropological journals that specialized in African studies, including for example, the journal, *Africa*, and the *Journal of the African Society*, later renamed *African Affairs*. Founded in the early 20th century, both journals remain important players in the production of scholarly discourse on African culture. The journal *Africa* deserves special attention because it featured more articles on the structure of African languages, on vernacular writing, and on native education than other Africanist publications such as the *Journal of the African Society*. *Africa* made its first appearance in 1928 in Britain as the main publication of an organization called the International Institute of African Languages and Cultures (IALC), which later became the International African Institute. The establishment of the Institute, based in London, was proposed at a conference of linguists working on African languages in September 1925 (Lugard, 1928: 8). The actual convening occurred at a meeting of interested Africanists, including missionaries, anthropologists, colonial administrators in June 1926 (Smith, 1934: 3). The IALC intended to differentiate itself from other anthropological bodies working on Africa by giving special consideration to African languages and literature in the vernacular in a time of social change. Its special concerns were reflected in the constitution of the organization, where the first item in the list of objectives indicated that the IALC was set up 'to study the languages and cultures of the natives of Africa' (Smith, 1934: 4).

The founding editor of *Africa* was Professor Diedrich Westermann who had earlier served as a missionary in Togo, before becoming a professor at the University of Berlin. Professor Westermann was a staunch supporter of African vernacular literacy, and widely recognized as a foundational figure in West African linguistics. Westermann the linguist is well recognized in African language studies; Westermann the cultural entrepreneur, less so in studies of the literature and the cultural politics of the colonial period.[10] The editorial inclinations of *Africa*, under Westermann's direction and his many publications on the subject of vernacular literacy provide numerous instances of the cultural entrepreneur at work. It was no surprise, given his predilections, and those of the IALC that the first three articles in the inaugural issue of *Africa*, dealt in passing, or extensively with the role of the vernacular in colonial Africa. Subsequent editions featured articles presenting linguistic findings on African languages, but also advocating vernacular literacy as educational policy. The IALC further established an annual competition for African vernacular literature in December 1928 to act as a stimulus for authors writing in indigenous

African languages (Westermann, 1937: 497). The canon of early African vernacular literature was largely formed from authors who first received recognition for their creativity through these competitions (Gérard, 1981: 184).

There were a number of related concerns linked to this campaign on behalf of the African vernaculars. In the first place, and looking through several articles on vernacular literacy and education in the early editions of *Africa*, it is soon apparent that distrust of the highly educated, and therefore Europeanized or 'denationalized' African served as the major premise for much of this discourse. In his article in the first edition of the journal, Carl Meinhof (1928), professor of African languages at the University of Hamburg explained how disregard of mother tongues resulted in the emergence of detribalized and untrustworthy Africans. Proposing a system of education based on respect for African tradition and the use of the vernacular in one of the early editions of *Africa*, Bryant Mumford, the Superintendent of Education in Tanganyika in East Africa, declared without hesitation: '... the semi-Europeanized Native, everyone agrees is a product to be avoided' (1928: 156). Frederick Lugard, chief architect of the policy of 'Indirect Rule' in British Africa, and variously High Commissioner and Governor-General in the colony and protectorates established in Nigeria between 1905 and 1919, was one of those who strongly agreed. His dislike of educated Africans was legendary and is well documented.[11] He favored the development of what he considered suitable education for the natives, which would include instruction in the vernacular. In his mind, missionary education was largely to blame for the emergence of 'denationalized' Africans, and though the majority of participants at the Le Zoute conference were missionaries, he gently chided them for the damage their endeavors had done to the true African.

Concern for the cultural integrity of the African was another component of this discourse. To quote Mumford (1929: 139) again: 'It is common knowledge that primitive peoples after continued contact with the white races almost invariably deteriorate in art, morale, and physique, and become discontented or idle.' Out of this concern for African cultural integrity arose an additional object of suspicion, the corrupting influences of trade and Creole languages, and of the lingua franca. And though there was disagreement about whether or not to promote vernacular literacy at the Le Zoute conference, the participants were apparently able to come to agreement on at least one point: 'No attempt... should be made to impose upon larger language units any African so-called lingua franca' (Smith, 1926: 113). The deficiencies of the lingua franca were eminently evident to supporters of vernacular (that is mother tongue) literacy. W. Schmidt (1930: 139) in a talk to the Executive Council of the IALC, impressed upon his audience, the need to avoid 'the spread of mongrel and stunted languages, such as Creole-French and pigeon [sic] English, and so on which constitute a serious obstacle to real progress and civilization.'[12] For similar reasons, many Protestant missionary groups in Tanganyika opposed the use of Kiswahili in elementary schools because it was not a mother tongue. And in those parts of Kenya where instruction in Kiswahili had been introduced, William Laughton (1938: 224) was of the opinion that educationists should 'deplore something which possesses as little cultural value as Pidgin English.'[13] A Congolese teacher working for the Swedish Evangelical Mission complained in the 1950s about the spread of the trade language Lingala to the detriment of Kikongo, the mother tongue of his people. 'I know Congo families,' wrote Joseph Samba (1952: 49), 'where Kikongo is not spoken anymore. Lingala has taken its place. Or what is even worse, they prefer the artificial language called Kituba (a rudimentary trade language based on Kikongo) . . .'

In the third place, support for African vernacular literacy was closely linked to statements acknowledging the value of real African culture, that is traditional culture, and of the African past in particular. On the surface, the discourse appeared driven by a kind of teleological purpose that would eventually lead Africans to modernity. But at the heart of the discourse on vernacular literacy was the postulation of an ineradicable gap between the African and the European that was both cultural and temporal. As individual cultures and peoples were called to individual destinies, so also they were assigned to their own temporal vocations. The vocation of Europe was modernity; that of the African, the past. It was not the past of antiquity, which too was European, rather it was some kind of intermediate stage, subsequent to European antiquity and prior to European modernity.

Thus, the Africanist discourse on vernacular literacy was like many other anthropological discourses of the time, predicated upon the principle described by Johannes Fabian as 'the denial of coevalness' defined as the 'persistent and systematic tendency to place the referent(s) of anthropology in a Time other than the present of anthropological discourse' (Fabian, 1983: 31). In an article on vernacular language literature in 1932, E. R. Hussey explained the connection between the vernacular and the African past for readers of *Africa*. The advocates of vernacular literacy, he said, dedicated themselves to this cause because 'they believe that African languages form an essential link between the people and their past' (Hussey, 1932: 174). The early resolutions of the Executive Council of the IALC made the case even clearer, invoking the ancestral environment of the African: 'we are of the opinion that no education which leads to the alienation of the child from his ancestral environment can be right . . . Neglect of the vernacular involves crippling and destroying the pupil's productive powers by forcing him to express himself in a language foreign both to himself and to the genius of his race . . .' (Smith, 1934: 10).

In the context of discussions surrounding vernacular literacy, this respect for the African past usually resulted in a tendency to elevate the older generation of Africans above the younger. Westermann (1926: 429) noted with concern that 'the younger generation is sometimes inclined to reject or to desert the indigenous forms of life altogether, and to adopt the western system indiscriminately.' And Mumford (1929: 153), whom we have quoted before, proposed the development of a school system relying on older African men: 'Older influential men who remember the old traditions and the state of affairs before the interference of the white man would be preferable to younger men who possibly might have more alert brains but who may be more prejudiced in favour of new-fangled ideas, rather than those of traditional value.'

Fourthly, it was understood that where higher education was offered to Africans, proficiency in European languages would play a significant role in such education. Westermann (1934: 259), like many other Africanists writing on the issue of native education, admitted that a small class of Africans would need to acquire Western education and mastery of English in order to become the vanguard for developing the entire community. The fact, however, that mother tongues would not be used in higher education acted as a real disincentive to further investment in vernacular literacy for the many Africans who considered higher education a route for escaping permanent subordination to Europeans in the colonies.

For their part, advocates of vernacular literacy frequently suggested that higher education be made available only to a small minority of Africans in every colony. Thus, the vast majority would have no need for higher education, and consequently no need to acquire literacy in European languages (Westermann, 1929: 350).[14] In the Lagos colony for example, the missionaries vigorously opposed the idea of education beyond the elementary level for Africans (Fajana, 1982: 34–6; Ajayi, 1965: 152–3; Ayandele, 1966: 286–9), and if secondary schools were eventually established, it was mainly in response to overwhelming pressure from African parents who demanded higher education and also raised the finances to support the schools. The missionary plan in contrast called for an education heavily weighted in favor of 'industrial' that is vocational and agricultural instruction. Parents were as opposed to these plans as they were to the idea of instruction in the vernacular, and for good reason. In Ajayi's words, the earliest missionary vocational schools did nothing more than 'produce masons and carpenters to build missionary houses and coffins' (1963: 519). But what most parents wanted was an education that would enable their children to compete for the best paying jobs in the colonial administration or to set up businesses independently of European control.

Finally, and in the fifth place, advocates of vernacular literacy assumed that if Africans educated in the desired manner engaged in literary activity, the result would be 'cultural' and 'traditional' rather than 'political' and contemporary in orientation, and primarily directed towards transcription of oral texts rather than analysis of contemporary reality. At any rate, it was certainly not anticipated in the founding of the IALC that the educated African who wrote in European languages would contribute in any way to the localizing discourses that were being produced about the continent in journals like *Africa*. In fact, a specific division of labor and language functions was envisaged. One series of publications titled 'African Studies' would publish the research and opinions of 'experts.' The second series to be called 'African Documents' and would consist of texts by Africans composed in their own languages before being translated into a European language. These vernacular texts would consist essentially of 'stories, songs, dramas, riddles, proverbs, historical and other traditions, descriptions of social institutions and customs, myths and religion in its every aspect...' (Lugard, 1928: 4). Literate Africans were to furnish diverse narratives for this series, preferably from the past, and preferably in their own languages, while the European experts would provide the theoretical interpretation of the texts.[15] It was a division of labor that was to dominate the discipline of African studies for decades to come.[16]

African Responses to Colonial Discourses of the Vernacular

If the colonial administrators and missionaries who were responsible for most of the education available in the British colonies up till the 1950s were so committed to providing instruction in the vernacular, how then did the use of English as a language of instruction ever become so widespread, not only in secondary schools, but also in elementary classes in many British colonies in Africa? The answers are several fold: on the one hand, the colonial administration required proficiency in English for prospective African workers in the civil service and this requirement created in itself an incentive to seek instruction in English in post-elementary education since those who had any formal education thought that they should be able to compete for such jobs. The fact that policies of this sort clearly negated the supposed objectives of colonial discourses of the vernacular only served to generate the suspicion that advocates of the vernacular within the colonial administration may have been more interested in disparaging those Africans who were already literate in English, than in instituting actual incentives for acquiring literacy in the vernacular under the colonial system.

Furthermore, and on the other hand, the facts show that African parents demanded teaching of English, particularly in those places where a previous tradition of literacy had not taken root before the arrival of the Europeans.[17] The missionaries were well aware of the fact that most African communities were indifferent, if not hostile to Christian doctrines, and would tolerate their presence only if they accepted to offer 'education' which had to include teaching of literacy skills in English, and the kind of accounting skills required for doing business with European merchants. Since missionaries in southern Nigeria were dependent on education as the main plank for evangelizing skeptical communities for the first half of the 20th century, they had little choice but to oblige African parents and communities by teaching English or lose the opportunity to make potential converts.[18] In hindsight, one cannot but be struck by the irony of the fact that subsequent generations of Africans have tended to attribute sole responsibility for the prominence of English in the school system to the missionaries, in much the same way as they have held missionaries responsible for privileging the humanities over instruction in vocational skills in colonial schools, even though that too was a calculated strategy adopted by Africans in the Lagos colony in the interest of competing with Europeans settled in the colony (Ajayi,1963: 522).

The resistance to vernacular instruction came as no surprise to European supporters of vernacular literacy who were well aware of the possible reactions that their proposals might generate among both literate and illiterate Africans. They had little reason to believe that Africans in the colonies would find the idea of vernacular literacy especially attractive. Dr Loram, who chaired the panels on education at the Le Zoute conference and was Commissioner for Native Affairs in South Africa, remarked during the discussion on this subject: 'The black people will finally say, we want to be taught in English and not in the vernacular' (Smith, 1926: 68). In anticipation of the expected reaction, Schmidt (1930: 139) proposed in a paper delivered to the Executive Council of the IALC, that African feelings on the matter be disregarded: 'It would be undesirable,' he wrote, 'to comply with any unwise wishes the natives themselves may express in favor of adding European languages to the school curriculum.'

The political repercussions of implementing all the components of the discourse of vernacular literacy for Africans were equally evident to those Europeans who embraced it. In Mumford's opinion, '[a]ttempts to preserve the old methods may be interpreted by many Africans as an attempt to keep them a subject race and to withhold the benefits of civilization' (1929: 154). Edwin Smith, who reported on the Le Zoute conference, further explained why educated Africans would probably be opposed to the idea of making vernacular literacy the sole form of literacy in the schools:

> Any attempt to adopt the vernacular as the medium of instruction would meet with the strong opposition of certain classes of literate Africans who would feel that the door of opportunity was slammed in the face of their children ... So strongly do Africans feel on the subject that if their mother tongue were made the basis of education they would open private schools for the teaching of English. (Smith, 1926: 68–9)

This, indeed, was the situation among the Igbo people of southern Nigeria, who confounded all efforts by the missionaries to make instruction in vernacular the norm, and were willing to pay additional fees for instruction in English (Fajana, 1982: 54). Nonetheless, British officials and missionaries continued to offer support for vernacular literacy, especially at the elementary level, and a tradition of writing in the vernacular did begin to emerge in many of the British colonies, making writing in several indigenous languages a viable option in places such as southern Nigeria. Indeed, both Yoruba and Igbo with the highest number of native speakers and literates had produced winning entries for the IALC competitions by the 1930s.[19] This fact notwithstanding, within a decade of these developments, a tradition of writing in English had begun to develop among college graduates within the very same language communities, and in time became so well established that authors of Yoruba and Igbo extraction now make up a disproportionate section of Nigerian novelists writing in English (Griswold, 2000: 41). Indeed, so significant was the willingness of Igbo writers to produce creative writing in English that according to Alan Hill (1998: 124), one of the former directors of Heinemann, the press that published Chinua Achebe's *Things Fall Apart* and launched the African Writers' Series, fully half of the first 20 novels published by Heinemann in the series were written by Igbo authors.[20]

And yet, there is every reason to suppose that the most prominent figures to emerge as English-language writers from southern Nigeria at the end of colonial rule had probably first acquired literacy in a mother tongue before moving on to English. Certainly the best-known writers were familiar with writing in the vernacular. Chinua Achebe, whose father was a catechist and teacher with the Anglican Mission, was undoubtedly conversant with at least one version of the Igbo Bible. For his part, Wole Soyinka was sufficiently well versed in reading Yoruba to translate the earliest masterpiece of Yoruba writing, a novel by Daniel Fagunwa, from Yoruba into English in the mid-1960s even though his autobiography suggests that he started learning English at an early age.²¹ My intention in this chapter is to explain why such educated Igbo and Yoruba authors ever turned to writing in English, given the prior existence of a successful practice of writing in the vernacular and their own exposure to writing in the vernacular. It is not enough, I would suggest, to know that a tradition of creative writing has developed in a particular language. To get a sense of its significance for both the producers and the audience, we must also map out the ways in which this practice aligns itself with various other cultural and political forces within the society.

And when we consider writing in English in southern Nigeria, we quickly realize that once historical, then journalistic, and later creative African writing began to appear in English, it often took positions that were at odds with those promoted in European discourse on African vernacular literacy. This concern for the vitality of indigenous African languages would have been entirely laudable, had colonial discourses of the vernacular not been so deeply implicated in projects of political subordination that were completely unacceptable to the educated African elite. The attempts to discourage Africans from seeking higher education, the condemnation of literary education and preference for technical and agricultural education, the emphasis on providing an education that would make the African fit for his or her subordinate status in colonial society, the denial of the validity of the claims for equality made by educated Africans, these were all aims that incurred the suspicion of educated Africans.²² If educated Africans were particularly hostile to Lugard during his tenure as governor of Lagos, it was not only because of the many repressive policies that he authored, it was also because of an awareness that he opposed everything that the educated African stood for.²³

I started this chapter with Dadié's fictional account of language and education in colonial West Africa, and would like to suggest at this point that in the British West African colonies in particular, ideas about 'Native education,' 'Indirect Rule,' and 'Vernacular Literacy' functioned as interrelated dimensions of a broad offensive directed by colonial officials against educated Africans from the 1920s onwards. All three strands of the campaign to discredit educated Africans came together in the works of figures connected either with education, language instruction, or administration like Lugard, Mumford, Hanns Vischer,²⁴ and Westermann, particularly in his 1934 book, *The African Today*. These were discourses and policies, specifically calculated in their privileging of the 'traditional,' to counteract and deny the legitimacy of any political demands made by the kinds of Africans who were being described as denationalized, and semi-Europeanized, in other words, educated Africans. In his book, Westermann (1934: 168) suggested for example that administration of

African colonies should preferably be entrusted to traditional chiefs than to native officials who were educated Africans. This was a view shared by the most fervent defenders of 'Indirect Rule' at the time who anticipated returning power to traditional chiefs and kings whenever colonial rule ended, completely bypassing those who had received formal Western education (Flint, 1969: 253).[25] Lugard no doubt had similar concerns in mind, when he spoke at the Le Zoute conference of the need to avoid 'producing imitation Europeans of a small section [of the African population] with a literary education crowned by a university degree' (Smith, 1926: 150).

While southern Nigerian nationalists rarely commented on proposals for vernacular literacy after the 1882 incident, they clearly recognized 'Indirect Rule' and 'Native education' as attempts to prevent educated Africans from acting as spokespersons for the African community. Writing in the 1930s, the then nationalist and future president of Nigeria, Nnamdi Azikiwe offered the following assessment of 'Native education' as envisaged by many colonial administrators:

> ... so long as the African would be content at menial tasks, and would not seek complete social, political, and economic equality with the Western world, he is deemed to be a 'good' fellow. But let him question the right to keep him in political and economic servitude, and let him strive to educate himself to the fundamentals of these modern problems, he is immediately branded as an 'agitator.' He becomes a 'bad' fellow for failing to stay in his 'place,' which of course, is in the background. (1934: 146)

The southern Nigerian nationalist Obafemi Awolowo (1947: 63) summed up the prevailing view about educated Africans among Nigeria's educated elite when he declared in 1947: 'It must be realized now and for all time that this articulate minority are destined to rule the country. It is their heritage.' Against this background, it is worth pointing out here, that much of the discourse on vernacular literacy produced by missionaries and colonial officials as from the 1920s unfolded alongside an increasingly articulate and combative practice of journalism in English in the British West African colonies. In southern Nigeria for example, 51 newspapers were established between 1880 and 1937, mostly by mission-educated men who had become disenchanted with the British through their professional encounters with Europeans (Omu, 1978: 26–8). Though there were a handful of very popular Yoruba-language papers, the overwhelming majority of the papers were in English.

Westermann who had lived in West Africa must have been aware of this tradition on the West coast, and Lugard, who was Governor in Nigeria was certainly aware of it. Indeed, he made the restriction of the powers of the local press one of his most urgent priorities while he was Governor in Lagos (Omu, 1978: 188–95). In fact it has been suggested that his dislike of the 'denationalized' African stemmed at least in part, if not substantially, from his experiences with Nigerian journalists who were vocal in their opposition to policies pursued by his administration (Omu, 1978: 48–9).[26] Given the context of the times, it is difficult to avoid the suspicion that vernacular literacy was so enthusiastically endorsed by some mainly in order to foster the development of an alternative to a growing, independent, and oppositional tradition of journalistic writing in English. These suspicions are further strengthened when one realizes that Westermann was the person entrusted with making the winning selections for the IALC competition in vernacular literature for several years after the competition was inaugurated.[27] In other words, following in the footsteps of some of his IALC associates who had been actively engaged in discrediting and suppressing West African journalistic writing in English, he took on the responsibility of single-handedly founding and compiling the canon of an acceptable African literature written in the vernacular.[28]

Major and Minor Discourses of the Vernacular

Probably because they have often constructed literary histories independently of larger political processes shaping the direction of colonial society, scholars of African-language literatures have tended to extend grudging or enthusiastic approval to the relative 'respect' accorded to African languages and cultures by the British colonial authorities and Protestant missionaries, in contrast to the apparent disregard for the African cultural heritage embodied in the French proposals for 'Assimilation' in their African colonies.[29] Such evaluations represent, in my opinion, a fundamental misunderstanding of the premises underlying the cultural politics practiced by European colonizers since the 18th century. Whether the preferred ideal was 'Assimilation' as with the French or 'Indirect Rule' as with the British, the cultural policy of these modern large-scale colonialisms was to establish the Other, the Native, the Negro, the Indian as unworthy of the privileges, rights, and protection enjoyed by citizens of the mother country under metropolitan law. Even where 'Assimilation' was the stated goal, it was rarely pursued as an end in itself and in a manner consonant with the eventual transformation of all Natives into Europeans. A consistent application of 'Assimilation' was possible mainly in colonies where a majority of the indigenous population had already been eliminated by war or disease, so that the on-going suppression of indigenous culture in policies of 'Assimilation' served to remind disempowered survivors of their fundamental otherness, manifested in their need for 'civilization.'[30] Such policies also had the advantage of providing a posteriori justification for the violence visited upon earlier generations of indigenous inhabitants of the colony. 'They were killed, not because it was their land, but because they were barbarians.'

In African colonies where a majority of the indigenous inhabitants survived the rigors of conquest and colonization, and where the colonial administration claimed to favor 'Assimilation,' only a handful of the local population ever acquired enough of European culture to warrant bestowment of French or Portuguese citizenship in half a century and more of active colonialism and contact with Europeans.[31] If the goal of 'Assimilation' was truly to transform most 'Natives' into Europeans, one can only infer extreme administrative lethargy in view of the unimpressive results obtained over several decades of activity designed to achieve this very result. Talk about 'Assimilation' in the African colonies, we must understand, was intended to maintain and reinforce cultural boundaries, and not to dissolve them.

Similar conclusions can be drawn about Britain's policy of 'Indirect Rule' as it was practiced in the African colonies. These were policies devised to fortify cultural and by extension, legal boundaries rather than policies inspired by an acceptance of African cultures as equals with European civilizations in the Western ratings of world cultures. If European culture and languages represented a higher stage of civilization as assumed by many European Africanists at the time, there was no need to insist on total African reliance on indigenous languages, except as a strategy for preserving the presumed disparity between civilizations and cultures.[32] As articulated in the British colonies, the discourse on vernacular literacy was a natural extension of the assumptions which informed the policy of 'Indirect Rule,' and thus it comes as no surprise that one of the most ardent British defenders of the principle of vernacular literacy, Frederick Lugard, was also the main inspiration behind the policy of 'Indirect Rule.'

The discourse on vernacular literacy developed by British colonial officials and Africanists involved with the journal *Africa* is, to my mind, a perfect example of a major discourse of the vernacular, a discourse developed by scholars and administrators who occupy positions of power in relation to the intended beneficiaries of the discourse. In its variable formulations, a major discourse on the vernacular is produced on behalf of subordinated groups and advocates the use of the mother tongue in formal educational systems as a way of protecting such subordinated groups from experiences of cultural alienation that have been precipitated in the first place by the violent intrusion within communities of new power structures dominated by foreigners. The fact is, the authority exercised by the advocates of the vernacular over diverse 'Natives' is often in itself, emblematic of the root causes of the condition for which a remedy is being proposed.

There is often in major discourses of the vernacular a kind of territorial logic at work, with the result that where vernacular literacy becomes government policy some type of fracturing of territory and administration is ultimately contemplated. Thus, when colonizers and other dominant groups develop a discourse of the vernacular on behalf of subjugated populations, it is usually because they envision these subjugated populations as residing in a place distinct from their 'home,' and where the laws governing life at 'home' no longer have any application. The process of elaborating a discourse of the vernacular in such circumstances inevitably implies a certain conception of space, requiring that those who speak separate languages inhabit separate spaces where they are subject to distinct laws and administrative procedures. In 20th-century Africa, the country that gave the most consistent support to the idea of vernacular literacy for subordinated groups was undoubtedly Apartheid South Africa.[33] It was also a country that increasingly moved in the same period towards excising the designated beneficiaries of this policy, Blacks, from the South African polity, first denying them legal rights and ultimately relocating them into homelands that were supposedly separate from white South Africa. But it is also interesting to note that where other African governments decided after independence in favor of what was described as 'mother tongue education,' such policies rarely took into account factors like the on-going process of migration, particularly from rural to urban areas, and the constant mingling of populations with different mother tongues within the same locality. Here as elsewhere, individual languages were correlated with individual territories in ways that presumed the existence of distinct and unchanging geographies for distinct mother tongues.[34]

Crawford (2000: 22) has argued that the visibility of the English-Only movement in the United States during the 1990s reflected more than concerns about language; rather the discourse enabled diverse groups in American society to articulate their fears about a number of issues, including immigration, welfare, civil rights and multiculturalism. Major discourses of the vernacular are similarly indicators of political trends and conceptions about foreignness and localness within a community. On the whole, these discourses are useful where some members of a dominant group derive benefit in making distinctions between 'home' and 'abroad,' between fellow compatriots and diverse foreigners. In addition, these discourses satisfy the need of professionals like missionaries and colonial administrators whose vocations are realized through travel to find difference at the endpoint of their journeys, thus justifying their own career choices. Major discourses of the vernacular likewise accommodate the fissiparous tendencies of Protestant missionary organizations and their proclivity for establishing distinct religious structures, supported by missionaries working independently of each other around individual language units and people groups as they are now more frequently known in contemporary Evangelical and Pentecostal circles.

I am by no means implying here that Protestant missionary organizations were or are insincere in their dedication to providing transcriptions and translations of the Bible into local languages, which is the main reason for their involvement in the production of discourses of the vernacular. Rather I wish to suggest that the investment in mother tongue literacy almost always requires as corollary acceptance of the idea of separate administrative arrangements for separate language groups residing in separate territories. Little wonder then that highly centralized religious organizations like the Catholic Church and centralized political systems like the French colonial administration showed such little interest in discourses of the vernacular in colonial Africa. Certainly in the French African colonies, there was a tendency to see *métropole* and *outre-mer* as part of an unbroken continuum in relation to administrative structuring and urban planning.[35] And though French colonial officials did begin to adopt policies showing greater respect for local cultures in the 20th century, this did not generally translate into the development of distinctive administrative structures for different ethnic groups and territories. At the same time, the monadic principle continued to hold sway in formal educational systems with French remaining the sole language of instruction admitted in most French African colonies.

Thus, organizations that deploy a uniform administrative structure over all the territories under their control, making no distinction between the metropolis and the periphery, and between different areas of the periphery in terms of administrative structures, appear to obtain minimal gain from pursuing a project of mother tongue literacy, since to do so would amount to an acknowledgement of cultural particularities, and provide a basis for questioning the universality claimed for the colonizer's culture, embodied inter alia in the practice of administrative uniformity for all colonized territories. In other words, major discourses of the vernacular have the greatest appeal where acknowledgement of cultural particularity can be used to justify asymmetries of power and administrative arrangement, especially in relation to marginalized populations residing in territories clearly demarcated from those identified as 'home' by the articulators of the discourse.

By contrast, individuals belonging to subordinated groups develop what I would like to describe here as 'minor' discourses of the vernacular in instances where their place of origin and residence has been incorporated as an integral element into the territory and 'home' of a dominant group.[36] The discourse on vernacular literacy then becomes part of a larger program to win political autonomy and possibly even territorial separation for the subordinated group. However, even in such instances, the proponents of vernacular literacy are usually those members of the subordinated community who are at the forefront of interaction with the dominant foreign culture.[37] They are frequently better educated than the norm, have lived longer periods outside their home community, have had more extensive contact with the dominant cultures. In consequence, they also have a more acute sense of impending cultural loss for the society that they hope to avert by advocating aggressive implementation of policies promoting mother tongue literacy. But the interesting fact when we consider many British colonies in Africa, is that the bulk of discourses of the vernacular produced during the colonial period emanated from European officials, and not from educated Africans. Even where Africans chose to write in indigenous languages, they rarely promoted vernacular literacy as essential to anti-colonial agitation. Educated Africans may have spoken their own mother tongues as a matter of course, but the usefulness of encouraging writing in all the vernaculars spoken in each colony as part of a program of resisting colonial rule was far from evident to them. The result is that discourses of the vernacular in colonial Africa, as an explicitly articulated project, were almost always the work of European administrators, missionaries, linguists and other professionals of education.

In explaining the failure of educated Africans to invest in discourses of the vernacular, one might begin by making a distinction between discourses of the vernacular and the 'natural' state of affairs in any community. Members of a country, of an ethnic group, of a religious community, will speak a first language, which may or may not be the language spoken by their immediate forbears.[38] In contexts of migration, prolonged contact with other cultures and especially of foreign domination, some kind of language shift is as much the norm as is language maintenance. Even though it may present itself as such, a discourse of the vernacular is in this situation more than simply a description of a 'natural' state of affairs. On the contrary, it is an active intervention calculated to precipitate change or to preempt changes that are already occurring in terms of language use in a given community, so that even where language is invoked as vernacular in nationalist discourse, the actual policies of the resulting nation-state will tend to privilege language as lingua franca, forcing some communities to undergo language shift. This in fact is the desired goal for cultural ideologues in many places: to transform the polity into a single nation, into an entity with a single culture. Thus almost everywhere one finds ethnic and linguistic minorities whose languages must be sidelined and marginalized if the cultural unity claimed for the emergent nation-state is to become lived reality.

Predicated as they are, on a fixity of languages and peoples in space, discourses of the vernacular generally have more to do with a particular vision of territory that can be used to advance a specific political agenda than with actual language practices within the territory, which will in all probability be in a state of constant flux. Only in rare cases of extremely isolated communities will discourses of the vernacular coincide to some degree with a reality on the ground. The key, therefore, to understanding the appeal of discourses of the vernacular does not lie in determining what the communities supposedly represented actually speak. Rather, discourses of the vernacular are best interpreted in relation to the tangible political benefits which they are expected to deliver by those who seek certain rights on behalf of residents of designated territorial units. In sum, both major and minor discourses of the vernacular will be embraced and promoted only where supporters can secure political, professional, and economic gain by marking difference through language.

Educated Africans in the British West African colonies began turning to English in part because they could perceive no such political benefit in endorsing discourses of the vernacular or marking cultural difference in this way. By the early 20th century, discourses of the vernacular rarely featured on the agenda of West African nationalist movements, and in the last years of colonial rule in Nigeria for example, the nationalist parties argued over whether to recognize only one or three languages as national languages after independence. This was, in other words, a debate about lingua francas and not about mother tongues.[39] Although members of these parties were interested in indigenous culture, the African nationalist movements represented more precisely as van den Berghe (1965: 215) has remarked, a form of territorialism, seeking self-determination for the invariably multi-ethnic and multilingual territory of the colony rather than for the single ethnic group with its distinctive language and other cultural attributes.[40] Among those authors who did write in English, similar concerns with transforming the colony into nation were at work as explained by the Nigerian writer, Achebe (1990: 32):

> Some of my colleagues . . . have tried to rewrite their history into a straightforward case of oppression by presenting a happy monolingual childhood brusquely disrupted by the imposition of a domineering foreign language . . . My position is that anyone who feels

unable to write in English should follow their desires. But they must not take liberties with our history. It is not simply true that the English forced us to learn their language ... We chose English not because the English desired it, but because having tacitly accepted the nationalities into which colonialism had grouped us, we needed its language to transact our business, including the business of overthrowing colonialism itself.[41]

The unwillingness to foreground discourses of the vernacular in resisting foreign domination is, from all appearances, entirely typical of movements for self-determination focused on territorial units rather than on individual ethnic groups. The few African leaders like those in North Africa, and Julius Nyerere of Tanzania who did make an African language the national and official languages of their countries after independence, were not, as is widely believed, unproblematic advocates of mother-tongue literacy. Kiswahili was no doubt widely understood in Tanzania in the 1960s, but it was not the mother tongue of most Tanzanians at the time when Nyerere made it the national and official language of the country.[42] Arabization policies pursued in North Africa similarly entailed disregarding the form of Arabic recognized by most North Africans as their mother tongue, and further marginalizing the mother tongue of linguistic minorities such as the Berbers. The intent, in other words, was neither to institutionalize instruction in mother tongues for the majority of the local population nor to practice vernacular literacy as I have defined it here.

In formulating their language policies, the leaders of these countries invoked the principle of the lingua franca, rather than that of the mother tongue, the demands of that emblem of modernity, the nation-state, rather than loyalty to traditional heritage and pre-colonial polities, the need to build anew rather than to preserve the past. In privileging the lingua franca over the mother tongue, these African states were not alone. Nationalists in former colonies outside the African continent, like Indonesia, also traveled the same road as part of the effort to make nation and new state congruent so that in time, the adopted lingua franca started to become the mother tongue of a new generation of Indonesians.[43] By contrast, colonial discourses on the vernacular placed emphasis on the construction of a supposedly authentic African culture from which educated Africans, nationalists and other dissenters from the colonial order were naturally excluded. The critical element to emphasize here is that, depending on the circumstances, support for vernacular literacy was as much a feature of colonial practice as was imposition of the languages of the colonizer.[44] And because both principles accommodated the larger goals of colonial rule equally well, resistance to colonial rule and a desire to reverse the cultural politics of colonialism did not always and naturally translate into support for mother-tongue literacy from the point of view of opponents to colonial rule.

There is no denying the fact that those educated Africans who did choose to do their creative writing in English had received much of their formal education and instruction in the same language, and that this experience had predisposed them towards writing in English.[45] But, since many of the English-language writers who emerged after the 1940s were critical of colonial rule, it might have been equally logical for them to advocate writing in the vernacular as a strategy for counteracting the effects of British rule in Africa, especially since this was a viable option for several languages in British West Africa. But the decision to write in a language other than the language of one's education is ultimately a political decision which becomes attractive only when it yields tangible and immediate political benefit. If many aspiring African writers in the period did not embrace this particular line of reasoning, and take advantage of the opportunity to write in indigenous languages, it was because the ideal of mother-tongue writing held as little strategic appeal for the creative writers as nationalists as it did for the politicians as nationalists. As I have argued in this chapter, discourses of the vernacular will in all probability fail to enlist the widespread support of local intelligentsias if their net result is to make the intended beneficiaries foreigners in their own land, i.e. to render them vulnerable to further political and economic subordination by an ethnically different dominant group. For self-appointed and elected leaders everywhere, the 'local' is not simply and exclusively that which is indigenous, rather it is every resource that can be mobilized in the cause of defending the interests of the local community. And in this instance, the recourse to English was a sign of the privileging of new and geographically more extensive imaginations of the local over earlier perceptions of the scope and constitution of the local.

The early West African writers in English belonged to a generation of educated Africans largely invested in the project of transforming the emergent states resulting from colonial rule into nations, that is making the state coterminous with some form of cultural solidarity. This meant for example addressing issues considered of 'local' interest from the perspective of its ramifications for the nation-state as a whole instead of from the perspective of its significance for individual ethno-linguistic units. It is clear for example that the works of authors like Christopher Okigbo, Onuora Nzekwu, Cyprian Ekwensi, or Chinua Achebe, to list some of the early writers of Igbo extraction, were not conceived by the authors as texts for advancing a specifically Igbo political or cultural agenda. To invoke Benedict Anderson's famous expression, the imagined community depicted by these writers and to which they addressed themselves was not one comprising the singular ethno-linguistic unit, but one constructed around the putative multi-ethnic and multilingual nation-state, visualized as sharing common interests, common goals, and common challenges. Though they wrote in English, the English-language writers did not envision the new nation-states as being largely English-speaking,[46] but they did view their own work as portraying issues pertinent to the entire nation-in-the-making, expressed in terms potentially accessible to all those similarly and effectively involved in the project of transforming the new states into nations.

Modernity, Contestation, and the Colonizer's Language

In the West African context, the emergence of English-language literary writing among the educated elite was not contemporaneous with, but rather subsequent to the development of indigenous-language writing. In other words, the increase in writing in English coincided with the last years of colonial rule and the onset of large-scale projects of 'modernization' initiated by local intelligentsias and diverse nationalists. From the point of view of African nationalists throughout the 20th century, a commitment to modernity has been a *sine qua non* for ending colonial rule and guaranteeing the political and economic independence of African states. These nationalists further envisioned the nation-state as the primary agent of modernity and modernization through the construction of roads, schools, hospitals, and the deployment of new political structures. To contribute to the strengthening of the nation-state was to invest in modernity. Both those who wrote in indigenous languages and those who wrote in English were implicated in these projects of modernization, but in rather different ways. To get a sense of the differences between these two strands of West African creative writing in the later colonial period I turn to the distinctions established by Ajayi (1961) in contrasting early and later African opponents to colonial rule. As Ajayi points out, the later nationalists who presided over decolonization did not define the objective of resistance to colonial rule as a restoration of the past, but as the establishment of a new order.

Major discourses of the vernacular, as we recall, were intended to lead colonized Africans in exactly the opposite direction. The focus in such discourses on the role of indigenous languages as essential components in preserving a valuable pre-modern African heritage is especially significant. Fabian's (1983: 16) contention that anthropology originated as a discipline using temporal categories to articulate otherness is relevant here, since colonial discourses of the vernacular enabled concerned Europeans to translate cultural difference into a temporal distance that justified the inequalities inscribed into the colonial order. Many educated Africans, on the other hand, increasingly perceived their role in colonial society as one of reversing these injustices and moving the society beyond the legacies of the past. As they understood it, successful resistance could not be undertaken without a commitment to the idea of modernity which in turn required the forging of new political structures and new alliances cutting if need be across existing ethno-linguistic lines.

To the extent that Western society itself was constructed as a model of modernity, African access to this ideal would be mediated at least in part through selective appropriations of the modalities offered by the Western world, perceived here as 'modern' rather than culturally Western in essence. In this connection, we would do well to remember, as Gikandi (1996: 17–18) has suggested, that it was imperial rule itself rather than European culture *per se* that figured in the minds of the nationalists as an adversary to be resisted. There was little doubt that European languages played a vital role in the formation of the novel political and economic structures associated with modernity and which were expected to ensure African emancipation from colonial rule. In these circumstances, continued recourse to English was a strategic choice made for the sake of constructing alternative modes of resistance to colonial rule.

For an important segment of West Africans who wrote in vernacular languages in the colonial period, producing a modern literature initially meant making folktales, proverbs and other forms of oral literature available in script. In the late 19th and early 20th centuries, such authors were usually intent on preserving African cultural patrimony by committing descriptions of customs, historical narratives and other forms of orature to writing. In the case of Asante Twi, one of the Akan languages in Ghana, Gérard (1981: 272) notes that the majority of writers in the 1950s and 60s were 'interested exclusively in the recording of oral lore, especially tales and proverbs . . .' During the colonial period and in the early years after independence, the pattern was identical for writing in other Akan languages like Akwapim Twi and Fanti. There were of course exceptions as in the case of Hausa writing (Furniss, 1998), but for the most part, early vernacular literature in West Africa was largely dedicated to the very goals outlined in colonial discourses on vernacular literacy, and in particular to the preservation of a pre-existing literary heritage.[47] This pattern in itself is not unusual: with the introduction of writing in many societies around the world, the earliest literary texts that appear in written form tend to be transcriptions of popular and widely circulated oral texts.[48] The problem with the scenario envisaged by proponents of colonial discourses of the vernacular in Africa is that they intended to keep creative writing in the colonies perpetually at that stage. The move towards writing in English was fueled

Colonial Encounters and Discourses of the Vernacular

at least in part by the desire to escape from the restrictions placed upon African vernacular writing during the colonial period.

The demands for real 'African literature,' understood as translations from the vernacular and transcriptions of oral texts, were seen as yet another attempt to deny the agency of the educated African and the legitimacy of the educated African's voice. Soyinka recounts his response to one British magazine's request for some authentic African literature during his student days at Leeds:

> I have, by lucky chance, a very recent example of this hankering after the non-creative literary transcription. A university publication in England asked me for translations of 'authentic' African tales and songs. I said I could give them short stories and poems written by me, but no, they were interested in 'authentic' stuff. Yes, I replied, but I do have material on folk themes, only I regret to say, they are original. No, they insisted, we must have translations. (cited in Lindfors, 1982: 144)

To satisfy this hankering for transcriptions on the part of Western readers, Soyinka produced a semblance of a folktale for the journal, replete with 'pseudofolk ingredients' (Lindfors, 1982: 144), thus reinstating his agency as author over the written text even if the editors of the journal in question failed to recognize it. Through their original writing, he and others who declined to consider transcriptions of oral texts as the only legitimate form for African literature, reclaimed the right to speak as individuals, bringing their personal judgment to bear on issues affecting the wider community when they acted as spokespersons for the African world.

But even where vernacular language writers during the colonial period were not engaged in producing transcriptions of oral literature, they tended to pursue a rather different kind of subject matter from those Africans who produced a non-commercial literature in English in the same period. In the case of Hausa prose writing in the 1930s, Furniss observes:

> On the evidence of these early Hausa novellas of the 1930s, the 'colonial encounter' is one rather insignificant component of experience during the colonial period. The writers of these novellas were deeply involved with the colonial education system . . . Clearly their daily experience was intimately bound up with aspects of a 'colonial encounter.' Yet at the level of imagination, as expressed in these narratives, it was the nature of their own notions of Hausa society which concerned them. (1998: 100)

By contrast, the colonial encounter itself was the central thematic concern of much early African writing in European languages. It provided the essential backdrop against which all other realities were to be explored, and against which Western ideas about Africans were to be scrutinized. So much has already been written in postcolonial theory about the practice of writing back that we might almost take for granted the single-mindedness with which the authors of such texts set themselves to engaging both scholarly and creative representations of Africans by Europeans during and following the colonial period. These were writers who made contesting European discourses on Africa their primary objective. For such authors writing in English, the pursuit of modernity consisted specifically in seeking to displace European scholars as the primary authorities on the African world and in responding to colonial discourse on Africa by inserting themselves within its very mode of production and circulation.

If the Africanist discourse produced by colonizers, represented like many other anthropological discourses of the time an epistemology 'whose referent [had] been removed from the present of the speaking/writing subject' (Fabian, 1983: 143), then writing in European languages provided a means whereby the referents (in this case Africans) could establish themselves as valid interlocutors, implanted in the same temporal location as the European Africanists who envisioned themselves as writing subjects *par excellence*. And since communication can only take place where coevalness has been established (Fabian, 1983: 30–1), this objective required that the writers situate themselves in the same Time as those who not only ruled, but claimed the power to define the compass and scope of local culture on the African continent. It also meant that Africans seeking to refute the diverse Africanist discourses being generated in the service of colonialism, would effect the required act of temporal relocation by consciously distancing themselves from the denial of coevalness signified inter alia by discourses on vernacular literacy.

It was therefore no accident that in the 1960s and 70s, English-language African writers produced some of the severest criticisms of the largely Francophone Negritude movement and its perception of a modern African literature. With its reification of the category of race, its allocation of completely separate vocations to different races, and its excessive attention to the past, Negritudinist art and discourse, especially in its Senghorian formulation, sparked recollections of an earlier discourse on African culture which English-language authors from the former British African colonies had learned to distrust and were committed to discrediting. In the 1960s, as more and more independent African governments began to reveal autocratic tendencies, Soyinka (1988: 19) pointedly reminded his fellow writers: 'The African writer needs an urgent release from the fascination of the past.' As many of those writing in English understood it, the vocation of the African writer was to interact with the authoritative discourses of the moment in which they lived, whether such discourses happened to be broadly colonial or created at the behest of new forms of dictatorship.

To be sure, some vernacular authors of the colonial period drew upon non-African literary practices and themes in producing their creative texts. For example, in addition to Yoruba mythology, Bamgbose (1974) lists John Bunyan, Daniel Defoe, Christopher Marlowe, *The Arabian Nights*, *Aesop's Fables*, and Greek classical literature among the many sources used by Fagunwa in his Yoruba-language novels. At the same time, and though Fagunwa drew equally upon the verbal traditions of the Yoruba in his writing, his work was much more tolerant of the ideologies associated with the Western presence in colonial West Africa.[49] In comparing Soyinka, also a Yoruba of a later generation, but who wrote in English, with Fagunwa who wrote in the vernacular, George (2003: 145) has noted the irony: 'It turns out, therefore, that the figure who writes in Yoruba lays no claim to a 'universal' audience, but is ideologically more overtly 'Western' – that is, Christian and 'pro-modern.' By contrast, the one using the English language is more 'Yoruba' (that is, pagan and anti-colonial) . . .'

In accounting for the orientation of many African vernacular language texts up till the mid-20th century, it is helpful to recall that much of the infrastructure for publishing African vernacular literature in Roman script during the colonial period remained firmly under the jurisdiction of missionary agencies and or colonial officials, with missionary presses (exercising an almost complete monopoly over vernacular publication), colonial Translation and Literature Bureaus, diverse linguists and missionary schools all affording a degree of oversight if not outright control over the style and contents of indigenous language writing throughout the colonial period.[50] Thus, the publication of Thomas Mofolo's *Chaka*, written in Sotho in southern Africa, could be delayed for 15 years by disapproving missionaries (Gérard, 1981: 191). For similar reasons in most of colonial Africa, African vernacular writing, to use Gérard's preferred term, remained at some remove from the nationalist movements of the later colonial period, in contradistinction to much of the writing in European languages, which often functioned as a kind of creative adjunct to the activity of nationalist politicians. In the case of Hausa literature for example, partisan politics, sectarian aspirations and the rivalry between leaders of different parties, rather than opposition to colonial rule appeared to have been the predominant concerns of political poetry in the last years of colonial rule in Nigeria (Furniss, 1996: 228–32). Despite the involvement of some Hausa politicians in creative writing, political considerations were even further removed from the newly emerging Hausa prose writing of the colonial period, fostered as it was by British cultural brokers eager to counter the English-language nationalist publications coming from other regions in Nigeria (Furniss, 1995: 15).

Paradoxically, activities conducted in English by graduates of both missionary and government run schools enjoyed much less interference from either colonial administrators or missionaries. Whether it was the literary clubs organized by young men in the coastal cities of West Africa (Newell, 2000), or the literary magazines founded on university campuses like Ibadan (Lindfors, 1982; Wren, 1991), or the publications put out by small African-owned presses in eastern Nigeria (Dodson, 1973; Obiechina, 1973), or the English-language press in colonial Nigeria (Omu, 1978), reading and writing in English offered one of the avenues in which educated Africans could freely pursue their own agenda without regard for the specific directives and concerns associated with colonial discourses of the vernacular. Given this state of affairs, the decision to write in English was more than an uncomplicated act of acquiescence to the might of British imperialism. On the contrary, educated Africans in the British West African colonies who sought the latitude to express themselves on matters of their own choosing without being subjected to the kind of division of labor anticipated by the editorial board of journals like *Africa*, were more likely than not to write in English.

I should make it clear, though, that I am not elaborating a theory of linguistic determinism here. Indigenous-language authors in colonial Africa were not predestined, as it were, to engage in transcriptions of oral texts, to avoid political themes, and to privilege moralizing interpretations of the reality of their times. In its configuration during that period, the institutional framework for the production of vernacular literature in print did, however, serve to advance the interests of colonial discourses of the vernacular and to exclude voices overtly critical of colonial rule. It is difficult to conceive, for example, that a Henry Townsend, who worked so relentlessly to prevent the rise of 'native leadership' in the Anglican church in Yoruba land in the mid-19th century, but also invested heavily in the promotion of writing in Yoruba, would have accepted for publication texts that directly called into question the right of people like himself to exercise both religious and intellectual authority over educated Yoruba Christians.[51]

This is not to say that English-language writing by West Africans during or after the colonial period was neutral, and if that were possible, value-free.[52] The authors were, however, able to address subjects other than those considered acceptable by the self-appointed guardians of the standards of vernacular literacy in colonial Africa. We are after all talking about books, and the critical element to keep in mind here is that published literatures do not emerge *in vacuo*. As such, it is the institutional framework for the production of any literature that informs the possibility of adopting certain ideological positions. To the extent that some institutional frameworks promote the use of certain languages and not others, language may become an important factor in assessing the ideological biases of the texts selected for publication and which reach an eventual audience. But as I have attempted to argue in this chapter, such institutional constraints can lead just as easily to the yoking of indigenous-language writing with a politically progressive agenda, as they can lead in more reactionary directions. Texts in indigenous languages are not necessarily progressive any more than texts in non-native languages are necessarily reactionary. And for this reason, we cannot, I believe, explain the shift towards creative writing in English among some educated Africans in the later colonial period in West Africa except we give consideration to the ideological orientations of the infrastructure of vernacular-language publishing in colonial Africa.

Ironically enough, for the latter half of the 20th century, and after the formal end of colonial rule in much of Africa, literatures written in indigenous languages that were not at the same time regional lingua francas, remained just as vulnerable to political repression and manipulation as had been the case during the period of colonial rule. After Apartheid policies began to be implemented in South Africa in the mid-20th century, for example, writing in indigenous languages increased several fold as a result of the support extended to principles of vernacular literacy. With the heavy apparatus of state censorship encroaching upon all areas of cultural activity within the country, however, Gérard (1981: 215) describes the results of this phase in South African vernacular writing in measured tones as 'more prolific, though less objectionable.' Those who could not but be objectionable, and who refused to conform wrote in English or went into exile, where their works were henceforth read mostly in English translation. A similar trend developed between the 1980s and the 1990s in Madagascar, where opponents to the rule of Didier Ratsiraka like the writer Michèle Rakotoson, either went into exile and or turned away from writing in the indigenous language, Malagasy, to writing in French.[53] In the case of Nigeria, Olatunji (1993: 31–2) references the harassment from government officials suffered by two Yoruba language poets, Adebayo Faleti and Olarenwaju Adepoju who were critical of the authorities in poems that were disseminated through radio and records in the 1980s. One poet lost his job with the government while the other was briefly detained.[54] The most widely publicized recent illustration of this pattern in African writing also comes unfortunately from Africa's best known advocate for indigenous language writing since the 1980s, Ngugi wa Thiong'o, whose own Gikuyu language works were for many years mostly read in English translation because of political repression in his homeland while Arap Moi was in power (Gikandi, 1991: 166).

The general pattern in the availability of literary texts in different languages to African audiences has not changed much since the 1960s. By virtue of being accessible to select audiences across a variety of borders, texts in both indigenous and non-African lingua francas and languages of wider communication have proved less amenable to the constraints occasionally imposed by the political, religious and other cultural codes of any one locality. Thus, if an author's intention is specifically to evade censorship and repression, the objective is more easily attained by targeting dispersed audiences who share the same mother tongue or dispersed audiences who share a language of wider communication in common.[55] By contrast, literatures written in languages spoken mostly by native speakers living among other native speakers, have of necessity to be more respectful of local conventions and complicit with the predominant ideologies of the states and regions where these native speakers reside in order either to gain acceptance or to avoid repression.[56]

Already by the first decade of the 20th century, English-language journalists in a colony like Nigeria were conscious of the possibility of addressing themselves on issues of major interest to an audience larger than that of fellow compatriots and local British officials.[57] The pattern continued after independence in many postcolonial contexts, so that where creative works could reach readers and critics located in places other than those represented within the text, they have been more difficult to suppress completely despite the fact of not conforming to social expectations or being at variance with prevailing social and especially political norms. In contexts of repression by the state or other local agents, oppositional writing survives as acknowledged oppositional literature to the extent that it is able to reach a dispersed audience located beyond the bounds of the repressive activity of individual states and particular authorities. Whether or not such texts are originally written in a language of wider communication, they will most frequently be read and accessed in a language of wider communication.

Where as has most often been the case, the postcolonial African state was for political reasons unable to select an indigenous lingua franca, creative texts in indigenous languages that function mainly as vernaculars have tended to operate within a specific number of configurations. The most popular forms have been realized within the context of oral performance as poetry or drama. In other words, popular indigenous-language texts, which may or may not reflect modernizing tendencies, are in the African context most likely to be heard and viewed in performance rather than to be read as written text.[58] I think here of examples like radio and television poetry in Nigeria or the political poetry associated with opposition movements in South Africa towards the end of the Apartheid era and beyond. The authors of such texts do on occasion initiate criticism of the local authorities and adopt an oppositional stance in respect of the local power brokers, but often with an awareness that if the authorities decide on repression of the creative text, this can be more fully and completely accomplished than would be the case with authors working in languages widely spoken beyond the borders of a single state.

In general though, and irrespective of language, the kind of stylistically innovative and thematically oppositional creative writing that attracts commendation for its literary qualities is most often read by relatively small audiences of committed and highly educated specialists in any society. Where such texts succeed in reaching a wider public, it is generally through the process of being incorporated into the school curriculum which consecrates the text's stature as 'Literature.' And in this respect, it is helpful to keep in mind the peculiarity of the texts that we designate as 'Literature' and how they are to be differentiated from commercially-oriented creative writing.

To the extent that they exist as written and published texts addressing certain kinds of issues, serious prose works in indigenous languages face similar problems with serious European-language literatures in Africa. That is to say, they will probably not succeed in attracting a socially diverse local readership even among those who can read the language. With few exceptions, serious literature texts in indigenous African languages have thus far been commercial failures, in part because like some of the works produced in European languages, they do not constitute a popular literature.[59] It is not just that low-income workers in the cities and farmers in the rural areas do not read the classics of 'African Literature' because they are written in a European language. As the record thus far shows, such texts would generate an equally restricted readership had they been written in an indigenous African language. The expectation that 'African Literature,' as a corpus of innovative and non-commercial texts, would ever attract an extensive and socially diverse readership is one founded on a misapprehension of the function of non-commercial writing in any society. Commercially-oriented texts in both indigenous African and European languages have, on the other hand, succeeded in generating a significant readership given the prevailing levels of literacy.[60] The production of Literature is still a business undertaking from the perspective of publishers, and if serious prose works in indigenous African languages are to attract the kind of critical attention currently directed at African literatures in European languages, it will largely be thanks to a practice of systematic translation into major African and non-African languages which makes the publication of such texts a viable option for publishers and thus acknowledges that the production of Literature does not end with the activity of a lone writer who chooses to write in this language or the next.

And yet, notwithstanding the cultural politics of colonial rule, it was certainly not inevitable that direct criticisms of colonial rule in the African context should have been written mostly in European languages. There have been instances outside Africa, in predominantly monolingual states such as Japan and Korea, but also in former multilingual colonies that adopted an indigenous lingua franca, such as Malaysia and Indonesia, where the commitment to constructing new political and social structures found expression in an indigenous language. Nor can we attribute the reluctance of many writers to using indigenous languages for their reflections about African society after colonial rule solely to the multilingualism of the new African states aspiring to become nations. In my opinion, the failure of educated Africans to transform indigenous languages into the primary vehicles for articulating the challenges of postcolonial society derives mainly from the lengthy shelf life of a vision of African writing first postulated in colonial discourses of the vernacular: that is the tendency to equate indigenous-language activity with a vernacular literature, a literature in mother tongues instead of a literature produced in an indigenous lingua franca.

Those Africans who wrote in English, and in French, or Portuguese both before and after independence certainly believed in the common destiny of the diverse peoples who were to become citizens of newly formed states. They did not reject their own mother tongues, but since their primary loyalty lay with the nation-state in the process of formation, they wrote in the languages associated with the development of this new identity rather than foregrounding older identities. Thus, while it was technically possible in the Nigerian case to write in several indigenous languages, one can understand that writers whose primary concern was with representing the difficulties of nation-building in a multi-ethnic and multilingual setting might decline to affiliate closely with activities tending to privilege the distinctiveness of individual ethno-linguistic units at the expense of the larger nation-state.

There have of course been movements that produced a renaissance of writing in indigenous languages in other postcolonial contexts, but I think a close examination will confirm that in almost every instance, writers involved in such movements envisioned the indigenous language of their choice either as lingua franca of the putative nation-state,[61] or were in fact more committed to the sovereignty of the individual ethno-linguistic unit, and to a restoration of previously existing administrative structures, than to cause of the emergent multi-ethnic nation-state. Their involvement with indigenous language writing was propelled by a commitment to a particular vision of the polity to be created and not by devotion to the principle of writing in the vernacular as an end in itself. If citizens of the future state they envisioned spoke different mother tongues, it will frequently be the case that such writers promoted writing in an indigenous language because they considered the indigenous language of their choosing to be a suitable lingua franca for the new state. On the other hand, if they did specifically speak of their own writing in an indigenous language by reference to the significance of vernacular writing, it will be because the polity they had in mind was one constructed around people sharing the same mother tongue. In other words, writers who do not postulate shared mother tongue as a significant basis for creating political community rarely become consistent advocates for the production of a literature in the vernacular. In this regard, Africans who write in European languages are not exceptional, but typical. It was only natural for them to turn away from discourses of the vernacular since they held firmly to the conviction that Africans could not escape enduring political and economic subjugation without creating new states whose citizens would necessarily be multi-ethnic and multilingual.

In contemporary societies with relatively high levels of illiteracy, a vibrant practice of literary writing in indigenous languages can rarely be fostered in any case without the active intervention of the state which authorizes the use of specific languages in government and educational systems, oversees processes of standardization for the selected languages, and legitimizes a specific orthography. This initial activity generates potential authors and readers for written texts in the selected languages and makes publication of books in such languages a viable undertaking. But when, in a multilingual polity, indigenous language writing refers only to mother tongue writing, and to the affirmation of ethno-linguistic identities other than those associated with the nation-state, then it becomes a practice that is necessarily marginal to a vision of modernity closely aligned with the project of nation-state formation, which in terms of language policy at the early stages, almost always entails in multilingual settings the privileging of a lingua franca where one exists, or of a selected number of mother tongues, especially within the educational system, because the cost of supporting advanced literacy in all the languages spoken by citizens would be prohibitive.[62] In effect, where writing in any one indigenous language is not directly implicated in nation-state construction, the state declines to provide the educational infrastructure for advanced literacy in the language, without which reading, writing, and publication in indigenous languages cannot be sustained.

The result is that indigenous-language texts became the principal literatures of a modernity focusing on matters of state and the postcolonial condition mainly where the language used had become the lingua franca either of an emergent nation-state, or of significant regions within the nation-state.[63] At a very basic level, the financial impediments to providing instruction up to at least the secondary school level for all but a handful of the indigenous languages spoken in any one country meant that there were few opportunities for would-be readers and writers to hone their skills. Furthermore, written responses to the modernizing discourses emanating from the state were more likely to be produced in the same languages in which the official discourses of the state had been realized. The African experience then is no different from the Asian examples to which I alluded earlier where indigenous languages could become vehicles for responding to the affairs of the new polity precisely because such languages served as the official language of the state as nation, and therefore functioned as a lingua franca for the many ethnic groups that formed the state. As a rule, the language used by the nation-state in implementing policies of modernization and social change, or the languages used by local populations in dealing with the consequences of the establishment of new political structures supply in the creative sphere the principal media to be used in writing the most visible and acknowledged departures from practices considered customary and traditional. In instances where indigenous languages are not used as official lingua franca of the nation-state, and are thus disassociated from the larger project of modernization and hence from the quest for modernity, indigenous-language writing as a mother-tongue literature is more likely to be recuperated under the emblem of a 'tradition' whose own modernity is left in abeyance.

Ironically, those African writers and critics who favored writing in indigenous languages after independence continued to frame the language debate with the very same tropes introduced by colonial advocates of vernacular literacy, invoking condemnation of educated Africans for their acts of cultural treason, respect for the past, preservation of cultural heritage and preference for the mother tongue so that each community would have access to a literature written in its own language. The persistence of commitment to writing in a mother tongue rather than to writing in an indigenous lingua franca accounts, to my mind, for the widespread ambivalence towards the possibility of writing in indigenous languages on the part of an African artistic community largely committed to a vision of modernity requiring various forms of territorial integration.[64] But for as long as the emphasis of indigenous-language writing remains on writing in the mother tongue, which few African states can afford to support in a comprehensive fashion, those African authors who feel that their primary responsibility is to shoring up the defenses of weak nation-states perpetually under assault, will probably continue to write in languages like English and French.

Autonomous and unsubsidized indigenous-language literatures will also remain unachievable for all but a handful of African languages with a large enough base of both native and non-native speakers and literates.[65] Indeed, I think it is safe to say that in many African states, the existence of an unsubsidized practice of indigenous-language writing can be envisaged only to the extent that such writing emerges in an indigenous lingua franca, or in the language of a linguistic majority within the state and the region.[66] Published literatures are simply not self-sustaining and commercially viable for all language communities in a multilingual, postcolonial state, especially when language communities are relatively small, largely rural, with low incomes, low levels of literacy, and without established pre-colonial traditions of creative writing to fall back on. The encounter between an author's draft and an eventual audience is always highly mediated, and the written text does not become the published and the read text unless the conditions are feasible. The conditions at this time are such that the book, literary or not, in contemporary Africa is most frequently a text produced in European languages.[67] African indigenous-language writing has undoubtedly survived and even flourished particularly among majority or favored language groups in the former British colonies, and did in time experience a diversification of themes and styles. But even in such instances, a sense of ambivalence has not entirely dissipated about writing in languages over which mother tongue speakers supposedly have exclusive claim, and which do not apparently serve to strengthen the new 'national' bonds to which at least some segment of the educated population is committed. As written text, European-language works have therefore remained even after independence and almost everywhere on the continent, the preferred arena for enacting a modernity dealing with the aftermath of colonialism and the challenges confronting the postcolonial state.

Conclusion

Thus, the emergence of literary writing in English by the educated elite in southern Nigeria was not solely and primarily about the repression of indigenous languages by colonial officials and sundry Europeans. Indeed, as I have pointed out earlier, by the early 1940s when literary writing in English began to appear, a variety of written literatures in indigenous languages already existed and were reasonably popular among the literate section of the population.[68] There were, it is true, several other instances in colonial Africa where indigenous languages were completely excluded from the educational system, but what the southern Nigerian experience and also that of South Africa, suggests is that even in the absence of such exclusion, the form of resistance that developed to colonial rule in many of those colonies ultimately ensured that some form of literary writing by educated Africans would still emerge in European languages. In general then, the language choices made by local intelligentsias and groups of authors in response to colonial rule and other forms of subordination are a function of the specific emancipatory purposes pursued by individual activist associations and not simply of the familiarity and even competence of local populations with the language chosen. Historically, the concerns have been for distinctiveness in essentially monolingual states, and for unity in essentially multilingual states. This may require in the one instance purging a language of familiar 'foreign' terms, to be replaced with unfamiliar indigenous expressions, or in other instances, adopting a language with symbolic currency, spoken only by the most educated, and which may be the mother tongue of only a minority of people in the state.

Nor was the decision of educated West Africans to write in the language of the colonizer particularly about becoming English or dissolving cultural boundaries even though the development of African European-language literatures has often been read as a sign of the surrender of a culturally alienated elite to the culture of the colonizers, a sign of their complicity with the hegemony of Europe over various spheres of life in postcolonial Africa. But being accepted as equals with other British writers was not really an option for educated Africans by the early 1940s when writing in English started in the British West African colonies, and is even less so today. In fact it was the realization that they would never be accepted as British and treated as equals with the British in their own land that fueled the anti-colonial movement among local intelligentsias all over West Africa. Properly understood, the onset of creative writing in English by educated West Africans referenced a larger movement unfolding on several fronts at once, intended to counteract the efforts of colonial administrators and other Europeans present in the colony to strip educated Africans of any claim to make political demands on behalf of the larger African community, and to deny cultural validity to any African anti-colonial texts being produced in European languages.

My argument in this chapter has been that texts written in vernacular languages are not necessarily more autochthonous in character than those produced in non-native languages. As a matter of fact, in the British African colonies, the entire complex that emerged to service a vernacular literature – including advocacy on behalf of vernacular writing and education, transcription and translation work, the establishment of printing presses and translation bureaus, the selection of texts for publication – represents one of the early examples of active European intervention in the production of what was being presented as indigenous African culture. Let me go even further by affirming that there is nothing inherently 'natural' about the initial emergence and development of creative writing in any language, even if it is a native language. Indeed, the initial encounter with a literature supposedly written in one's own language, is always experienced as a moment of estrangement.[69] While the written and especially the published text generally exists at some remove from the spoken word, the perceived distance between the written text and its designated audience is even greater where written grammars have not yet begun to dictate the standards that govern acceptable forms of speech.

In the early stages, the idea of writing and reading in the vernacular or mother tongue is often to some degree a contradiction in terms. For, notwithstanding the atavistic premises on which advocacy for vernacular literacy is often predicated, such projects necessarily involve extensive processes of standardization and suppression of dialectal variants that result in situations where at least some of the designated beneficiaries are either unsettled by or do not even acknowledge the language of literacy to be their own mother tongue.[70] By postulating language shifts as inherently anomalous and deviations from the norm, many proponents of discourses of the vernacular deny the very processes of change to which they themselves contribute through the production of written grammars and ultimately literatures. Thus, while the disappearance of the speech forms of any community represents a regrettable diminishing of the world's cultural patrimony, I remain unconvinced that modification of language repertoires for the purposes of adapting to a changing world is by its very nature inimical to the best interests of any community.[71] The fact is, populations migrate, foreigners intrude, invade, and dominate, economies diversify and in the course of these very typical human experiences language repertoires are modified. As Eastman (1984: 260) has so succinctly put it: [c]hange happens,' and the most strongly entrenched vernaculars today have both benefited from and advanced such changes in language repertoires.

Defining local culture is, we need to keep in mind, always a matter of strategic functionality for different groups positioned in different ways at different points in time in relation to the local culture in question. Or to quote Chinua Achebe (1964: 55) again from his famous novel, *Arrow of God*: 'The world is like a mask dancing. If you want to see it well, you do not stand in one place.' How local culture is imagined usually depends on where one stands. Where cultural distinctiveness supplied the main argument for demanding equal rights under the law and greater political autonomy from within a single state, local elites in subordinated communities have thrown their support behind discourses of the vernacular. However, where cultural distinctiveness provided the basis for denying civic rights to communities located beyond the 'home' envisioned by the colonizer, local elites have been much less enthusiastic about discourses of the vernacular. In any case, since most states are multilingual and multi-ethnic in composition, the idea of a judiciously applied vernacular literacy often becomes at some point incompatible with the standardizing agenda pursued by many contemporary nation-states, especially in the earlier stages of nation-state formation. Sooner or later, in seeking to reconcile the reality of linguistic diversity with the desire to develop economies of scale, rulers in nation-states become, on matters of language, defenders of the ideal of the lingua franca. African elites after independence were no exception. Whether they were able to find an indigenous language to play this role, as happened in Tanzania, or eventually resorted to European languages, as happened in the majority of African states, political leaders have declined in practically every instance to implement a systematic policy of vernacular literacy.

Notes

1. See Appiah (1992: 53) for a reference to Sony Labou Tansi's recollections of his experiences in the schoolroom.
2. Such experiences have also been recorded in a variety of non-African contexts where attempts were made to suppress minority languages in favor of a local lingua franca in the educational system. Baron (1990: 164–5) lists examples from within France, Great Britain, Norway, Sweden, Turkey and the United States. As a native speaker of English in rural England, Simpson (1986: 5) likewise recalls his own memories of the schoolroom and painful efforts to master Received Pronunciation.
3. Although this position has been contested by several other linguists (see for example Dimmendaal, 1989), who argue that language does not always function as the most significant symbol of ethnicity, I have started here with Fishman's point of view since it is the major premise that informs the positions taken by most scholars of literature and cultural studies in their discussions of language and cultural activity in postcolonial contexts.
4. See Seton-Watson (1977) and Swietochowski (1991) on earlier language-based nationalisms in Eastern and Central Europe, Landau (1996), Perry (1999) on the post-Soviet Union, Brown (1992) on South Africa, Baron (1990) and Crawford (2000) on battles over English in the United States.
5. This is not to deny the constraints imposed by colonial systems on colonized elites. But as Zachernuk (2000: 184) remarks, 'To dismiss colonial intellectual life as merely dependent and derivative discourse misses the point. The ... colonial intelligentsia were also active, self-interested participants in the construction of Africanist knowledge ... And it is their creations and creativity – their inventiveness that need to be stressed, instead of continuing to stress their dependence.'
6. Several studies of the educated elite in Nigeria during the colonial period have

been written, including Smythe (1960), Ajayi (1965), Ayandele (1974), Cole (1975), Echeruo (1977), Mann (1985), Zachernuk (1991, 2000). Most of these studies have been produced by historians and are extremely helpful for tracing the various ideological shifts among the educated elite from the late 19th century to the 1960s. My work here draws upon these earlier studies, while focusing particularly on one of the discourses that contributed to the intellectual climate in which the educated elite operated in colonial Nigeria.

7. See Fajana (1982: 50–55), Omu (1978: 107-8), Awoniyi (1975: 62–7).
8. See for example Zachernuk (2000: 56–7), Ajayi (1965: 234–64), Ayandele (1966: 246–51).
9. See for example Ward (1941) The Provision of Vernacular Literature for Africa, *Oversea Education* 12 (4), 162–73; Vernacular Text-book Committees and Translation Bureaux in Nigeria, *Oversea Education* 3 (1931), 30–3.
10. Much of the work published on Westermann has been written in German and for this reason is probably inaccessible to those scholars in African studies who work primarily in English or French. For example, Onovoh's (1998) discussion of one of Westermann's publications provides useful material on Westermann's cultural politics from the point of view of African studies, shedding light for example on the connections between his professional activities in language studies and his involvement with Nazism, but since this book too is written in German, it may go unnoticed in future evaluations of Westermann's impact on African language studies among scholars writing in English and French.
11. See for example, Zachernuk (2000: 105), Omu (1978: 188), Perham (1960: 593), and Fajana (1982: 121)
12. In actual fact, it was often impossible in areas of significant linguistic diversity to adhere rigidly to this position in providing formal education. In northern Nigeria, for example, most of the government activity on behalf of the 'vernacular' was concentrated around a single language, Hausa, since there were well over a hundred vernaculars spoken in some areas of the region (Paden, 1968: 203). The fact that government officials and missionaries worked so readily with the lingua franca where systematic mother tongue literacy was impracticable makes their insistence on the corrupting effects of 'foreign' languages all the more suspect within the context of colonial West Africa.
13. Such views rapidly became commonplace among educated Africans particularly when they belonged to somewhat larger ethnic groups whose language was not being considered as a possible lingua franca. In colonial Uganda, for example, representatives of the Baganda resisted the introduction of Kiswahili, a 'foreign' language, but not of English, which was no doubt equally and perhaps more foreign (Gorman, 1974: 419). The Gikuyu in Kenya were likewise opposed to the wider dissemination of Kiswahili at the expense of their own vernacular (Whiteley, 1956: 347). And since, with few exceptions, educated Africans have continued to direct interest in indigenous languages towards mother tongues rather than towards indigenous lingua francas, European languages have remained and been strengthened in their position as the major languages of wider communication among Africa's educated elite.
14. The connection between the discourse on vernacular literacy and a certain conception of 'Native education' was not merely fortuitous, and does lead back to a distrust of the educated African. Westermann is once more a useful source of information. Speaking about the education of Africans, Westermann (1934: 221)

recommended that 'their education should be as little as possible a matter of book-learning, but a training that will suit the needs of the future peasant or craftsman.' In Kenya in the 1920s, a representative of the British settlers both echoed and anticipated Westermann when he declared that he could not conceive of a more incongruous situation than that 'we should introduce the language (English) to large numbers of people, ... whose proper education is to work in the fields ...' (Gorman, 1974: 417). Similar views evidently formed the basis for Apartheid South Africa's later emphasis on vernacular literacy in its program of Bantu education. In a well-known statement, one of the main spokespersons for this policy, Dr Henrik Verwoerd, criticized earlier education programs which 'drew [the native child] away from his own community and misled him by showing him the green pastures of European society in which he is not allowed to graze'; appropriate education, he suggested, 'must train and teach people in accordance with their opportunities in life...' (Gérard, 1971: 89). Commenting specifically on the West African situation, Fajana (1982: 137) has explained the origins of such proposals for practical African education in the early 20th century from the Tuskegee experiment and plans for agricultural education for African-Americans in the United States. At the same time, Westermann like other proponents of vernacular literacy mentioned here, was highly critical of educated Africans, writing that 'the 'primitive' African is not uneducated. Many Africans, men and women, who have never been to school nor in contact with Europeans, show such dignified and tactful behaviour, and refinement in what they say and do that they well deserve to be called 'educated'. On the other hand, 'uneducated behaviour is at times met with among people who for years have been under intensive European influence and in schools conducted by Europeans' (1934: 206).

15. Naturally, this activity too would be carried out under European supervision. Westermann (1934: 251) declared: 'The task of creating an interest in the heritage of the past and producing a vernacular literature cannot be left to the Natives alone. The white man must take the lead.'

16. Even in Francophone West Africa, where the discourse on vernacular literacy had far less appeal, a similar division of labor apparently came into effect in anthropological circles. Thus, the Malian writer, Hampâté Bâ eventually turned to creative writing in French in order to find possibilities for self-expression beyond that of the almost invisible native informant that he had played for many years as an assistant to French anthropologists (see Aggarwal's analysis of Bâ's professional trajectory). Somewhat similar considerations animated the discussions on African philosophy that took place among African philosophers during the 1970s, and best represented by Paulin Hountondji's well-known work, *Sur la philosophie africaine*. In that instance too, there were concerns about finding a space where the educated African could transcend the role of native informant, functioning instead as an individual among peers in the theorizing of African philosophy.

17. To consider a few examples from southern Nigeria, chiefs in Bonny sent a letter to missionaries in Liverpool as far back as 1848 requesting teachers to provide instruction in English for their children (Ajayi, 1965: 56). Parents in such communities had minimal interest in either the religious instruction or the vernacular literacy that the missionaries proposed. And so when missionaries began providing instruction in the vernacular in Efik communities also in the southeast, school attendance actually suffered a decline (Zachernuk, 2000: 25).

Colonial Encounters and Discourses of the Vernacular 41

The situation was not much different in Yoruba-speaking territory, also in southern Nigeria, once schools began to be established. Much against the desire of the missionaries, the parents demanded the teaching of English (Awoniyi, 1975: 50). Parents who consented to receive adult literacy lessons in Yoruba insisted on English-language instruction for their own children (Awoniyi, 1975: 54). And in Fajana's words (1982: 55), the desire to learn English may have been the sole incentive for even attending school in this period. Finally, when Yoruba officials took over the educational system as from 1952, a full eight years before independence, they encouraged research into the Yoruba language, but did not make it the compulsory language of instruction even though it was the mother tongue in large sections of what was then called the Western region. Indeed, according to Awoniyi (1975: 136–7), in an initial period, the syllabus actually made greater provision for the teaching of English than the teaching of Yoruba.

18. Though the Igbo of southern Nigeria represent perhaps an extreme case in terms of their desire for English, their experience is relevant, especially since many of the early and later Nigerian novelists writing in English have been Igbo. Writing about their response to missionary education, Ayandele (1966: 292) reports: 'Outwardly the pupils conformed to the compulsory routine of worship at school but only wanted English education. Outside the school the children neglected the vernacular Bible and literature. Ibo children went to the extent of complaining to the C.M.S. that they had enough religious instruction in the church and Sunday schools and wanted to have no more of it at school. Thus, much against their intention, the C.M.S. had to provide English education to Iboland so that they might not lose ground to the Roman Catholics and contact with the people.'

19. *Omenuko*, written by the Igbo writer Pita Nwana, and published in 1933 won the competition as did *Ogbójú Ode Nínú Igbó Irúnmalè*, published in 1938 and written by the Yoruba author, Daniel Fagunwa. Both novels were widely read within their respective language communities and reissued several times over (see Lindfors, 1982: 3, and Emenyonu, 1978: xiv, 33). Such was the popularity of Fagunwa's novels among the Yoruba that Lindfors (1982: 13) claims that he may have been 'the author with the largest reading audience in Africa . . .' The success of these novels certainly confirms the existence of a viable readership for creative writing in some of the indigenous languages of southern Nigeria, particularly during the colonial period.

20. Creative writing in English emerged from two centers at once in southern Nigeria, one tradition was associated with elementary school graduates in the city of Onitsha in southeastern Nigeria, and the other with graduates of the newly founded University of Ibadan in southwestern Nigeria. These college graduates form the nucleus of the group that I describe here as the educated elite, and it is their move towards writing in English that I would like to focus on in the rest of this chapter.

21. Ngugi may have had few models to turn to when he first attempted prose writing in Gikuyu in the 1970s, but this was certainly not the case for Igbo and Yoruba writers from southern Nigeria from the 1930s onwards. This fact is significant when we consider the fact that southern Nigerian writers account for an important proportion of contemporary African literary writing in English.

22. Literary histories of southern Nigeria will often mention for example, the founding of the first Yoruba newspaper, *Iwe Irohin* founded by the British C.M.S. missionary, Henry Townsend in 1849 in the city of Abeokuta. But liter-

ary scholars usually fail to locate Townsend in the context of his politics. Such omissions undermine our full understanding of the circumstances surrounding his activities on behalf of vernacular writing. In Townsend's case, the circumstances do include his relentless opposition to the promotion of educated Africans to positions of leadership in the church hierarchy. His lengthy battle against the promotion of Samuel Crowther, an African, to the position of Bishop of the Niger, which eventually translated into a lifelong battle against the Crowther family and children is well documented. See for example Ajayi (1965: 180-96). In such circumstances, it is easy to see why educated Africans could not always readily associate themselves with the vernacular initiatives of the missionaries in the colonial period.

23. See, for example, Fajana (1982: 121), Omu (1978: 219–20).
24. Hanns Vischer, another foundational member of the IALC, and fellow traveler with Lugard in northern Nigeria in the early 20th century, was likewise a proponent of education suited to the circumstances of the natives. As first Director of Education in northern Nigeria, Vischer tried to ensure that the northern Nigerians would not become exposed to the corrupting influence of radical southern Nigerians, who had been 'miseducated' in the missionary schools. He developed a curriculum for northern Nigerians placing emphasis on acquisition of vocational skills and instruction in the vernacular. As late as the 1970s, scholars of education from southern Nigeria were still heaping criticism on the 'racial educational theories' of both Lugard and Vischer. (See Fajana, 1982: 111–18).
25. In another example of this line of thinking, Hugh Clifford, who succeeded Lugard as Governor of Lagos Colony, mocked the political aspirations of the local intelligentsia, declaring in an often-quoted 1920 speech: 'It can only be described as farcical to suppose that... continental Nigeria can be represented by a handful of gentlemen who in the safety of British protection have peacefully pursued their studies . . . whose eyes are fixed, not upon African native history or traditions or policy, nor upon their own tribal obligations and duties to Natural Rulers . . . but upon political theories evolved by Europeans to fit a wholly different set of circumstances, arising out of peoples who have arrived at a wholly different stage of civilization' (Zachernuk, 1991: 153–4).
26. In fact, writes Omu (1978:189), Lugard came to the conclusion that 'education had not brought happiness or contentment to Nigeria if the performance of the newspapers was taken as criterion.'
27. This was revealed by Lugard (cited in Westermann,1934: ix).
28. And thus, when Westermann evoked the possibility of the Native 'speaking for himself', he was thinking primarily of the native informant (1934: 15) who would provide the European anthropologist with material for study. He was, by contrast, much less enthusiastic about the opinions of educated Africans whom he described as lacking in leadership qualities (1934: 298).
29. See for example, Gérard (1971: 382; 1981: 176–8); Michelman (1995); Sanneh (1993: 77); Zabus (1991: 25). Ngugi (1981a: 26), too, comments on the activities of the missionaries, though he does not specify whether these are Protestant missionaries working in British colonies.
30. I am thinking here in particular of colonization in the Americas.
31. In the early 20th century, Associationism, which involved greater respect for local cultures and partly inspired British policies of Indirect Rule, tended to supplant Assimilation as the preferred mode of operation among French colo-

nial administrators. The impracticability of implementing assimilation where a large proportion of the indigenous population had survived may be one reason among others for this shift in thinking.
32. For example, Westermann (1934: 259), like many other Africanists writing about native education, believed that development could not occur in the African community except some Africans, at the very least, had access to advanced Western education and mastered English. At the same time, because instruction in European languages 'constituted one of the powerful disintegrating factors in African life' (1934: 260), the teaching of European languages was to be discouraged particularly at the elementary level, which was as much education as Westermann considered adequate for most Africans. In other words, the gap between civilizations would be maintained to the extent that his African contemporaries remained faithful to their vernacular languages.
33. Apartheid South Africa's support for vernacular literacy for Blacks is not incompatible with the legislation requiring instruction in Afrikaans that sparked the Soweto uprising of 1976. In 'South Africa' as defined by the Apartheid authorities, instruction was to be in Afrikaans, while in the Black homelands, education would continue to be provided in the Black vernaculars. The problem of course was that townships like Soweto were not located in homelands.
34. In Accra, Ghana for example, Ga, the language of the indigenous inhabitants of Accra, also known as Ga, was selected as the language for mother tongue instruction. Although the Ga remain one of the largest, if not the largest single ethnic group in Accra, there has been a steady influx of people of other ethnicities into Ghana's largest city throughout the 20th century so that by 1960, the Ga constituted only 54% of the inhabitants of central Accra (Kropp Dakubu, 1997: 46). In some neighborhoods populated mainly by migrants to Accra, Ga was the mother tongue of only 36% of the children in selected elementary schools. Not only was Ga not the mother tongue for most children in schools in this area, the majority of teachers since the 1970s were themselves not Ga and some had only limited proficiency in the language (Kropp Dakubu, 1997: 64-5). To the extent that the policy of using Ga was actually implemented by some teachers, instruction was occurring in an indigenous language which may or may not have been familiar to many students and teachers, but it certainly was not mother tongue instruction by any stretch of the imagination. Such are the inconsistencies of indigenous language policies based on discourses of the vernacular and their tendency to construct static relationships between individual mother tongues and individual territories. I think it certainly makes sense to encourage instruction in Ga even among the children of migrants to Accra, since it is a language that is widely spoken in Accra and will ultimately prove useful to the students. However, the failure to acknowledge that this is not in fact mother tongue education only serves to further perpetuate the kind of confusion on which some discourses of the vernacular thrive. Once we begin to recognize that 'mother tongue education' is often in contemporary urban African settings instruction in a second or third language, we might be in a better position to begin to assess the wider implications of turning to indigenous and non-native languages of wider communication in Africa apart from the sole perspectives emphasizing cultural imperialism under colonial rule.
35. Wright (1991: 54) notes for example how in the French colonies in the early decades of the century, policies for colonial cities provided French architects

and urban planners with an opportunity to find solutions for problems that afflicted French cities. She further observes (1991: 135): 'Between the two world wars Morocco provided a foil to architecture and urbanism in France. One textbook on urban design compared Casablanca, Paris, and Marseille on the same terms, without suggesting that the North African example was in any way distinct.' This to my mind represents a way of conceptualizing space in both the metropolis and the colony that does not highlight the disjunctions between these spaces to the same extent that we find in British colonial policies.

36. I think here for example of the connections between Czech language movements and the development of Czech nationalism (see Seton-Watson, 1977: 150–4) or the symbolic importance of the Irish language for Irish nationalists (see Edwards, 1985: 53–65).

37. In the Irish case, Edwards (1985: 55) notes, for example, that members of the organizations founded to revive and protect Irish were often 'upper-middle-class individuals.' The same observation would be valid for Africa where advocates of vernacular literacy are often highly-educated scholars and other professionals.

38. Edwards (1985: 47–98) provides useful summaries of many instances of language shift where communities no longer speak the language of their forbears, but retain a sense of distinct identity. Brenzinger et al. (1991) discuss related issues with specific reference to African examples. M. Kropp Dakubu's (1997) discussion of language repertoires in Accra, Ghana, offers one of the most up-to-date accounts of the very dynamic language situation in urban West Africa where polyglottism is the rule and children frequently acquire competence in languages that are not the mother tongues of their parents and in which their parents have limited or no competence. In extreme cases, children actually have as a mother tongue a language that is not the language of either of their parents.

39. See Paden (1968: 204–5). And indeed, far from investing in mother tongue literacy, as Paden points out, political parties in northern Nigeria for example, sought to extend the use of a single language, Hausa, as part of a policy of 'northernization' that was to strengthen them in their competition for power with parties based in southern Nigeria.

40. Most of the nationalist movements that developed in the latter years of the colonial period were territorial in orientation, though there have been language-based nationalisms in Africa, such as that of the Oromo (see Bulcha, 1997), and of the Afrikaner (Webb & Kriel, 2000). A resurgence of language-based nationalism across the continent cannot be ruled out for the future, as an expression of growing disenchantment with current political arrangements.

41. Writing in 1949, another Nigerian writer, T. M. Aluko (1949: 1239) likewise identified the opposition to writing in the vernacular as 'nationalist' though he himself declined to take a firm position in that article on whether or not West Africans should write in their mother tongues. As we now know, Aluko, who was Yoruba, subsequently went on to write novels in English. Similar positions were taken by some advocates of English in India who proposed English as the only possible pan-Indian and therefore 'national' language because it imposed an equal handicap on learners from all regions of the country, unlike Hindi, the favored indigenous lingua franca which put southern Indians at a disadvantage (Rajan, 1992: 14–15). Given the widespread publicity generated by Ngugi's decision to begin writing in a mother tongue in the 1970s, it is worth pointing out that some scholars specifically credit the Gikuyu, Ngugi's ethnic group,

with advancing the fortunes of English as lingua franca in Kenya in the last years of the struggle against colonialism as a strategy of the nationalist movement after having initially embraced vernacular literacy as a form of resistance (Gérard, 1981: 308–11). Gikandi (1996: xix) confirms this state of affairs in his recollection of growing up in a part of central Kenya where the population was fiercely anti-colonial, but also at the same time desired education in English for its children.

42. It is thus not surprising that Walter Bgoya, a leading authority on African publishing, and who is himself Tanzanian, showed much less enthusiasm for the Kiswahili policy than most other African observers of the Tanzanian case who tended to speak of Kiswahili in Tanzania as if it were a mother tongue. Writing in 1996, he remarked, 'A policy, for example, that is unspoken in Tanzania but which is there all the same would sacrifice all languages in favor of Swahili. This is an unacceptable policy that cannot be defended, precisely because no argument, no matter how dressed up – national, progressive, or revolutionary – can justify the loss of any language' (1996: 172). This is a reminder of the fact that even in Tanzania, there are those who still hold strongly to the ideal of a vernacular literacy rather than a literacy based on the lingua franca.

43. Writing about Indonesia, Anderson (1991: 134) remarked, 'Thirty years ago, almost no Indonesians spoke bahasa Indonesia as his or her mother-tongue; virtually everyone had their own "ethnic" language . . . Today there are perhaps millions of young Indonesians, from dozens of ethnolinguistic backgrounds, who speak Indonesian as their mother-tongue.'

44. British policies and official statements on the subject of language of instruction varied not only from colony to colony, but also from one decade to the next. Gorman (1974), for example, provides a detailed account of the continual shifts in direction of the language policy in Kenya under colonial rule. In early 20th-century East Africa, the decision was to use the regional lingua franca, Kiswahili, in what was then Tanganyika (Gérard, 1981: 134), to promote a few vernacular languages and English in Uganda, while in Kenya '[m]any Europeans settlers regarded the teaching of the English language to "natives" as a potentially subversive force. Social distance between master and subject had to be maintained through linguistic distance' (Mazrui & Mazrui, 1998: 141). Thus we find in the East African sub-region at the same time, support for mother tongue instruction, for an indigenous lingua franca, and also for English. We also find changes over time since the initial support for an indigenous lingua franca in most of the sub-region and for vernacular literacy in Kenya eventually gave way to policies favoring instruction in English by the 1940s. Likewise in colonial India according to both Pennycook (1998) and Viswanathan (1989), where the debate raged for some time among British officials on the language of instruction, both partisans of Orientalism who favored emphasis on vernacular literacy and the Anglicists who supported instruction in English were equally complicit in the project of colonial rule. Based on British practice in Africa, I certainly agree with Pennycook (1998: 93) when he argues that we cannot assume that imposition of and instruction in English was the sole policy in matters of language in the British colonies.

45. But we must understand what this education signified within the context of discussions about vernacular literacy in the British African colonies. With their university degrees mostly in the humanities and European literary studies, early Nigerian writers like Achebe, John Pepper Clark, Flora Nwapa, Christo-

pher Okigbo, Wole Soyinka, Gabriel Okara and others represented just the kind of educated African despised by European proponents of vernacular literacy. Furthermore, by writing in English and producing works that were not transcriptions of traditional oral texts, these writers were projecting a vision of what local culture could be in a postcolonial society that was unlike the ideal cultivated by European supporters of vernacular literacy. Achebe, for one, was clearly aware of the antipathy felt by some Europeans towards educated Africans. A full 15 years after Nigeria became independent, he was still speaking about the colonial attitude towards educated Africans. In this connection, he remarked: 'To the colonialist mind it was always of utmost importance to be able to say: I know my natives... Meanwhile a new situation was slowly developing as a handful of natives began to acquire European education and then to challenge Europe's presence and position in their native land with the intellectual weapons of Europe itself... Now did this mean that the educated native was no different at all from his brothers in the bush? Oh no! He was different, he was worse. His abortive effort at education and culture though leaving him totally unredeemed and unregenerated had nonetheless done something to him – it had deprived him of his links with his own people whom he no longer even understood and who certainly wanted none of his dissatisfaction or pretensions...' (1975: 5).

46. The attention given to translating proverbs and other local idioms, in addition to generally representing indigenous languages using English clearly suggests this.

47. I am mindful here of Barber's objections raised in her 1995 article on African-Language writing where she criticized the tendency among critics using the postcolonial lens to present vernacular-language literatures in Africa as an extension of oral traditions and to equate literatures in European languages with the expression of modernity. And yet, I would argue, such perceptions are not limited to contemporary critics working with postcolonial theories in mind. On the one hand, early authors and producers of indigenous-language texts in colonial Africa self-consciously styled themselves as renovators of tradition, and to that extent they saw themselves as advocates of modernity. And yet, they also saw themselves as custodians of tradition and were thus following in the very paths anticipated by European advocates of vernacular literacy.

48. I trust that readers are sufficiently familiar with examples of this trend in world literature, from Biblical writing to *Beowulf* among many others. In the Yoruba language, following the success of Fagunwa's novels, several other authors adopted the same narrative structure that he had used, which was loosely based on the Yoruba folktale (Bamgbose, 1974: 5). Gérard (1981) records a similar preoccupation with transcription and preservation of traditional lore in the earliest indigenous-language texts produced in other parts of West and Southern Africa. More recently, Williamson's (1993) survey of minority-language publications in Nigeria revealed that out of a total of 117 minority languages with publications, only 40 had produced any publications in creative literature. Of these 40 languages, only three, Ibibio, Idoma and Efik had more publications of what Williamson described as 'modern' literature than of 'traditional' literature, including folktales, transcriptions and the like. These trends have even crossed over into film so that a preoccupation with traditional values and with traditional verbal arts remains an important component of contemporary Yoruba-language film in Nigeria.

49. Olatunji cites as follows Barber's assessment of Fagunwa: 'The values emphasized by Fagunwa have been described by Karin Barber . . . as solidly conservative bourgeois.' These values coincided with those emphasized by the missionaries in order 'to maintain the status quo and promote the smooth functioning of the colonial machinery.' Bambgose (1974: 24–8) too notes the strong Christian element in Fagunwa's narratives. By contrast, one of the authors of Onitsha market literature complained that the moralizing and religious references in his work had been removed by the publisher before publication (Dodson, 1973: 183–4).
50. A case in point: Fagunwa's first, and highly successful novel, *Ogbójú Ode Nínú Igbó Irúnmalè*, was first published by a missionary press belonging to The Church Missionary Society. See Westley (1992) and Peires (1979) for further references to missionary interference with the subject matter of vernacular writing.
51. I refer readers back to note 22 of this chapter for some further information on Townsend.
52. For example, Dodson (1973) shows clearly that the publishers of the mainly English language Onitsha chapbooks had their own agenda. Even though Dodson's research on the publishers of Onitsha market literature was carried out in the early 1970s, I believe the findings are valid for the period before the 1960s. For his part, Moore (2002) discusses efforts made starting from the early 1960s by the CIA to cultivate the friendship of African writers, many of them writing in English as part of the ideological battle being waged against the Soviet Union. By providing an outlet for artists to express themselves and at least some of the funding for the activities of African writers and artists during the 1960s, the Transcription Centre in London, which was the locus of these activities, became one of many gatekeepers for African writers, enabling certain kinds of authors to achieve public recognition for their work.
53. In the words of Michèle Rakotoson (1994: 11–12): 'Pour ceux qui, à partir des années quatre-vingt, se mirent à écrire en français, qu'il s'agisse de Jean-Luc Raharimanana, de Charlotte Rafenomanjato ou de l'auteur de ces lignes, ce choix revenait à s'inscrire dans une tradition de contestation. Madagascar avait, à l'époque, opté pour une malgachisation radicale, l'île s'était renfermée sur elle-même et l'idéologie 'socialiste' tendait à nier l'individu. Ecrire en français, c'était réclamer la liberté d'expression dans une langue librement choisie, affirmer le droit de parler de soi-même.' 'Those who from the 1980s began to write in French, whether it was Jean-Luc Raharimanana, Charlotte Rafenomanjato, or the author of these lines, were identifying themselves with a tradition of contestation. At that time, Madagascar had opted for a radical policy of promoting the Malagasy language and for the socialist ideology. The island had become too withdrawn and inward looking. The socialist ideology tended to disregard the individual. Writing in French was a way of reclaiming freedom of speech in a language freely chosen, of affirming the right to speak of oneself.' (My translation).
54. These two were certainly not the only verbal artists ever persecuted by successive Nigerian governments, but had the government so desired, it could have more effectively stopped the circulation of their works than would have been the case with texts produced in or translated into languages of wider communication.
55. I am speaking here primarily about the effective circulation of the author's texts.

No matter what language he or she writes in, the author can become a victim of imprisonment or torture under a repressive regime. But the probability that his or her texts will continue to be read, does in large part depend on their being made available in a language read beyond the borders of the state in which the author has been imprisoned. When those in power stop the circulation of a text written in a language spoken only within the national borders, and untranslated into other languages, they effectively prevent the text from functioning as a work of literature. I refer readers to the comparative fates of two Malagasy authors during the colonial period, Jean-Joseph Rabearivelo who wrote in French and Ny Avana Ramanantoanina who wrote in Malagasy. Both were critical of colonial rule in different ways. French repression of the movement to which Ny Avana belonged was so successful during the colonial period that his publications remained out of print until the late 1980s even within Madagascar, and were largely unknown elsewhere in the world. By contrast, Rabearivelo went on to become a famous national and international author, who continued to be read. See Adejunmobi (1994; 1996) for details.

56. Writing for example about Yoruba drama in the 1970s, Adéèkó (1998: 68) observes: 'Overtly ideologically engaged drama has never been a strong point for the Yorùbá-language theater companies, which, unlike the university-based and state-supported elite English-language groups, must always be concerned with box-office earnings.' Although Adéèkó specifically refers to the commercial dimension, he also describes both university-based troupes and state-supported activity as a single type. I would like to suggest that university-based productions, which, through publication could reach different kinds of audiences within and outside Nigeria, were frequently more overtly political than state-supported dramas created for 'cultural festivals' and television. The point in any case is that texts dependent financially and otherwise on a single and highly localized type of audience can often ill afford to be excessively experimental and critical of the status quo.

57. When for example, a bill was passed in 1902 restricting freedom of the press, local newspaper editorials began addressing their appeals to '"all lovers of freedom" in England and elsewhere who had always championed "the cause of the down-trodden and oppressed in Africa"' (Omu, 1978: 179). By the 1940s, West African journalists were sending delegations to Britain to submit proposals for independence directly to the British government (Omu, 1978: 247).

58. Thus, many African indigenous-language texts have been written, but few are accessed primarily in written form. As a performance, the Luganda play, *Oluyimba lwa Wanoko* by the Ugandan, Byron Kawadwa, remains popular with Ugandan audiences, but is published only in the English-language version (see Ntangaare, 2001). Four of the chapters in Bodunde's (2001) edited volume on African-language literature in the 1990s refer to live drama and poetry forms. In Adejunmobi (1998), I discuss other instances of works written in indigenous African languages but published and read only in European-language versions because there are limited possibilities for publishing in those languages. In Adejunmobi (1996), I also refer to texts originally published in indigenous languages, but which have been out of print for several decades and are to all intents and purposes inaccessible for any kind of audience.

59. See Adejunmobi (1994) for a discussion of some examples of this trend in African publishing.

60. Chakava (1988) provides information on sales of popular fiction, African-

language titles, transcriptions of oral literature, books by Ngugi wa Thiong'o, and co-edited books in Kenya between 1985 and early 1987 by Heinemann Kenya. The figures for sales of three of the four popular literature titles listed were in the thousands compared to sales in the hundreds and less for the other types of publications.
61. In India for example, the interest shown by nationalists in Hindustani towards the end of the colonial period had more to do with their desire to promote the language as lingua franca of the future state than with any commitment to mother tongues as such (see Das Gupta and Gumperz, 1968: 157–63).
62. Ethiopia offers an early and controversial model of privileging one language (Amharic) and marginalizing other mother tongues (see Bulcha, 1997). For brief periods in time, Sudan pursued a similar policy with Arabic (see Miller, 1986). Tanzania, meanwhile, serves as a more recent example of the deliberate promotion of a 'national' language, in this case, Kiswahili.
63. I am not suggesting here that indigenous-language texts are irretrievably bereft of modernity. There is no doubt that many indigenous-language texts in Africa today deal with contemporary concerns and exhibit stylistic novelty. It is true, however, that texts produced in the languages of the state and especially of its school system (whether such languages are African or non-African) are more likely to be perceived as effectively contributing to the advent and construction of modernity.
64. But since the colonial period, advocacy on behalf of indigenous languages has been most appealing to local intelligentsias in Africa when it was linked to projects for modernization. I think here for example of the Vy Vato Sakelika movement in colonial Madagascar which supported writing in Malagasy, and looked to Japan as a model for modernization that did not require giving up local identity. (See Adejunmobi 1996 for further details on this movement).
65. The Executive Council of the IALC acknowledged as much in a 1928 article: 'a small language cannot maintain a [written] literature except by artificial means ... The only alternatives are either a vernacular literature in a limited number of important languages, or no vernacular literature at all' (1928: 19). Yet scholars, administrators, and missionaries continued to speak in other publications as if vernacular literatures were possible for all African languages, largely I would suggest because of the ideological significance that the idea of vernacular literacy had come to assume as a means for countering growing anti-colonial agitation among educated Africans. Their main objective of course was to discredit the politically-motivated writings in English by educated Africans. Writing almost 70 years later, Altbach (1999: 4) drew a similar conclusion about African countries, noting 'Only a few countries have languages spoken by large enough segments of the population ... to support a viable publishing industry.' The interesting fact though, is that in the past 30 to 40 years, indigenous lingua francas have begun to emerge in several African states. I think here of Wolof in Senegal, Dyula in Ivory Coast, Twi in southern Ghana, Pidgin in southern Nigeria and Western Cameroon, Sango in Central African Republic, Lingala and Kiswahili in Congo, and Kiswahili in Tanzania and Kenya, to name a few. However, few writers have committed themselves to developing written literatures in those languages in those states, probably because most continue to envision indigenous-language literature principally as a mother tongue literature.
66. To take a few examples of unsubsidized indigenous-language writing from

around sub-Saharan Africa today, Hausa and Yoruba are the languages of majority ethnic groups in Nigeria. Kiswahili, especially in Tanzania, but also increasingly in Kenya is a lingua franca. Amharic formerly occupied a similar position in Ethiopia, and though non-Amhara groups are now challenging the prominence of Amharic, the language still benefits from a pre-existing infrastructure which supported writing in Amharic.

67. Altbach (1999: 1) confirms this: 'The large majority of books published in Africa appear in English, French, Portuguese, or other non-African languages.'
68. In attributing the emergence of European-language literatures in Africa solely to repression of indigenous languages by colonial authorities, we have tended to generalize based in particular on accounts by Francophone authors and Anglophone writers like Ngugi wa Thiong'o. My suggestion is that the situation may have been somewhat more complex than is usually acknowledged, no doubt involving repression in some cases, but also deliberate choice in others.
69. I owe this insight to Vicente Rafael who made the comment in response to my presentation of a draft of this chapter at a conference on language and the nation at UCLA in June 2002.
70. This is to be expected especially in dispersed non-urban communities where extremely divergent dialects of the same language are in use, since the introduction of vernacular literacy will often involve processes of standardization of the language, adoption of orthographies, dissemination through schooling, compiling of dictionaries, that may unfold over several generations. During that time, and even afterwards, there are many in the language community who may not recognize the standard form as their own mother tongue. The long search of the C.M.S. missionaries for a pre-existing Igbo standard during the 19th century is a case in point. Samuel Crowther, from Sierra Leone determined that the so-called 'Isuama' dialect, based on the form spoken by Igbo receptives in Sierra Leone constituted 'proper Ibo' (Bersselaar, 1997: 277). However, attempts to communicate with communities in Igbo territory using what was supposedly the people's language encountered considerable resistance (Hair, 1967: 75, 94). And when eventually, a new standard was constructed for the Igbo in the early 20th century by the missionaries, people in some Igbo-speaking areas such as Onitsha, refused to accept this language which was supposedly 'their' language, because, according to a C.M.S. missionary, the average man 'was fondly clinging to the absurd idea that his dialect is not Ibo at all, but a distinct language' (Bersselaar, 1997: 285). A century later, an Igbo standard has come into existence, thanks in part to the work of missionaries which enabled communities separated from each other by considerable distances to begin communicating using a language that they did not initially recognize as their own.
71. Although this book is not largely devoted to questions of language in education, I should state, for the avoidance of all doubt, and given the arguments that I have advanced thus far, that to the extent that is financially possible, I feel that instruction at the elementary level should start in a language in which a majority of students already have some competence. However, it is important to recognize that in the emergent multilingual and polyglot communities of the contemporary world, the language in which the greatest number of students has some proficiency may not necessarily be a mother tongue. Furthermore, if the aim of formal education is to equip students for effective participation in a multilingual society, if not on the international stage, education that does not at

some point begin to provide students with a strong basis in at least a regional language of wider communication, must be recognized as leaving students with significant disadvantages for integration into the newer sodalities which may be essential to their future attainment of some degree of self-sufficiency in the present age.

Chapter 2
African Literature, European Languages and Imaginations of the Local

I begin in this chapter with an account by the critic, Russell Hamilton, of a conversation he witnessed in Mozambique not long after the country gained independence. Hamilton recalls:

> In May of 1979, José Craveirinha, the celebrated Mozambican poet and I were returning to Maputo after a short visit to Swaziland. The driver of our government-owned Land Rover was a young Mozambican soldier, in civilian dress. A few minutes after crossing the border we stopped at one of those ubiquitous military checkpoints where a guard, barely out of his teens, asked to see our papers. The driver and the guard, revealing their common ethnic origins, exchanged a few sentences in the Ronga language. Suddenly, the guard switched to Portuguese, and with obvious annoyance, asked the driver: 'Oh pa, tu és moçambicano?' (Say, are you Mozambican?). The driver assured his interlocutor that he was indeed a native born Mozambican. 'Entao, porque não falas português?' (Then why don't you speak Portuguese?), challenged the guard. (1991: 313)

Hamilton suggests nowhere in his essay that the majority of Mozambicans at the time or since had achieved mastery of the Portuguese language. Nor does he fail to record the Mozambican poet's reaction to the exchange between the guard and the driver, noting that Craveirinha did not particularly approve of the guard's opinions, though as we know, Craveirinha himself does his writing in Portuguese. Nonetheless, this association of the space of Mozambique with the language of Portuguese is significant and offers a useful starting point for my efforts to unravel the significance of a community's use of a non-native language in certain kinds of activities.

For the most part, denunciations of the impositions of colonial rule and affirmations of the power of native languages have continued to feature prominently in discussions of the language question in African and other postcolonial literatures produced in the languages of former colonizers.[1] Following in the same logic, the significance of native languages is invoked in terms which imply that nativeness is immanent to languages, while identities associated with such languages are irreplaceable and exempt from further modification. Language shifts become a deviation from an uninterrogated 'norm' and polyglottism a possible betrayal of the native tongue. These are assumptions whose premises need to be questioned.

We do well to acknowledge the impact of colonialism on the contemporary language situation in Africa, but in acknowledging imposition of colonial languages as a historical fact we have not yet begun to address appropriation of colonial languages as an on-going reality and to probe the motivations underlying such acts of appropriation. In the previous chapter, I alluded to a certain conception of modernity as one of several possible reasons for the appropriation of the languages of the colonizer by educated Africans in the imaginative and other spheres. The point of the present chapter is to explore some of the other motivations for these acts of appropriation and to argue in particular that the movement towards using non-native languages in the production of imaginative texts offers much more than a trace of colonial and other impositions. In fact, such changes can also signal a modification of the scope and parameters of the local, thus allowing us to track the displacements, contractions and expansions of the space of the local. Perhaps, therefore, the best way to explain these developments is not in connection with the sole fact of colonialism, but in terms of their role in the elaboration of changing alliances, affiliations, and communities.

In the previous chapter, I sought to understand why most of the educated elite in European colonies in Africa did not embrace writing in mother tongues, and discourses of vernacular literacy as a strategy for resisting colonial rule. In this chapter, I start out with a different question: having made the decision to write in a European language, why did a generation of educated Africans, starting from roughly the 1930s not simply perceive and describe themselves as European writers? Though it seems unlikely in the immediate and foreseeable future, it is certainly possible that indigenous African languages will one day completely give way to European languages as mother tongues of a significant proportion of the African population. But even if such an improbable scenario were to unfold in the language practices of the majority of contemporary Africans, would these Africans become therefore by association 'European,' would they begin to think of themselves as British, French, Portuguese and Spanish because they had changed mother tongues? I think not. They probably might begin to identify themselves differently if they changed mother tongues; however, the adoption of new mother tongues is not necessarily and always an indication of identification with the ethnicity of previous mother-tongue speakers of the same language.

Where populations do not actually experience a change of location and of social or civic status, a complete shift in mother tongues may not immediately occur despite long-term contact with other languages; rather a prolonged state of co-existence between languages acknowledged as native and non-native may persist over several generations. The use of what remains a non-native language for certain kinds of activities is in these circumstances rarely indicative of a desire to completely relinquish a previous identity or even to acquire what is perceived as a hybrid identity. Instead, the decision to begin undertaking imaginative activity in non-native languages often points to a subsuming of an earlier space of distinctiveness within a larger framework, and an expansion of the territorial compass associated with the idea of the local. It signifies a redrawing of the borders of belonging in order to reflect the acquisition of new affiliations spread over a wider territory than previous affiliations. It marks a shift in the determination of what henceforth will be considered a prominent or primary place of belonging. The question to be asked here is not so much, how have foreign languages affected local culture, but what do those who consistently use non-native languages as a medium of cultural activity experience as 'local?'

Unless we specifically spotlight the role of such languages in the constitution of home territory and the local, the significance of these languages for the construction of new sites of belonging will often go unremarked. For too long we have foregrounded the function of language with regard to the specific ethnicity of historic mother tongue speakers over the fundamental operation of language in the formation of affiliations, ethnic or otherwise. Thus we have failed to recognize that in the African context, the emergence of imaginative writing in European and other non-native languages correlates in the first place with the emergence of 'Africa' as a major site of belonging and provides evidence of the growing prominence of new types of affiliations viewed as local, but not necessarily native and 'traditional.' The significance, therefore, of the recourse to particular non-native languages in the area of cultural production is in the indications it offers of the willingness of some individuals to privilege new sites of belonging embodied in such entities as 'African' literature, 'African' identity and many other things 'African' in the present age, which were initially constructed and given substance largely through a discourse produced in European languages.

Of course one cannot completely rule out the possibility that those who adopt a new language will in the end identify with mother tongue speakers of the language in question. But there is in my opinion a distinction to be made between the kinds of individuals whom Echeruo (1977) describes as constituting a Victorian society in the Lagos Colony, and the generation of writers who as from the 1930s onwards committed themselves to the creation of an entity to be subsequently known as African literature.[2] Some members of Lagos high society in the late 19th century probably did see themselves as one with the British 'nation,' but that certainly was not a conviction shared by those who took the lead in producing creative writing in English in the same location by the mid-20th century. And even for those populations on the West African coast whose use of English referenced a more wide-ranging identification with British citizens and their way of life in the late 19th and early 20th centuries, it was simply a question of determining what henceforth would be considered 'local' culture for them.[3] They did not identify with Britain as a foreign nation but as their own newly chosen home nation.

A similar concern with defining the new terms of locality comes across in many of the statements made in the support of the English language elsewhere on the continent around the same period. Much has been made, for example, of the attitudes of some of the early diasporan intellectuals on the West African coast towards indigenous African languages.[4] But even an Alexander Crummell, African-American missionary in Liberia, who spoke so disparagingly of African vernaculars entitled his famous speech on the subject, 'The English language in Liberia.'[5] In other words, his concerns here did not pertain primarily to England where he received his higher education or the United States where he was born, but to Liberia, and thus to Africa as a recommended site of locality for Black people around the world.

Likewise, the famous Pan-Africanist and diasporan intellectual, Edward Blyden, came down on the side of the English language, mostly on behalf of a putative 'African' nation, noting in an equally well-known declaration: 'English is undoubtedly, the most suitable of the European languages for bridging over the numerous gulfs between the tribes caused by the great diversity of languages or dialects among them' (1887: 212). Later generations of writers in West Africa clearly situated and envisaged local culture differently from the Lagos Victorians, and in a manner that more closely resembled Crummell and Blyden. But for them too, these choices were made with an intention to defining the new limits of locality. Home for the later writers in English was not Britain but Africa, and Africa rather than simply Igboland or Eweland if such a territory might have been said to exist. This specific choice of locality and home territory was to a large extent the major factor that prompted their willingness to use languages like English and French as a means of cultural expression.

Generally speaking, when a significant minority or even a sizeable majority takes on an additional language, the initial justifications are mostly pragmatic. One learns a new language because one is compelled to, in order to secure better jobs, or to accommodate changes in the political dispensation, or as a consequence of emigration and so on.[6] But except these non-native speakers of a second or third language can gain effective and full entry into the community of native speakers, they will have little incentive to identify culturally or politically with the native speakers of the prevailing languages of power. Even in a world of movement and displacement, the concept of a home space remains powerful though greatly modified. Among other definitions, Rapport and Dawson (1998: 21) propose that home might be the 'environment (cognitive, affective, physical, somatic . . . in which one best knows oneself, where one's self-identity is best grounded – or worst, or most freely, or most presently, as one deems fit . . .' If non-native speakers are attracted to a language of power because of the relative opportunities guaranteed by proficiency, but cannot find acceptance and a home within the community of native speakers, the very inequities and exclusions of the system ensure that they will ultimately pursue alternative sites of belonging even as the exigencies of political resistance often require them to fall back on the same languages of power. Thus, in colonial Lagos, many in the Lagos Victorian community eventually realized that they would never experience full equality either with the Europeans in the colonies or with those back in the metropolitan centers, and ultimately they began to seek other forms of self-identification even as they pursued education in English.

Wherever the gates of civic rights and power and economic advancement are locked to a sizeable proportion of non-native speakers of a language, the pattern of seeking home and self-identification elsewhere will apply. People will continue to expand their language repertoires by stocking them up with additional languages of power if that is the price to be paid for survival and success. When, however, they begin to use these newly acquired languages of power as a means of cultural expression, though they have other languages at their disposal, and though they derive no benefits from seeking admission or can never gain full admission into the community of native speakers, we can safely assume that what we are witnessing in such circumstances is the emergence of a new vision of the local.

African Languages and African Literatures

My subject matter in this chapter is the category of 'African literature' and my focus relates particularly to territorial identities with special reference to some of the modalities involved in affirming an 'African' identity. I think it useful to start out by differentiating some of the ways in which we use the adjective 'African' in our discussions of the diverse cultures represented on the continent. A ritual performance organized, for example, by a rural Senufo community in northern Ivory Coast to mark the beginning of the harvest season will be described as 'African' in the sense that the performers originate from the African continent and are carrying out an activity perceived to be 'traditional.' But Africanness here is latent rather than active, imputed rather than self-consciously appropriated. All things being equal, members of this hypothetical Senufo community probably might not use the term 'African' in their own acts of self-identification. My interest here relates more so to those cases where African identity is a matter of self-ascription than to instances where Africanness is latent and attributed. As a self-aware and activated form of identification, African identity provides a platform for organizing such entities as 'African literature,' 'African music,' 'African cinema' and depends for self-realization on communication networks established in languages of wider communication. It is these pairings of geography and culture that I would like to examine here, keeping in mind Katz's (1994: 68) caution about the dangers of making sites vessels for holding cultural attributes.

While terms like 'African literature' are used as a matter of convenience, I feel there is insufficient recognition of the particular modalities involved in such pairings of geography and cultural activity. Critics occasionally speak as if these terms corresponded to an actual space of cultural unity existing independently of interventions by certain individuals in various domains, and independently of communication networks in particular languages. Thus, the willingness of all verbal artists on the continent to identify with an 'African culture' and with an 'African novel' or 'African performance,' rather than with some other kind of category is taken for granted no matter what languages they use in their creative works. At the same time, the constructed dimension of the languages at their disposal and the role of these languages in postulating zones of cultural continuity is often disregarded.

Consequently, indigenous African languages are sometimes presented in literary analysis as a category *in situ*, an outpost of unsullied Africanness that survived the colonial encounter virtually intact. But this is a picture that overlooks the active role of missionaries, foreign anthropologists and linguists in the naming and classification of Africa's languages, while also failing to recognize the possibility that the cultural configurations imputed to colonial and later post-independence territory were informed, inter alia, by prior decisions made by the same foreign agents in respect of Africa's languages. In different ways, both official classifications of language and the changing patterns of language use affected the kind of relationships established between territory and culture. Instead, therefore, of interpreting any changes in existing language patterns simply as betrayal of the culture of a pre-constituted community with 'its' own home territory, it might perhaps be more instructive to consider how successive changes in language patterns point to on-going reconfigurations of the relationship between territory, culture, and identity.

Fabian's (1986) study of the activity of both church and state with regard to the spread of Kiswahili in the Belgian Congo is one of several pertinent works that addresses this reality. Fabian highlights the manner in which territorial ambitions impacted upon linguistic realities, resulting in a process he describes as 'grammaticalization' (1986: 83). In effect, missionaries and colonial agents, confronted by a disturbing variety of linguistic idioms attempted to impose some form of spatial organization on what they perceived as the linguistic wilderness of the new domains under their control. The project was not dissimilar to, and indeed paralleled the course of territorial conquest and delimitation of rigidly defined spheres of influence associated with colonial rule. Thus, according to Fabian (1986: 79), Belgian missionaries approached unfamiliar African languages in central Africa as 'strange regions to be explored, as bounded systems to be graphically described, as the possessions of territorially defined groups (so that linguistic, ethnic, and geographic labels could become interchangeable).' From this perspective, one could almost say that theories about particular languages gave legitimacy to particular territorial units. The classification of languages provided in the first instance a framework for mapping territory and as a by-product, also postulated spaces of cultural affinity. The politics of language involving both official edicts and changing language repertoires resulted in the formation from above and below of corresponding geographies.

In matters of language, it is perhaps best, then, to start off by acknowledging that nativeness is neither destiny nor unchangeable vocation. Languages and the identities associated with them are by no means imbued with permanent tinctures of nativeness. Occasionally, the opportunity for missionary implantation in some locations worked to strengthen existing divisions with somewhat unfortunate consequences for the future development of literary writing in the concerned language or languages. In what is now Ghana, for example, the accessibility of the German Basel missionaries on the one hand, and the British Wesleyans on the other, to locations either close to the coast, or suitable for European habitation ensured that Akwapim Twi and Fanti emerged as separate written languages and not as one single language to be used by all Akan communities, despite a significant level of intelligibility between the idioms spoken by different Akan communities.[7] Neither written 'language,' as it turned out, was acceptable to the numerically dominant Asante, whose territory further inland had not proved as hospitable for missionary linguistic work as had the Akwapim hills or the coastal region. As a result, Akwapim Twi, Asante Twi, and Fanti continue to be taught as separate subjects in Ghanaian schools, and this fact has no doubt served to privilege a sense of distinct identity for each group where the emergence of a unified Akan identity might have been just as conceivable.

In southern Africa, to take another example, Harries (1988) attributes the emergence of Tsonga as a language distinct from Ronga, mentioned at the beginning of this chapter, to a power tussle between two Swiss missionaries, Henri Berthoud, and Henri Junod, both sent out by the Free Church of Vaud to work in Southern Africa. Despite opposition from Berthoud who was responsible for early work on the language that became known as Tsonga, Junod insisted that Ronga was a separate language and that his vocation was to provide this separate language with written grammars and a suitable orthography. Junod persisted in his convictions resulting in the publication of written grammars for Ronga. His activities probably contributed at least in part to later acknowledgement of the Ronga as a separate ethnic group, presumably speaking its own language, by both Portuguese colonial and Mozambican authorities. However, the story does not end there. According to Harries (1988: 51–2), Junod's own son, Henri-Philippe, was later to deplore the splitting of Tsonga and Ronga into separate languages. Speaking in a tone of admiration for his father's opponent, Henri Berthod, Henri-Philippe Junod wrote in 1939: 'He [Henri Berthoud] had understood that the Ba Ronga only formed a small part of the great Tsonga tribe, and that this eccentric dialect could not reasonably be allowed to grow at the expense of the fundamental unity of a language spoken by more than a million individuals' (Harries, 1988: 52). In his major work on African-language literatures, Gérard too refers in passing to both Tsonga and Ronga, noting that 'Mention should be made at this point of the abortive attempts made in the 1930s towards the formation of a written art in two dialects that are so closely related to Tsonga as to be mutually intelligible: Ronga and Tswa . . .' (Gérard, 1981: 343). The encounter of Ronga speakers with the Portuguese language, alluded to earlier in this chapter, would seem therefore to represent only the latest twist in a history of interventions relating to language experienced by speakers of a language now known as Ronga.

In yet other cases, and as suggested in the previous chapter, populations just as readily appropriated formerly 'foreign' languages as they abandoned previously 'native' languages. In the late 19th century for example, according to both Bamgbose (1991: 14) and Hair (1967: 4), residents of

Freetown, Sierra Leone, who spoke different varieties of the language now known as Yoruba, declined to identify themselves as Yoruba, preferring terms understood in contemporary usage to represent dialectal sub-groupings of the Yoruba, such as the Ijesa or Ijebu. In their opinion, the term 'Yoruba' reflected the aspirations of a distinct group with which they had no desire to be identified. Indeed the uncertainty about whether the Yoruba constituted a single ethnic group or several different ones appears to have persisted until the late 1940s (Law, 1996: 73).

Be that as it may, within the context of contemporary Nigerian politics, a Yoruba identity certainly exists as of now, albeit under constant strain, an identity shared by a population speaking a wide variety of dialects that are not always mutually intelligible. Fagunwa, the most celebrated of the early Yoruba authors, wrote in the Yoruba language, or more precisely, the Oyo dialect, which had been chosen as the standard for the written language by the missionaries, and differed substantially from the variety that he would have learnt as a child, given the fact that he was not himself from Oyo.[8] To all intents and purposes, however, he considered himself a Yoruba, in a way in which citizens of his place of birth might not have done in previous generations. The emergence of a Yoruba identity is undoubtedly related to the activity of early Yoruba cultural nationalists, many of them educated in missionary schools and or descended from the population of Yoruba recaptives of Sierra Leone. They in turn were influenced, inter alia, by transcriptions of a certain idiom by C.M.S. missionaries, identified as the standard for a language henceforth called Yoruba by the same missionaries, by the translation of the Bible into this idiom, and by the naming of a wide swath of territory inhabited by populations speaking several different dialects as Yoruba country.

But notwithstanding its origin in the cultural manipulations of non-natives, this identity has spawned Yoruba states within the contemporary Nigerian polity, Yoruba political parties and organizations, Yoruba churches and many more embodiments that cannot be listed here but which together constitute a powerful force in Africa's most populous state. Missionary activity in this case and many others did not simply consist in discovering and documenting pre-existing linguistic and territorial units recognized as such by the local populations. Rather, as Fabian (1986: 76) rightly indicates, missionary linguistic work very rapidly progressed from 'descriptive appropriation to prescriptive imposition.' Missionaries established native tongues, named languages, determined the territorial scope of languages in keeping with all kinds of considerations, not all of them linguistic. According to Ansre (1971: 696), the ensuing standardization of African languages, in particular, was largely the work of foreigners. Having been named and standardized, these 'native' languages were then promoted and enforced through an educational system dominated by missionaries and other foreigners. The resulting formation of an identity around the linguistic activity of these external agents should come as no surprise, for as Amselle (1998: 33) has argued, 'there are cultures that have the power to name other cultures, and to circumscribe their own field of expression, while others are only capable of being named.' Identities are apparently no less real just because the scope of the languages linked to those identities has been constituted and imposed by foreigners in fairly recent time.

Given such patterns of language change as have been documented in Africa and elsewhere in the world, we cannot be satisfied with simply noting that any one language is a native language. Rather, we might also wish to inquire: how and when did this particular group of people begin to recognize this language in its present form as their native language? What does the willingness to use this language tell us about how the space of the local and the native is being envisaged? And what does it tell us about the geographic coordinates of these spaces at this point in time? In what discursive context do invocations of the nativeness of particular languages occur? What ideological purpose do such invocations of nativeness serve within that specific context? These are some of the questions that I will address in the remainder of this chapter.

African Literature as a Pan-Africanist Practice

Since the early 20th century in the African context, the elaboration of the emergent nation-states and the continent itself as a space of cultural coherence and common political destiny has been irrevocably tied to activities performed in what are, for the most part, non-native languages of wider communication. The idea of an 'African' literature represents one such example of the elaboration of the continent as an area of cultural continuity and common destiny manifested in the creative work of authors from diverse corners of the continent and with diverse mother tongues and cultural backgrounds. In this light it would perhaps be more accurate to describe this entity as 'Pan-African' literature to underscore its close involvement with the Pan-Africanist project and ideology. From the same perspective, the most consciously African or Pan-African of Africa's literatures have been written in non-native languages, and in particular in European languages. By and large, Pan-Africanist commitments all over the continent are expressed through cultural practices and texts in either non-native languages and or languages of wider communication. By this I mean that Africans who actively identify the diverse cultures of the continent as related cultures, will frequently seek out activities by 'fellow'

Africans conducted in languages which are not their own mother tongues, and in languages which are used across considerable distances as languages of wider communication.

African literature is, like Indian literature, or Canadian literature and other similar entities created elsewhere in the world in relatively recent time, an artificial construct with a traceable history, and one which like others in the same company was not in its foundational configuration fully representative of the entire spectrum of verbal arts produced in the location supposedly covered by the term. There were evidently texts written in indigenous languages that did not make the first cut of 'African literature' between the 1930s and 1960s, just as there were texts in European languages that likewise did not make the cut. Fiction in French that was supportive of the colonial encounter such as the Malagasy author, Edouard Bezoro's novel *La Soeur inconnue*, or that was ambiguous about colonialism like Bakary Diallo's *Force Bonté*, were ignored in the early discussions of 'African' literature, as were examples of popular literature by authors like the Togolese, Félix Couchoro.[9] At the same time, authors like the Malagasy writer, Jean-Joseph Rabearivelo, who described himself as 'Latin among the Melanesians' would probably have been astonished to learn of his subsequent and posthumous incorporation into an African canon, for he evidently did not define himself as such while he was alive.[10] Indeed it is one of the great ironies of the Malagasy literary scene that though the majority of the population has remained decidedly ambivalent about the usefulness of assuming any kind of African identity, Malagasy writers have for the most part achieved prominence only to the extent that they have allowed themselves to be incorporated into an African and or Francophone literary pantheon largely dominated by dark-skinned people of African and Caribbean ancestry.

The problematic selections, omissions and exclusions noticeable in the early history of the construct of 'African literature,' and which persist in varying degrees till the present time are not simply indicative of an oversight to be easily remedied through gestures guided by retrospective intent; rather they tell the story of this particular construct and point to the circumstances of its emergence and continued existence, or what one might describe as its conditions of possibility. Given the continued reification of African languages in their capacity as mother tongues, excluded, therefore, from the functions of languages of wider communication which in postcolonial states are seldom mother tongues for a major proportion of the local population, those conditions of possibility, I will now suggest, have been, and continue to be very firmly enmeshed with creativity in European languages. In other words, European languages are not simply and as is sometimes assumed a foreign imposition on the entity of 'African literature.' On the contrary, as the historical record clearly demonstrates, the entity of 'African literature' took shape in, and was constructed upon the bedrock of African writing in European languages.

To be sure, there were authors in West Africa, for example, who long before Achebe and Ayi Kwei Armah were writing in indigenous languages and whose works belong in a representative corpus of African literature. But these earlier authors undertook few recorded actions suggesting their recognition of authors from within their sub-region or other parts of the continent as associates engaged in a common endeavor. Though they submitted their manuscripts into the 'African literature' competitions organized by the IALC, they either did not have the resources or did not perceive the usefulness of engaging in collaborative discussion with Africans who wrote in languages other than their own.[11] Whatever the reasons, we know that the first conferences dedicated to discussing African literatures in their plurality, and organized by Africans themselves were established by those writers who wrote in European languages. We know that the first journals founded by Africans themselves for the criticism of African literatures in their plurality were founded by authors and critics writing in European languages.

English and French were, and still are the major languages used to conduct business in conferences organized to discuss African literatures in their plurality, both in and outside Africa. English and French were, and still are the major languages used for debating about African literatures in their plurality in journals founded on the African continent such as *Abbia, Black Orpheus, Ethiopiques, The Horn, Okike, Okyeame, Penpoint, Transition,* among several others, which have at one time, or another, provided an outlet for the criticism of African literatures in their plurality by Africans themselves. This, then, is the critical point. The emergence of the construct of 'African literature' as an autonomous category of creativity comprising texts and authors that were presented as being somehow related to each other, cannot be disassociated from the commitment of certain writers to establishing networks of communication involving authors who did not share in common the same mother tongue, and from the activity of well-placed editors in publishing houses, critics, and educational professionals who likewise decided that a selection of texts of their own choosing deserved to be promoted as 'African literature.'

As is well known, the diverse verbal and other arts created in various locations around the world do not in and of themselves produce the kinds of entities represented by terms like 'African literature.' Nor do these arts naturally generate their own audiences without the active intervention of powerful cultural brokers. Potentially, all those who are literate in the language of any text have access to the text and could eventually constitute an audience for the text. But, this is not the same thing as saying that the author writes only for those who speak the language in question as a mother tongue. Nor does it mean that those who speak the language as a second or third language are automatically excluded. Literacy in a non-native language is still literacy, and in some regions of the African continent, it may be the only form of literacy at a people's disposal. The African author who writes in a European language is not simply giving up a local audience for international fame as has been variously argued by Gérard (1981: 312) and the Tanzanian writer Mlama (1990: 7) among many other critics. What is also at stake and often ignored is the struggle between competing visions of the local, between a concept of the local as coterminous only with those that share the same mother tongue and a vision of the local as inclusive of those who inhabit a specific geography and with whom one shares only non-native languages in common. Such literatures in non-native languages are indeed 'minor' literatures in relation to the texts produced by the socially dominant native-speakers of the language, to borrow the formulation suggested by Deleuze and Guattari (1986). However, minor literatures are also literatures of the local. And especially in instances that do not involve permanent emigration and or geographic contiguity, the local as envisioned by writers in non-native languages will not frequently coincide with the local as defined by mother-tongue speakers of the same language.

Though I will address questions relating to language and audience in greater detail in the next chapter, I would already like to make some initial observations here and in particular to distinguish the audience of the text from the community of those who are proficient in the language used, if only to point out that all those who are literate in a given language do not in fact end up reading every text in that language. They constitute a potential but not an actual audience. Thus, language proficiency alone does not an audience make. It is sometimes implied that many African literature texts would naturally attract a more extensive local readership if only they had been written in indigenous African languages.[12] As Ricard (2000) points out with regard to the Tanzanian writer Ebrahim Hussein whose works are written in Kiswahili, this may well turn out to be an unsubstantiated assumption.[13] Texts that are not written primarily for commercial gain will not succeed in generating a widespread local readership without significant institutional intervention by political and other agents among native speakers of the language used. Whether such backing comes from religious bodies requiring literacy in a particular language, or from the state working through the educational system, or from powerful professional and or cultural associations, it is essential. No doubt, many writers continue to produce texts without regard to these institutions, but such texts do not acquire a sustained audience until they enter into the systems of cultural transmission established by such institutions. Whether these institutions have good reasons to promote and support literacy in a given language will in turn depend on a number of other factors.[14]

By and large then, the establishment of audiences for texts located outside the scope of African urban popular culture is especially dependent on the political choices of institutions like universities and ministries of education, and on the activities of those publishers, scholars, and critics who have a professional stake or interest in the classification of certain groups of texts as separate categories. As such, they are read in Africa and abroad not simply because they are written in a familiar language, but mostly because they feature within a socially significant institutional framework designed to advance particular political, professional, and cultural agenda, including, for example, the projection of a territory and a community as a plausible zone of historical and political continuity through the educational system. We are not far off the mark in affirming that the activities of varied cultural brokers working through the systems at hand both create the literary category and generate the relevant audience either in the language of original composition or in translation. It is the fact of being adopted by such cultural brokers that creates an audience for these high literature texts rather than the fact of being written in a local language.

We might further describe the texts in question, their authors, the critics and publishers who determine the initial boundaries of this corpus, as constituting a field of interactions carried out in a limited number of shared languages with the intention of confirming the selected texts, and by implication the highlighted territory, as a plausible continuum of cultural affinity.[15] Whatever the mother tongues and other languages spoken by those who participate in the established field of interactions, in the end, significant communication within that sphere occurs for the most part in one or two languages shared in common by those who are active participants in the field. There may, for example, be perceptive and instructive articles being written about 'French literature' in Polish, and there may be skillfully rendered translations of texts by French authors available in the Polish language, but no one doubts that the canon for that category is being largely determined, and that the agenda for critical discourse on the subject is being mostly circumscribed through communications carried out in French and secondarily in English. Likewise, for example, the category 'postcolonial literature' has had much less resonance in the French-speaking world, and has included fewer discussions of works originally written in French except in instances where such texts have been translated into English. To all intents and purposes, the category of postcolonial literature and postcolonial theory is intimately connected with texts originally written in English or available in English translation to networks of communication conducted primarily in English. Given the constraints of time and ability which prevent any one participant in a particular transnational field of interactions from learning all the languages spoken by all the other participants, the establishment of these literary categories as on-going fields of interaction depends in effect on the adoption of a restricted number of languages as the predominant languages of critical discourse and as the predominant languages through which acknowledged texts are to be accessed.

For 'African literature,' that field of interactions was inaugurated and continues to operate primarily in French and English, with languages like Portuguese, Arabic, Kiswahili among others serving as secondary languages of communication. In the interest of accuracy, it might be best to recognize that languages like English and French have not been simply superimposed upon a substratum of genuine African literature; rather these languages might be said to provide the linguistic matter used for the establishment a category that came to be known as African literature. It is certainly true on the one hand that the canon of 'African literature' has since the 1970s been considerably expanded to make room for texts composed in indigenous languages. But on the other hand, indigenous-language texts that are not translated into the founding languages of this entity, and that do not become the object of critical discourse in these languages rarely gain entrance into this field of interactions. They may exist, and even be popular with certain audiences, but they will not feature in the anthologies, journals, curricula and discussions that purport to represent 'African literature' unless they are translated into the languages that predominate in the circuits of communication which together constitute and literally produce the category of 'African literature.' Indeed, just as the ideology of Pan-Africanism took shape around a discourse in European languages, so also did the idea of an 'African literature' take shape around a discourse in European languages.

If the category in question were not in fact 'African literature' but 'Zulu literature' or say, 'Ewe literature,' a category defined by a single language rather than one defined by a territory where diverse languages are spoken, communication might have been possible without recourse to a language of wider communication. And the barriers to constituting the category 'African literature' as a specific field of interactions in indigenous languages are not insurmountable, provided a broad understanding prevails that one or two African languages will become the predominant languages of communication in this field despite the fact of not being the mother tongues of a sizeable proportion of participants engaged in discussion around the texts. Writers like Ezekiel Mphahlele (1963) and Wole

Soyinka (1988) have indeed spoken out in support of the idea of a lingua franca for African literature, but they are in the minority. Since the majority of Africans committed to the project of an 'African literature' continue to envision indigenous African languages mostly in their function as mother tongues, reliance on non-native languages of wider communication remains inevitable wherever communication is required between parties that do not share the same mother tongue. In other words, and as a corollary, unless a commitment develops to the identities linked to various mother tongues as ends in themselves, minimal energy is likely to be directed at sustaining indigenous-language literatures on the African continent by those committed to a Pan-Africanist agenda.

Thus, the idea of an 'African literature' as an object of study, as one series among others offered by groups of publishers, as an additional item in school and college curricula, and as an entity so acknowledged by particular writers, emerged largely in connection with texts definitely read and almost always written in a select number of languages of wider communication which happen as a result of the colonial encounter to be European languages. This is not surprising since the concern with 'African' identities and cultural production is itself a response to the complex history of Western interaction with peoples of African descent from the Atlantic Slave Trade to the political and economic configurations of the present day. The African situation cannot in this respect be considered especially peculiar. Since the monolingual character of a territory and a state can rarely be guaranteed, a politically determined field of interactions is often constituted around texts in one language, to the detriment of texts in other languages whose existence is simply elided in the majority of instances around the world where geography rather than language provides the basis for these literary classifications. Only recently, for example, have efforts begun to be made to acknowledge the consistent exclusion of texts in languages other than English, including other European languages, Asian and Native American languages from the established canon of 'American literature.'[16] English is the language of the field of interactions that we describe as 'American literature' but it is not the only language in which literary activity has historically been carried out within the United States.

The situation of Western Europe is somewhat more ambiguous with qualifiers initially referring to language conveniently extended to cover territory.[17] There has been frequent reference for example in discussions of the language situation in Africa to the fact that scholars and creative writers in Western Europe abandoned Latin for 'vernacular' tongues during the Renaissance and Reformation periods.[18] The languages adopted for writing may have been the mother tongues of well-placed individuals who turned away from writing in Latin, but they were not in fact the only languages in use within the shifting borders of the state whose cultural interests these individuals claimed to represent. The chosen languages may have been the vernacular for some communities and social classes, but were certainly not the vernacular for all residents of the nation as defined at the time.

Thus the decision to write in 'French' was also a decision not to write in Provençal, Basque, Breton and later still Alsacien among varied languages that have not completely disappeared and continued to be widely used within the borders of 'France' well into the 19th century. The recognition of literary writing in English proceeded alongside efforts to suppress Welsh, Irish, and Scots Gaelic to name only a few of the other languages spoken within the British Isles for centuries after the historic turning to the 'vernacular.'[19] And as Hobsbawm (1994: 61) has pointed out, when Italian nationalists proclaimed Italian as the national language in the early 20th century, most residents of the polity and territory so designated did not in fact speak Italian, even though the language had certainly been in use by the elite and by writers for several centuries. Indeed, in some parts of Western Europe as in many other regions of the world, where the language selected was the language of a dominant group within the state, these literary categories became one important means among others for both promoting and enforcing the fiction of a monolingual territory particularly within the educational system. If it is true that some Western European writers celebrated in official literary histories turned away in their writing from the languages of an external colonizing power, it is certainly also true that their choices legitimated a new round of linguistic impositions emanating this time from within rather than without of the national territory.[20] The cultural history of Western Europe on these matters teaches us about the conditions in which vernacular literatures successfully take root, but also serves as cautionary tale about the ends for which ideologies of the vernacular have been historically mobilized.

The peculiar characteristic of these terms that correlate geography with culture in a conjoined expression, then, is to postulate the territory in question as a zone of cultural affinity and to crystallize a sense of community around a specific geography. Thus, the dynamic literary categories that I have been discussing here do not merely operate as metonymic figures for the cultural unity imputed to a territory, they literally engender it by becoming textual embodiments of such concepts as 'American' culture, 'French' culture and 'African' culture with local intelligentsias long before the same concepts have acquired any form of substantive resonance among other segments of the population living in the territory circumscribed within the construct. Categories like 'African cinema,' 'African performance,' 'the African novel' and even 'African studies' elaborate and incarnate spaces of cultural affinity that are far from self-evident to local populations outside of the texts and practices signified by these terms. The cultural congruence implicit in these terms exists mostly in relation to particular sets of discursive and performative practices and is only selectively acknowledged by inhabitants of the designated territories who regularly target fellow residents of the same territory with whom they supposedly share a related culture as foreigners and cultural outsiders.

To a large extent, the geocultural zones produced by these categories are not conceivable apart from the field of interactions mentioned earlier, and the field of interactions itself flourishes only to the extent that its activities are realized in a limited number of languages or supported by an extensive infrastructure engaged in continuous translation. As such, these literary and other constructs mobilized to postulate territories as zones of cultural affinity effectively constitute selective circuits of mainly verbal communication which cannot be operative unless certain languages, even non-native languages, are shared in common by those who intervene in these circuits of communication. The critical element in this entire configuration is not so much the languages spoken by residents in the territory supposedly represented by the geocultural construct, as the ability of the relevant cultural brokers to communicate among themselves. These cultural brokers cannot be said to have simply given up their membership of a native community in order to align themselves with colonial culture; rather they form part of what Sorensen (2000: 19) describes as a 'transnational linguistic community' who stand in a position of some privilege in relation to those who have not mastered the standard form of the dominant transnational language whether in the former metropolitan center or in former colonial peripheries. It is this group's language of inter-ethnic communication rather than the languages spoken within the designated territory that determines the predominant and effective language in which these constructs are generated and accessed. This fact in a sense explains the contradictory signals at work in the continuing debate over the language of African literature. Concerns over the language of this body of writing emanate largely from critics and writers committed to defining African literature as a composite body of texts distinct from Western literatures. But continued dependence on European languages is inevitable in the absence of an indigenous lingua franca among its proponents, and for as long as the movement involves a broad-based commitment to 'African literature' rather than localized activity in support, for example, of Amharic writing or Bemba literature. Given its insistent focus on the destiny of an 'African' literature, this campaign to promote writing in indigenous languages has little choice but to perpetuate the very condition it proposes to eliminate.

The possibility that African writers who use the vernacular will in the future make the constitution of a field of interactions around the idea of an ethnic or vernacular literature their primary objective can certainly not be ruled out. Alternatively, the desire for continued and sustained interaction with authors and critics from elsewhere on the continent and who write in other languages might lead them to undertake systematic translation of vernacular language texts into other vernacular languages and into languages of wider communication, so that critics who do not speak particular vernacular languages have effective access to texts in these languages. Until that begins to happen, vernacular language literatures will probably remain a marginal presence in a field of interactions specifically dedicated to the discussion of texts from around the continent as a related body of works.

It is not a mistake, therefore, to begin a history of 'African literature' with references to Senghor's 1948 anthology and to Heinemann's African Writers Series among others. Heinemann did more than create an image of African literature in its selections (Venuti 1998: 168), Heinemann created the category 'African literature' through its series, as a body of texts largely written in English, and comprising translations from the French and Portuguese, and very occasionally texts from indigenous languages. These publications did represent a watershed moment, and significantly altered the parameters to be henceforth invoked in assessing responses to imaginative texts produced by Africans on and away from the African continent. There is a real sense in which 'African literature,' as pan-Africanist practice, begins here and not with earlier or later authors whose creative careers rose and fell in isolation from authors elsewhere on the continent and abroad within the same time frame. 'African literature' comes into existence when particular writers from different parts of the continent begin to communicate with each other about their work, even if some of the initial interactions occur away from the African continent in locales such as Paris and Rome. Indeed the kind of indignation later expressed over the earlier exclusions of indigenous-language authors from the canon of 'African literature' offers perhaps the best evidence of the extent to which the premises informing the construction of this category have taken on a life of their own. Consequently, the formative components of the category are not always acknowledged as such, with the result that the systemic character of these exclusions is often obscured.

Imaginations of the Local in Critical and Creative Writing

Numerous signs of the quest for alterity or what I would call the desire for alternative sites of locality in European-language writing by Africans can be found in the critical literature on the one hand, and in the ways of using language and talking about language on the other. According to Bishop (1988), language was an early and recurrent concern in efforts to determine critical standards for category of African literature. And as is well known, debates over language have continued to animate discussions of 'African literature' ever since it emerged as a distinct area of study and creativity. Not surprisingly, the list of African authors and critics who reflected on matters of language and its significance for African literature is fairly extensive.[21] In fact, almost every major African writer has had to address this very question at one time or another, and some more frequently than others. When the Malagasy author Jacques Rabemananjara, a participant at the 1959 Second Congress of Black Writers and Artists in Rome, described the gathering as a conference of 'language thieves' (Wauthier, 1979: 31), it represented one of the early shots in what was to become a public and recurrent lamentation over African literature's 'language problem' among writers and critics. The subject was to receive greater attention at the Conference of African Writers of English Expression that took place in Kampala in 1962. Ngugi (1981a: 6), who attended the conference, recalls that the first item on the agenda for the conference was a discussion of the following question: 'What is African literature?' Obiajunwa Wali's thought-provoking rejoinder to the question followed shortly in *Transition* magazine, as did comments from other African writers in the same journal and discussions at later conferences. Ngugi's 'Farewell to English' in *Decolonising the Mind* first published in 1981 spurred a new and continuing wave of expressed support for writing in indigenous languages from diverse African writers and scholars. His own practice and comments on the subject have become the major symbol worldwide of attempts to foster an African literature in indigenous African languages. In 1990, the African Literature Association based in the United States again took up the question at its annual meeting with the theme, 'Tongue and Mother Tongue: African Literature and the Perpetual Quest for Identity'[22] while *Research in African Literatures*, a leading journal in the field, dedicated a special issue to the subject of language and African literature in 1992. The most recent of the major conferences on the subject was probably the Asmara conference in 2000, entitled 'Against All Odds: African Languages and Literatures into the Twenty-first Century.'

Essentially, the authors and critics who addressed this question were trying to come to grips with the implications of cultural production in non-native languages. As far as I can tell, where authors did not actively rule out the practice of writing in European languages, the consensus was to emphasize the distinctiveness and non-Europeanness of African writing in European languages. In discussing the texts written roughly up till the 1980s, a discourse about translation became one privileged method among others for dealing with the perceived language problem of African writers and constructing a literature of difference, a body of texts seeking to be identified as 'African' but written in European languages. The importance attributed to the activity of translation in this context is directly related to the persistent nostalgia for 'origins,' 'original languages,' and most significantly for 'original' or what might be better described here as distinctive and local identities. In a well-known and often quoted article for example, the Nigerian writer, Gabriel Okara declared:

> As a writer who believes in the utilisation of African ideas, African philosophy and African folk-lore and imagery to the fullest extent possible, I am of the opinion that the only way to use them effectively is to translate them almost literally from the African language native to the writer into whatever European language he is using as a medium of his expression. (1963: 15)

Writers like Ahmadou Kourouma have provided similar explanations for their distinctive use of language in some of their works. It is important to note, however, that Okara, like many other African writers who experimented with language in their work, rarely attempted to represent the indigenized forms of French and English actually spoken in West Africa.[23] To do so would be to imply the legitimacy of European languages as one linguistic form among others used in the African context. But this would also have complicated the efforts in the early years to differentiate writing by Europeans from writing by Africans in the same languages, which was clearly the prime consideration. By invoking instead the practice of translation, both authors and critics could continue to signify derivation from indigenous-language originals, further justifying the claims of a distinct identity for these texts read and written in European languages.

Yet other authors chose instead to evacuate their real authorial presence by appropriating the posture of translators, mere mediators between a supposed indigenous-language original and a European-language version. For example, several early narratives in French are presented as texts originally recounted by an indigenous-language narrator and subsequently transcribed and or translated into French. Hampâté Bâ, Ferdinand Oyono, Birago Diop, and Jean-Joseph Rabearivelo have had recourse to this technique in their novels. Zabus (1991: 106) has rightly questioned the appropriateness of the term translation as a description for the kind of practices described by Okara, on account of the absence of an original version in indigenous African languages subsequently translated into a European language. But I am concerned here not so much with the accuracy of the claims made about translation in respect of these texts as with the motivations underlying the reference to translation and what this tells us about the attitudes of both writers and critics to the language used in the creative text. The deployment of a discourse about translation in the absence of an actual original is clearly intended to call into question any ready assimilation of these European-language texts into European literary traditions. As we are well aware, a translated text always encodes a cultural referentiality beyond the language in which the text is being read, and every translation is an exercise in locational politics. If we accept, as the authors and critics would have us do, that they are in fact translations, then we cannot attribute European identity to the texts even though we read them in European languages. Here again, the objective is to invoke an alternative identity and refute certain kinds of deductions about the category to which the text belongs from the language of its composition.

However, there are cases where an original version of the text does exist in indigenous languages, and this points us to yet other dimensions of the interplay between European and indigenous African languages in the construction of an 'African' literature. Elsewhere, I have described these types of translations as 'authorized translations' to distinguish them from instances where the text was composed directly in European languages even if the authors ascribe their technique to the practice of translation (Adejunmobi, 1998). To consider a few examples of such 'authorized translations,' Mazisi Kunene, Okot p'Bitek, and Ngugi have all written texts in their mother tongues and subsequently translated some of these texts into European languages.

As a rule, many of the texts existing in multiple versions demonstrate a reasonably close connection with African oral traditions. They are deliberately modeled on traditional songs, poetic forms and oral narratives. Speaking about Mazisi Kunene's poetry, for example, Goodwin (1982: 173) remarks: 'The world of discourse of his poems is a Zulu one, and the philosophy, the imagery, and the rhetoric rely heavily on the oral traditions of Zulu poetry.' Ngugi (1981a: 77–8) similarly has this to say about his first novel written in his mother tongue: 'I . . . borrowed heavily from forms of oral narrative, particularly the conversational tone, the fable, proverbs, songs and the whole tradition of poetic self-praise or praise of others.' And yet if these texts were initially written in indigenous African languages from the perspective of foregrounding their formal and thematic non-Western affiliations, they have ironically been translated into European languages in accordance with the Western norms of fluency. Venuti (1995: 1) has identified fluency as the dominant convention of contemporary Euro-American translation, suggesting that 'a translated text, whether prose or poetry, fiction or non-fiction, is judged acceptable by most publishers, reviewers and readers when it reads fluently, when the absence of any linguistic or stylistic peculiarities make it seem transparent.' He (1995: 5) further adds that 'a fluent translation is immediately recognizable and intelligible, 'familiarized,' 'domesticated, and not 'disconcerting[ly] foreign.'

Fluency has remained the dominant strategy in translations of most African-language texts into European languages, both in instances where such translations have been undertaken by the author of a written original, and or with a view to incorporation of a text originally written in indigenous African languages into the entity of 'African literature.' Comparing Mazisi Kunene's translation into English of certain traditional poems in the Zulu language with a different translation of the same poems, entitled *Izibongo: Zulu Praise Poems*. Goodwin had this to say:

> The *Izibongo* version seeks to keep close to the Zulu parts of speech and word order... Kunene, while preserving these qualities as far as possible, is prepared to sacrifice them at times in the interests of making sense or achieving a more rolling oratorical rhythm. Where the *Izibongo* versions sometimes read like word-for-word cribs in which the meaning has to be elucidated by a footnote, Kunene's versions show the selective freedom and judgment exercised by someone thoroughly familiar with both languages, having a scholarly and imaginative insight into meaning and poet's way with words. (1982: 186–7)

That is to say, Mazisi Kunene's translations eschew linguistic difference and can be read practically without consciousness of the fact that the poems were first written in Zulu. Taban Lo Liyong's comments about p'Bitek's *Wer pa Lawino*, originally written in Acholi, and the author's translation of the same text into English as *Song of Lawino*, do not exude the kind of commendation implicit in Goodwin's remarks on Mazisi Kunene. In essence, though, they amount to an identical assessment of the English-language translation of the Acholi original. Lo Liyong (1993: 88) states for example that '*Wer pa Lawino* was watered down in translation to *Song of Lawino*,' and then he expatiates on this further by suggesting that 'Okot produced a simplified version of *Wer pa Lawino* in English – all proverbs, wise sayings, and puns were rendered into sarcastic English. So the depth and erudition of the Acholi original were passed over in favor of flowery and colorful English' (1993: 89). Gikandi's reflections on the 'eloquent' English-language translation of Ngugi's *Matigari Ma Njirũũngi* are even more explicit. Certain proverbs are omitted in the English translation, he suggests,

> possibly for the sake of fluency, and replaced by a simpler alternative... This translation captures the spirit of the original, but fluency is only attained by effacing the linguistic difficulties that give the Gikuyu

language its power and identity. Such effacement makes the English translation of the novel into a simplistic, sanitized version of the original. (1991: 165)

Authorized translations thus tend to be the least foreignized of African texts existing in European languages. The translation seeks to convey the meaning but not the language of the original. Linguistic peculiarities are avoided or altogether omitted. In Friedrich Schleiermacher's famous formulation, these authorized translations seem to move the author towards the European-language reader.[24] Attention does not focus on the translating activity itself. Indeed, were it not for indications contained in prefaces and title pages, one might easily conclude that these texts were originally composed in European languages. So normalized are these translations that they bring back a cultural other, in Venuti's (1995: 18) words, 'the same, the recognizable, even the familiar.'

Nonetheless, the fact of being translations remains significant for many African writers and their critics, even if the target versions adhere to a mode of translation that seems to suppress the alterity of the original text in indigenous languages. In this instance as elsewhere, the existence of these original versions serves by inference as a guarantee of the genuine Africanness of these texts, which would seem to imply that only texts in indigenous African languages can be considered truly African. No study of Kunene, p'Bitek, or Ngugi is thus complete without reference to the existence of these original versions in indigenous languages. Mazisi Kunene speaks for himself and many other writers and critics when he concludes:

> ... writers who write in a foreign language are already part of foreign institutions; to one extent or another, they have adopted foreign values and philosophical attitudes, and they variously seek to be a member of that culture. They cannot be said to be an African cultural representatives who write in another language because, in spirit, at least, they speak from the perspective provided for them by the effective apparatus of mental control exercised by the former colonial power. (1992: 32)

However, statements made in this vein usually overlook the fact that the said texts, by and large, function as a literature – texts that are read and critiqued even within the mother-tongue community of the author – only in their normalized European-language translations. Speaking about Kunene, Goodwin (1982: 173) therefore concedes that 'by a paradox of contemporary publishing opportunities, Mazisi Kunene, who writes in Zulu and then translates some of his poetry into English, has had much more of his work appear in translation than in the original.' In other words, not only is Mazisi Kunene widely read in translation, Mazisi Kunene is read essentially *only* in translation.

Another East African publisher makes reference to p'Bitek's magnum opus, the *Song of Lawino*, in his comments on the difficulties of publishing literary texts in indigenous African languages: 'titles published in the indigenous languages were all a 'financial disaster', even though one of them was a prize winning novel in Luo and the other a translation back into original of Okot p'Bitek's *Song of Lawino*' (Zell, 1980: 1071). This observation suggests that the well-established reputation of p'Bitek's text is founded on the initial publication of the English-language translation rather than on the subsequent publication of an indigenous-language 'original.'

Ngugi's texts in Gikuyu, however, seem to constitute something of an exception to this trend, to the extent that they did achieve popularity within the author's mother tongue community. But even in the case of Ngugi, as Gikandi has pointed out, the act of translating a text like *Matigari Ma Njirũũngi* into English further exposes the disjunctions in status between the original text and its translated versions. He (1991: 167) further notes that the 'sanitized' nature of the translation encourages the tendency to read the text as if it were a novel in English, since it effaces all signs that would remind readers of their 'inability to master the original and to negotiate the untranslatable aspects of the Gikuyu language.'

It is not mere coincidence that a number of the texts mentioned here are read mostly in English-language translation and have at the same time regularly featured in discussions of 'African' literature. Literary texts are being written in any number of languages in contemporary Africa, but the subject matter of the scholarly discourse generated around 'African literature' continues to be constituted and accessed mainly in English and French. Texts that are translated gain entrance into this specific arena of discussion, while those that are untranslated circulate within a different economy of assessment. Thus, the texts in question are read, as are most 'African literature' texts, in particular European languages, while the fact of initial composition in indigenous languages, conveniently precludes them from incorporation into non-African literary canons and once again enables authors and critics alike to claim a non-European identity for texts that are effectively read and function as literature in European languages. Indeed, so successful have been these references to derivation from indigenous-language originals that some critics actually speak as if writing in indigenous languages constituted the norm from which the category of 'African literature' has lately departed, when in fact writing and reading in European languages provided the organizational basis for the production of an 'African literature.'

The desire to construct an alternative identity for the European-language African literature text likewise explains the recurrent engagements with the representation of indigenous languages in texts for which indigenous-language originals did not in fact exist. As mentioned earlier, African authors have expended very little effort on gaining acceptance for the indigenized forms of European languages spoken around the continent. Rather in their literary works, deviations from European standard forms are presented, not as authentic local idioms, deserving respect, but as aberrant speech forms to be deplored and mocked. Texts, for example, like Soyinka's *Death and the King's Horseman* and Bâ's *L'étrange destin de Wangrin*, where the narrative unfolds in the colonial era, make a clear distinction between the voice of at least three different types of characters. There are those who speak an indigenous language, officials of the French and British colonial administrations, and characters who mediate between the first two groups in their capacity as translators and all-purpose servants.

In Soyinka's play, the speech of Pilkings, the British District Officer, comes across as colloquial, exuding a certain familiarity and ease with the English language itself, and not just with those who serve him. Amusa, the Nigerian sergeant employed by Pilkings, on the other hand, is heir to a long and shopworn tradition of nativespeak associated with imperial literature. These are characters whose mastery of the colonizer's language remains forever suspect, forever incomplete, when in imperial literature their speech is not reduced to mere grunts and noise. He is to be differentiated from Olunde, another Nigerian character who has been a student in England, and whose English can best be characterized as very correct. But the unaffected ease of Pilking's speech, the faltering English of Amusa the servant, and the absolute correctness of Olunde's diction contrast with the poetic texture and cadences of statements supposedly spoken in Yoruba by other characters in the play. In the speech of the Yoruba characters, parallelisms proliferate as do rhyme, alliteration and assonance. Aphorisms, almost always expressed in figurative language, typify the speech of the Yoruba-speaking characters, as does the use of such words as 'lest' and 'tryst' that have a more archaic flavor to them.

We find comparable distinctions of voice in Bâ's *L'étrange destin de Wangrin*. The speech of the French *commandants* in the novel alternates between a Pilkings'style colloquialism and an officious administrative register. Excepting Wangrin, the protagonist of the narrative, all intermediaries between the colonial administration and the African population express themselves in what the narrator describes as 'forofifon naspa,' a form of French in which we are told the verbs had neither tense nor mood, while substantives were not differentiated according to gender or number

(1973: 32). We recognize in this ungrammatical French the language impairments of the subordinated native. In this novel as in Soyinka's play, eloquence is reserved for those whom we are made to understand speak the local language, in this case, Bambara. This is particularly true of the griots, and the marabouts who intervene at critical junctions in this narrative to pronounce magic formulae or to declaim in figurative language the praises of the central character.

I would like to describe this particular voice and form of speech as archaic, especially in relation to other voices present within the same text. The declamatory character of the dialogues in question, their highly patterned and rhythmic quality, the anchoring of thought to concrete images, local historical references and proverbs, the occasional recourse to archaisms in the lexicon, all of these serve to impart an impression of antiquity to certain voices in the text. But it is at the same time a situational register whose value and force derives from the contrast it presents with the plain colloquialism and functional utterances of some characters and with the linguistic incompetence of others in the same text.

However, even when writers differentiate characters by idiolect, with few exceptions, these characters tend as individuals to inhabit linguistically bounded worlds. As such, we are given to understand that an urban protagonist like Fama in Kourouma's *Soleils des indépendances* speaks Malinke rather than a mixture of Malinke and Français populaire ivoirien. Code-switching, possibly the most salient feature of African urban speech, is alluded to rather than depicted given not only the difficulties of representing two languages, but also the problems involved in recognizing that urban African characters are probably not monolingual.[25] At the same time, the connections between social deviance and implied linguistic deviance remain strong. As noted by Zabus (1991: 66), the 'first full-fledged Pidgin-speaking character' in West African literature in English was a prostitute, and partially Pidgin-speaking characters that appear in later works like Ken Saro-Wiwa's *Sozaboy* and Ahmadou Kourouma's *Allah n'est pas obligé* still tend to emanate from marginalized social groups. The fact that Pidgin is more likely to be represented as a substandard and ungrammatical form of English (Elugbe & Omamor, 1991: 66) serves a similar purpose in presenting whatever is not in indigenous languages as a deviation. Thus, even where no claims of translation are made, and no nativization strategies are attempted, a number of factors work together to foreground indigenous languages as the only proper speech forms for African characters. These factors include the representation of local varieties of European languages and creolized forms as evidence of linguistic deficiency, signs of cultural if not of moral inadequacy, and the association of indigenous languages with eloquence, with respect for grammar and for cultural heritage.

The significance of these diverse practices is not in the occasional claims made by either writers or critics to the effect that some authors originally wrote their texts in indigenous languages, or that they successfully modified the structure of various European languages to accommodate the speech patterns of their mother tongue, or that certain poems originally existed as oral texts in indigenous languages. Clearly these texts are mostly written and read in English or French as the case may be. Rather the significance of these claims and the specific language practices themselves lies in the further evidence they supply of the authors' manifest desire to have their writing located in a category other than British literature or French writing. In other words, they did not write in European languages in order to be identified with European literary traditions and canons however imperfectly constituted. On the contrary, the purpose of these indigenizing practices and the discourses generated around them is to provide legitimacy for affirmations of belonging to a literary category of a different order, and to demonstrate the authors' ongoing engagement with an evolving sense of the local. There can be no doubt that for African authors since the 1930s, writing in European languages has not primarily been about aligning oneself with British or French culture: it has been about representing and giving substance to the fact of belonging to an area other than Europe, on the one hand, and larger than the spaces associated with 'traditional' ethno-linguistic identities on the African continent on the other.

Debating Language

In assessing the import of questions pertaining to language in the critical discourse produced around the entity of African literature, one fact stands out: most of the creative writers, critics and other African scholars who reflected on the problematic status of indigenous African languages in a postcolonial Africa did *not* in fact end up writing in those languages. Though there were some like Ngugi and Wali, who chose to begin writing in an indigenous language, they constituted the exception rather than the rule. For his part, as an example, Jacques Rabemananjara, who was one of the first to refer to the language question, continued to write in French throughout his career, despite the existence of a well-established tradition of writing in Malagasy, his mother tongue.[26] The majority of those who commented on 'the language problem' did likewise, and made few recorded attempts to abandon writing in European languages or to systematically encourage writing in indigenous African languages.

In re-examining the relationship between the debates on language and the actual practice of those who wrote in European languages, one is led to conclude, therefore, that the debates did not generally function as a prelude to action, a sign of a radical and impending departure in matters of creative and or critical writing. On the contrary, the fact of commenting on the language of African literature hardly ever correlated with a decision to begin writing in indigenous African languages. The significance of these comments and their relationship to creative practice is perhaps best explicated then in somewhat different terms. From my understanding, it would seem that the concerns expressed about the impact of colonialism on the status of African languages, prominent as they were, did not generally take precedence over a number of other equally important considerations and objectives that had hitherto structured the practice of the acknowledged 'African' writer. It is worth asking then what purpose was served by these periodic expressions of angst over using the colonizer's language if they were not indicative of a definite intention to write in an indigenous African language.

I would like to propose that the first and major function of these debates was to distinguish African writing in European languages from Western writing in European languages. Having made the decision to write in European languages, and having made the decision to assume an identity other than that associated with writers in the Western canon, those involved in the establishment of the category of African literature needed a means by which their activity in European languages would be distinguished from the activity of writers from the Western world. Debates about language, and the entire critical apparatus that was mobilized to track traces of indigenous African languages in European-language texts functioned as only one of many strategies deployed to achieve this particular goal. Indeed, the recurrent discussions over language constituted one of the founding discourses of the genus of African literature, a body of texts largely composed in European languages and which required differentiation from texts composed in the same languages by writers from other parts of the world. The highlighting of the truly African credentials of these texts in European languages was certainly important to the writers themselves in the early years after independence, given the persistence of the tendency to question the commitments and identity of educated Africans generally, and of those who wrote in European languages in particular, a trend which as I have observed in the previous chapter was probably inaugurated in conjunction with colonial discourses of the vernacular.

I would also like to suggest, though, that one of the main reasons why many of those who expressed a concern over the fate of African languages never did make that transition to writing in indigenous languages was, precisely, because their commitment to the category of 'African' literature in the area of cultural production continued to supersede their commitment to entities such as Zulu literature or Akan literature and to the identities associated with their diverse mother tongues.[27] One of the most fascinating characteristics of the literature of advocacy for indigenous-language writing, therefore, is its frequent appeal to the adjective 'African' rather than to qualifiers of the specific languages, such as say, Shona or Ga, on whose behalf a campaign was being launched. Indeed, Ngugi (1981a: 1) explicitly cautions his readers against adopting so-called 'tribal categories' in interpreting the various crises on the continent. The activism of Ngugi and others like him who have spoken out on behalf of indigenous African languages in the literary field clearly differs in intention then from that of those European nationalists over the past few centuries who embraced mother tongue writing as part of a pursuit to obtain political autonomy for a specific territory and an envisaged monolingual state. While the other African critics and writers who have likewise spoken of the importance of writing in native languages do not necessarily adhere to Ngugi's political agenda, they too conduct their advocacy primarily on behalf of 'Africa,' and only secondarily in support of their regional linguistic and ethnic identities. Thus Wali's well-known critique of African writing in European languages does not so much address the challenge of writing in any one indigenous language, as that of defining 'African literature' as a body of texts with its own specific attributes, distinct from those associated with European literatures. Mazisi Kunene (1992) likewise speaks of 'African' philosophies, beliefs, institutions in his defense of writing in Zulu, while others make consistent references to the infirmity and obligations of 'African' writing. Given his own clear commitment to the space of 'Africa', rather than simply to Gikuyu nationalism, it is not surprising that in the end, even an Ngugi has been forced to continue producing theoretical writings in English on the present condition of the 'African' author and 'African literature.'[28]

In the area of creative literature, the word 'African' as part of the description or title of literary texts produced by Africans first appears in texts written and or read in European languages. Titles such as *Contes et légendes d'Afrique noire* by Ousmane Socé Diop (1938), and *Légendes africaines* by Maxmilien Quenum (1946) were fairly typical of literary production in Francophone West Africa from the 1930s. The title of Senghor's trailblazing *Anthologie de la nouvelle poésie nègre et malgache de langue française* reflects a similar homogenizing intent in its use of the word *nègre* (Black) which on some occasions functioned as a synonym for the term 'African' in the colonial context. Congresses of 'Black' writers soon followed in Paris and Rome where the languages of interaction were European, while the founding of a publishing house appropriately named Présence africaine, provided an outlet for the swelling stream of 'African' texts, invariably written in French. For those who wrote in English, conferences of 'African' writers such as the one organized at Kampala in 1962, the creation of the African Writers' Series under Heinemann Educational Books, as well as the publication of English-language journals like *Transition* and others mentioned earlier in this chapter, provided an identical institutional framework through which to disseminate a body of related 'African' texts. Certainly for the first half of the 20th century, African authors writing in European languages were as a group, the first creative writers, and often the mostly likely writers to use the term 'African' in respect of the identity of their work. We are of course justified in applying the adjective 'African' to the work of those who wrote in indigenous languages during the same period, as long as we also recognize that for many of them, Africanness was more often imputed to them by others, than self-assigned.

The second function of the debates over language was to challenge the domination of foreign scholars in African studies by critiquing the body of Africanist scholarship produced by non-Africans, many of whom were not proficient in the languages spoken in the communities on which they had produced so much knowledge and founded their often illustrious careers. These discussions about native languages fed into a larger project and discourse whose intention was to undermine the claims of universality made on behalf of Western scholars and Western scholarship especially as related to their reading of African cultures. A slew of articles dealing partly or substantially with the subject of universality and African literature began to appear as from the 1970s.[29] Among the creative writers, it was perhaps Achebe who spoke most forcefully on the matter. Writing in exasperation over the standards to which African literature written in European languages was expected to conform by some Western critics at the time, he objected,

> [i]t would never occur to them to doubt the universality of their own literature. In the nature of things the work of a Western writer is automatically informed by universality. It is only others who must strain to achieve it. So and so's work is universal; he has truly arrived! As though universality were some distant bend in the road which you may take if you travel out far enough in the direction of Europe or America, if you put adequate distance between you and your home. I should like to see the word *universal* banned altogether from discussions of African literature until such a time as people cease to use it as a synonym for the narrow, self-serving parochialism of Europe, until their horizon extends to include all the world. (1975: 9)

Both within and outside the literary field, the reservations expressed in respect of the 'ideal' of universality were further manifested in a distrust of theory, viewed as another attempt to foist the same principles in the form of a universal grammar designed within the realm of academic work about Africa to marginalize local subjects, their concerns and interventions.[30] Calling into question the results of fieldwork carried out by foreign researchers with limited or virtually no competence in the languages spoken by the communities on which they claimed considerable expertise, the Ghanaian anthropologist, Maxwell Owusu, also writing in the 1970s, noted the tendency for such scholars to interpret their distance from the material at hand as scientific detachment and to subordinate the ethnographic data to the supposedly more significant and rigorous imperatives of theoretical interpretation.[31] 'Alas,' he notes (1978: 317), and despite the appearance of intellectual complexity, 'the "theory" or "theories" generally turn out, on closer inspection, naturally to be well established, fairly orthodox Western views of society and culture, their origins and development, based on European academic and popular philosophical thought and experience, which are then applied to the whole of humanity.' Owusu maintains that 'theory' cannot be a substitute for a thorough ethnography and that no one can claim to have truly studied a people 'whose language he does not speak, read, and understand, and hence, whose world view he cannot truly share' (1978: 327). Ultimately, Owusu recognizes the questions he raises in his essay as pertaining to the distribution of power within the discipline of African studies, and calls for an open dialogue between foreign and native Africanists.

Nonetheless, there is little reason to conclude that in advancing this position, Owusu and others who have spoken about the significance of African languages in their writing are to be located in the same camp as those who would doubt the African credentials of all writing by Africans in European languages. Indeed, it is worth noting that these are generally authors who have come to terms with the necessarily multilingual space of Africa as a site of belonging and have continued to do most of their own writing in European languages. If such authors problematized matters of language, it was not with the intention of enabling the existence of a monolingual community forever closed to those who did not speak the native language; rather it was with a view to challenging the discourse on universality as it informed the dominant epistemologies in the fields of African literature and African studies writ large. By providing a more accurate and dependable interpretation of information initially offered in indigenous languages, African scholars who spoke the local languages and those non-Africans who bothered to learn these languages not only showed up the inadequacies of certain 'theories,' but also enhanced the value of their own work.[32]

As such, Owusu does not propound theories of ineradicable difference based on the figure of the vernacular. To the contrary, he calls attention to the constantly shifting linguistic situation of African communities that necessitates the learning of not one, but several local languages, and thus his preference for the acquisition of what he describes as 'polylinguistic skills' (1978: 324). If the existence of different languages points to the reality of unbridgeable cultural gulfs, then there is no need to seek proficiency in diverse African languages as Owusu clearly recommends for both African and non-African scholars. It is precisely because cultural translation is possible though difficult that he advocates learning of local languages as a prerequisite for studying foreign communities. In a general sense, his concern in this article has more to do with the tendency to privilege certain kinds of theoretical abstractions above a more substantive engagement with specific local communities, and thus to marginalize non-Western scholars whose strength lay in their ability to speak of and for these communities from within. It is clear then that unlike those who produced colonial discourses of the vernacular, Owusu and other Africans who spoke in a similar vein with regard to Africa's languages, were pursuing a rather different agenda and did not seem particularly committed to ideologies of cultural containment and purification. To further substantiate the case, I turn to Kourouma's *Soleils des indépendances*, a text that is especially rich for understanding the larger goals of the African scholars and writers who wrote in European languages but also spoke about indigenous African languages.

Kourouma's famous novel is a text that has been often examined from what I would like to describe as the recovery-of-the-indigenous-trace perspective, stressing the continuity of indigenous modes of speech in modern African cultural production. Kourouma's distinctive use of the French language is noted in practically every discussion of this text. And Kourouma himself has spoken at length on the subject in the many interviews he has conducted, giving the following explanation for his modification of the rules of the French language in this work: 'I think in Malinke and write in French . . . I have thus translated Malinke into French by breaking up the French language so as to recreate an African rhythm.'[33]

Even without the benefit of the author's clarifications linking his idiosyncratic practice of French in this novel to a desire to reconstruct the structures of the Malinke language, the attention given to an ample representation of a specific culture and homeland identified as Malinke culture is clearly evident in the narrative. Kourouma's decision to write in a style that can be recognized as culturally distinct is clearly motivated by a desire to have his fictional work identified with a place other than that usually associated with the French language, namely France. Kourouma's language practice does then serve to bolster and confirm his chosen identification as an author with another place, either Africa, Ivory Coast, or perhaps, the territory of those speaking the various Mande languages.

At this point, however, we must sort out and distinguish between multifarious forms of the politics of place energized by a diverse cast of actors and directed at divergent goals, bearing in mind the fact that the claim of translation is as much an exercise in locational politics as the act of translation. My suggestion, here, is that this writer's identification of his writing with a specific place does not necessarily signal affiliation with more exclusionary ideologies of place that may have wider political currency. Hartmann observes, in this connection, that some of the most exclusive and xenophobic nationalisms have originated in particular ideologies of place, noting with reference to the European Romantics:

> In the political sphere, unfortunately, simplification and demagogic exploitation make the appeal to the (lost) land and landed virtues, to native soil, *pays, patrie, Heimat, Heimatland*, a dangerous weapon of the revolutionary (i.e. counterrevolutionary) Right. The land and the dead buried in it combine to create a powerful topos of demagogic lamentation. Spirit of place (the genius loci) becomes not only a nostalgic subject of study but also a source for retroactive nationalistic, or identitarian claims. The Left, too, even when 'green' rather than 'red' in outlook, does not manage to articulate a philosophy of culture that escapes sentimentality or the suspicion that it is merely incubating another fanaticism or impractical political religion. (1997: 184)

The dangers pointed out by Hartmann are real and one might legitimately inquire whether Kourouma's own politics of place, evidenced in his references to translation, is mobilized for the benefit of such causes. Examining the specific novel in question, it does not seem to me that this is Kourouma's aim, although some readings of his interest in indigenous languages are crafted in terms which might suggest a potentially problematic nationalism. But before concluding that Kourouma's recourse to the strategy of translation in *Soleils des indépendances* is indicative of a non-negotiable commitment to writing in the vernacular, it is helpful to remember that texts like Kourouma's novel make sense only in a foreign language. Many of the strategies deployed would have been superfluous had the text originally been composed in Malinke for a presumably Malinke-speaking audience. These strategies do not actually amount to a statement of intention to write in an indigenous language. Rather they explicate indigenous culture to a non-native audience. Furthermore, we do not see exemplified in Kourouma's narrative many of the other ideological positions that Hartmann identifies with European artists committed to the genius loci. These include celebrating the landscapes of specific localities, the ideal of rootedness, cultural purity and faithfulness to cultural roots, notions of organic connections to place, disappearing rural culture, and the expression of antipathy towards urban 'modern' civilizations. In other words, Kourouma's statements about language do not apparently translate within the narrative itself into a certain kind of politics of place.

The central character, Fama, who we are told is a pure Malinke and legitimate descendant of the princes of the Doumbouya dynasty, who are rulers of Togobala village, is sterile. Nor is this simply a domestic matter, for Fama is otherwise unfruitful in every undertaking and endeavor, whether it be conjugal, commercial or political. Sterility is the defining trait of this embodiment of Malinke ethnicity who becomes the very personification of a narrow nationalism and devotion to the genius loci in this novel. While the European Romantics may have celebrated rural landscapes and lifestyles in their poetry, the narrator in this text takes care to point out the physical and moral desolation of Fama's place of birth, Togobala, in the countryside. The countryside is not here the obverse of a decadent urban setting, for despite his noble ancestry, Fama lives as a beggar in the capital city, and does as much on his return to his native village where he depends on his so-called servants, the griot, and the medicine man for sustenance and support. Furthermore, by providing readers with conflicting versions of foundational myths of Togobala, the narrator manages to cast aspersions on the claims to the territory made by Fama's Malinke ancestors. Organic connections to place are deconstructed here rather than being reified and consolidated. Furthermore, this is not the only instance in which we are made to distrust declarations made by the Malinke. The narrator compounds this distressing view of Malinke culture and its homeland with repeated references to the duplicity and deceptions of the Malinke. Since the narrator self-identifies himself as Malinke, these declarations can only generate among readers a distrust of the Malinke voice that the author is supposedly committed to reconstructing.

Given Fama's constant invective against the illegitimate independences, it is surely ironic that one of those who does survive where Fama has failed is his griot in the village, who is provided for in his old age by the two illegitimate grandchildren that his daughter had while she was a mistress of a French official in the colonial period. Thus, the character who best epitomizes the kind of commitment to cultural purity and places of origin that Hartmann associates with the Romantics, is the one who in this text remains sterile and ultimately dies a needless death. If, therefore, Kourouma's modification of the French language may be taken to signal a deliberate engagement with the politics of place and identity, it does not by association amount to an endorsement of an ethnocentric cultural nationalism. To take Kourouma as an example, the representation of sites and cultural practices that are recognizably traditional by some African authors, does not necessarily reference an alignment with ideologies of cultural purity. The fact that the most ardent defenders of the old order tend to be anti-heroes consigned to problematic deaths suggests a pervasive ambivalence towards 'tradition' in much of African writing in English and French.

In short, references to translation are the means by which this author intervenes in and contributes to the elaboration of a particular geo-cultural construct: namely African literature in French. Representations of specific sites in an imaginary Mande territory give density to these claims of translation, but do not amount to a corroboration of ideologies of place with a premium on notions of cultural purity. Kourouma, and I would suggest Owusu, are clearly not disciples of Herder or Fichte, and of those who insist on use of the mother tongue alone to the exclusion of all other languages. These are authors and scholars whose agenda consists not so much in recovering a linguistic status quo ante, or some kind of pre-lapsarian standing for indigenous languages, as in opening up a space of self-expression for educated Africans within existing configurations of power and given the conditions surrounding the production of knowledge about their communities in a postcolonial world. Certainly, within the field of criticism, a concern to explicate the oral, the vernacular, and the traditional, in relation to texts read in European languages developed among African scholars and alongside the emergence of African literature as an autonomous area, enabling such scholars to present themselves as privileged interpreters specifically on account of their familiarity with indigenous languages and cultures. Deploying the local, which is what these writers were engaged in through the positions taken, then becomes one strategy in the midst of other strategies for challenging political practices and epistemologies that systematically marginalize particular sites and communities under the rubric of a false universality.

Conclusion

Ngugi's description of the literature produced by Africans in European languages as 'Afro-Saxon' rather than truly African is familiar to most critics of African and postcolonial literatures. It is by now quite evident that I am not as inclined as Ngugi to question the African identity of this body of writing. On the contrary, I would like to suggest that we pay serious attention to the claims made by producers and or audiences that these cultural manifestations in non-native languages are indeed 'theirs' and attend to their needs in some way. In dismissing these texts as inauthentic or corrupted samples of African culture because they are written in non-native and by extension foreign languages, we miss what I consider to be perhaps the most noteworthy dimension of this development, and that is the significance of these non-native languages in the elaboration of a new site of affiliation and network of communication, namely in this instance 'Africa.'[34]

Ali Mazrui (1975: 11), Ngugi's compatriot, was perhaps the first to use the expression 'Afro-Saxon' in describing a new generation of African native speakers of English in a perceptive and often overlooked discussion of language and identity in Africa published several years ahead of Ngugi's *Decolonising the Mind*. Although Ali Mazrui approached the phenomenon of the Afro-Saxons with considerably more empathy than Ngugi, on occasion his arguments did seem to anticipate the directions later pursued by Ngugi. On the one hand, Mazrui highlights the contribution of shared languages among the educated elite, in particular English, but also French, Kiswahili and others to the development of African nationalist consciousness, and Pan-Africanist ideology in the last years of colonial rule and early years following independence. In this respect, he calls attention to what he describes as the 'detribalizing' properties of learning the English language, noting for the colonial period that '[i]f one found an African who had mastered the English language, that African had, almost by definition, ceased to be a full tribesman' (1975: 48). On the other hand, however, the very choice of the term 'Afro-Saxon' with reference to situations where a complete shift in mother tongues had occurred almost seemed to imply that populations which experienced such shifts became at the very least partially English, and developed some kind of hybrid identity. Ngugi's description of some African writers as Afro-Saxons for writing in non-native languages betrays similar presumptions.

Although I am primarily concerned in this book with instances where the 'foreign' language does not in fact become a mother tongue, I would like to point out that acquisition of English in Africa has not for the greater part of the 20th century resulted in identification with metropolitan English culture. As a matter of fact, it is increasingly the case that in cultural terms, either as a mother tongue or mostly as secondary language, English is deployed in contemporary Africa in relation to the culture of an African nation-state, in connection with a diffuse pan-Africanist sentiment, or global Black culture, and a host of other forms of non-English identifications. Learning an additional language does not merely give the speaker an ability to transcend particular sites of belonging as manifested in existing racial and ethnic boundaries (Ali Mazrui 1975: 70). It certainly can do that, but perhaps more importantly, changes in language repertoires generate a framework for constituting new ethnic and racial categories, new alliances and sodalities as part of a reconfiguration of the borders of what henceforth will be considered local. Though the point is not always explicitly articulated in this particular work, Mazrui himself gives examples of precisely such a development in his discussion of the relationship between language and the political practices associated with both African nationalism and the Pan-Africanist ideology.

The emergence of Africa as a potential site of affiliation and cultural continuity for Africans and non-Africans alike goes to the very heart of the arguments that I am making in this book about the nature of local culture in the contemporary world. As Anthony Appiah (1992: 174) has so quaintly put it, 'To speak of an African identity in the nineteenth century ... would have been 'to give to aery nothing a local habitation and a name." Even today, it is likely that outside of urban centers, many Africans still do not particularly think of themselves or define themselves using this particular qualifier with all that it presupposes in shared ancestries, cultures, outlook and so on. If the consciousness of a shared African culture and identity has now become lived reality for some segments of Africa's population, especially urban dwellers and the educated, it is initially and largely thanks to a field of interactions where business is conducted in what are for the majority of African participants non-native languages shared in common. In this instance as in others around the world, communities and identities are defined, not only through particular practices, but also through communication networks where dialog and interaction occurs in selected languages over matters of common interest. Without this field of verbal interaction, Africanness as a self-assigned identity claimed by thousands of people on opposite ends of the continent, could not exist.

Africanness in the sense of origination from the continent does continue to be largely incarnated in 'native' or vernacular languages, but when Africans are theorizing Pan-Africanness in writing, that is speaking of Africa as an area of cultural and political coherence, using a system of verbal signs where intelligibility is a requirement for communication, this activity is almost always carried out in a language that is not a mother tongue except in those instances where the mother tongue is also a language of wider communication employed by many different communities. And despite the misgivings expressed by some in regard to the continuing reliance on European languages, in particular, in the area of creative writing, these constructs in non-native languages have contributed enormously to naturalizing the idea of Africa as a space of mutually legible cultures inhabited by populations sharing a common destiny. The fact that some educated and urban Africans today define their primary identity as 'African' almost without second thought, is a development that we can trace back to a lifetime of familiarity with these practices in non-native languages which both exemplified and postulated notions of a shared destiny and vocation in respect of a territory designated as Africa.

'African literature' exists, then, in the first place, as a field of interactions and a communications network where the languages of communication are non-native languages of wider communication. The reliance on languages of wider communication is in this setting inevitable since the entity that provides the basis for this field of interactions is circumscribed by reference to geography, by reference to a territory where diverse mother tongues are spoken, rather than to language. As I have argued in Chapter 1, these languages of wider communication do not in fact have to be European languages. But in order for African languages to serve the function of language of wider communication for these categories constructed around geography and territory, African scholars, critics, and writers will have to develop alternative kinds of discourses and practices around indigenous languages, discourses that focus on the strategic importance of indigenous languages of wider communication instead of on the authenticity of mother tongues. That they have largely failed to do so, even within individual states, is a testimony to the enduring power of discourses of the vernacular in conversations pertaining to the language of literature in Africa since the 1940s. Except the entity to which a field of interactions refers is a territory whose inhabitants are by definition monolingual, writing in the vernacular is necessarily antithetical to the development of a communications network constructed around the idea of belonging to a territory. In the end, those who profess equal commitment to an identity defined in relation to a shared mother tongue, and an identity defined in terms of belonging to a territory encompassing communities that do not share the same mother tongue, must produce the discourses which embody this territorial identity in a language of wider communication that will be a non-native language for most of the participants in this field of interactions.

West African languages like Yoruba are clearly major world languages, spoken by millions of people living predominantly in southwestern Nigeria, and in variously sized communities across the West African coast and elsewhere in the world. The same observation could be made for several other languages spoken in West Africa and other regions on the continent. But, and this is a critical point, the majority of speakers of Yoruba till date are mother tongue speakers. In this regard, Yoruba does not play a similar function in people's lives as languages like Krio, Nigerian Pidgin, Hausa, Twi or Dyula that are now being used and acquired by an increasing number of non-native speakers in West Africa. It is this specific function that European languages have played for those individuals who committed themselves to producing an 'African' literature. These languages are not simply foreign languages or the languages of the colonizer, they are specifically in this context, languages of wider communication. By this I do not mean that they enjoy a wider popularity around Africa than many vernacular languages and mother tongues. Rather, it is the case that those who choose or desire to create new kinds of associations and to communicate beyond the communities constituted around today's 'native languages' will have recourse to languages that enable them to communicate across the borders and barriers which exist at the present time. Taking this argument to its logical conclusion, I would like to propose at this point an additional definition for the well-known linguistic concept of the language of wider communication: it is a language that enables the formation of sodalities whose members do not necessarily share in common the same mother tongue or primary site of belonging, and where therefore imaginations of the local are subject to reformulation.

Obviously, mother tongues that are not at the same time languages of wider communication continue to play an important role in many spheres of life in contemporary Africa. However, the resiliency of cultural production in both indigenous and non-native second and third languages as media of communication along other kinds of social axes, suggests that notwithstanding the diversity of their political affiliations, there are significant and growing constituencies in contemporary Africa including for example the urban youth, certain types of religious groupings, and the highly educated who choose as part of their cultural repertoire a deliberate identification with cultural forms that are at once 'modern' and at the same time local, in the sense of not being Western, and that are almost invariably expressed in indigenous and non-native languages of wider communication, including Hausa, Pidgin, Kiswahili, Lingala, but also French, English, and Portuguese, among other languages. Such forms of identification are not simply deviations to be deplored and wished away; rather they present us with some of the new faces of community in contemporary Africa.

Imaginations of kinship and shared ancestry are frequently the hallmark of an acknowledgement of sharing the same mother tongue. By contrast the affiliations that emerge in non-native languages will in all probability be explained by reference to other kinds of convictions. With multilingualism and polyglottism likely to remain the norm in contemporary Africa for the foreseeable future, we can certainly envisage the development of many more politically and culturally significant sodalities that may not necessarily invoke myths of shared ancestry. In expanding one's language repertoire to include such languages, it is not so much a question of giving up a native identity as of reformulating the spatial coordinates of belonging and the character of belonging. The kind of considerations which led some educated West Africans to begin describing themselves as 'Yoruba' and using a standard reconstructed and reified by missionaries at the end of the 19th century are the very same kind of considerations that have led a different generation of West Africans since the mid-20th century to begin describing themselves as 'Africans' using yet another medium of wider communication to bring this sodality into existence.[35]

Languages exclude but also include. Non-native languages in Africa generate both new zones of exclusion and fresh zones of inclusion. From the perspective of the arguments that I am developing in this book, debates about language are also ultimately debates about new sites of inclusion and new types of affiliation. If the alliances that are adjudged politically expedient for a given age can be constructed in languages recognized as mother tongues, then there is no need for debate and no grounds for recourse to a language of wider communication. Where new alliances become imperative for political survival, new imaginations of the local are likely to follow, and in the absence of indigenous languages of wider communication, these new imaginations of the local may very well be fashioned in non-native languages. The elaboration of Africa as a site of belonging and shared destiny, in and through literary texts in European languages, among other means, is thus a prime example of the kind of maneuvering that results in the designation of certain activities and practices as local culture, even though it is clearly understood that these practices are neither indigenous nor traditional. Local culture in this formulation is frequently correlated with the necessity on the political front of creating additional associations and alliances in response to the most recent challenges faced by communities.

Thus far, in this chapter, I have used the expressions native and local culture almost interchangeably. I find it useful at this juncture to begin making some distinctions. There are practices in the contemporary world which may be viewed as exemplifying local culture, to the extent that they are deployed on behalf of spaces envisioned as legitimate sites of belonging, but which cannot be considered native or traditional culture since their novelty and indeed modernity is just as clearly indicated. In asserting ownership of these practices, and constructing through them sites of belonging, the intent is not so much to repudiate the space of native culture as to extend the range and territory in respect of which belonging and shared interests can be invoked, inclusive of but not limited to native culture. It is this expanded site of belonging that I describe here as local culture. Envisaged this way, the local is not simply the obverse of the global, or just another term for distinguishing between the foreign and the native. Rather it is a claim to distinctiveness that may entail dissolving old boundaries between the foreign and the native while establishing fresh border posts between newly designated insiders and outsiders, between acknowledged affiliates and those located outside the chosen fold.

And given the considerable amount of interest manifested in transnational cultural flows as one dimension among others of a globalizing age, it is perhaps useful to reiterate that the rise of this global age has not resulted in a dissipation of the sense of the local, of a sense of belonging to a circumscribed territorial unit. While there are obvious overlaps in meaning, I am not referring here simply to the perpetuation and intensification of the social phenomena described by Appadurai (1996) as primordialisms which may involve activism on a transnational scale but where the geographic framework of the local remains basically unchanged. When people from the African continent who might have described themselves using other terms, identify themselves as Africans and invoke 'Africa' as a site of cultural affinity in contrast to other possible and more restricted sites of belonging, the space of the local is in this case expanded. Changes in language repertoires are one indication among others of this on-going modification of the geographic coordinates of the local.

Participants in the field of interactions generated around entities like 'African literature,' Africans and non-Africans, alike, form a geographically dispersed transnational community, responding to each other's discourses, meeting occasionally at international conferences, holding conversations about an expanded site of belonging through channels established in selected languages. Though they are widely traveled, well educated, speak several languages and are familiar with several African and non-African cultures, many of the African participants do not appear to fit the profile developed by Hannerz (1990) in his discussion of 'cosmopolitans' among other kinds of mobile subjects. For one thing, they hardly ever embrace the framework of cosmopolitanism in their acts of self-identification. Indeed, if true cosmopolitans have lost the ability to feel 'at home' even at home, these African writers and critics never quite lose a sense of connection to a home in Africa, even abroad.[36] As with previous generations of long-term African exiles and expatriates, the term 'Africa' gradually becomes interchangeable with the name of a village of origin, of an ethno-linguistic unit, a region, or even a state. The constantly renewed experience of marginalization in diverse locales dims the appeal of the principle of hybridity for all but a select few, despite the continuing need to use non-native languages for communication with 'fellow' Africans. Instead, such Africans have shown a preference for the principle of clearly bordered but geographically expanded attachments, and membership of a territorially circumscribed community. In other words, their acts of self-identification have been constructed around the idea of the local, and a locality situated outside of metropolitan centers.

Colonial languages, like all languages of power, are fated to acquire a large company of non-native speakers, and more often than not, the operative languages in the constitution of expanded sites of belonging in postcolonial contexts have been colonial languages. In theory, any language, and not necessarily languages of colonizers, could have served the purpose since as Anderson (1991: 133) has observed, '[m]uch the most important thing about language is its capacity for generating imagined communities, building in effect *particular solidarities*.' In practice, colonial languages have tended to play a determinant role because colonialism provided the context, forum, and structures in which communication became imperative and initial encounters took place. As a rule then, many of the constructed kinships and affiliations elaborated around geographically dispersed populations today are established using colonial languages, languages systematically deployed beyond the territory of their own native speakers as part of the necessary infrastructure in a process of internationalization which continues to gather pace in the contemporary political and economic realm.

Erlmann (1999: 8) has suggested that '[t]he formation of modern identities always already occurs in the crucible of intensely spatially interconnected worlds.' In highlighting the inevitable contribution of non-native languages to certain constructions of the local today, however, I do not merely seek to call attention to the hybrid character of the identities and cultural classifications in question, but to underscore the continuing appeal of a sense of distinctiveness even to groups of people whose professional, creative, and other lives unfold in non-native languages and at this intersection of connected worlds. If it is true that the local has always been constituted in relation to and in connection with the non-local, it is also the case that both entities are always on the move and their scope of application is continually subject to revision.

Obviously, the languages I have been concerned with here are in the main European languages, but simply speaking about imaginations of the local in European languages would not shed light on the difference between an Australian writer for whom English is a mother tongue, and an Indian or African writer for example, who frequently has another mother tongue and may speak additional indigenous languages. An author who writes in a mother tongue which also happens to be a global language does not necessarily make a choice to venture outside the circle of alliances forged on the basis of communication via the mother tongue. We cannot presume that the author's sense of the local differs markedly from that of previous generations of compatriots who were engaged in cultural production in the same mother tongue. An author who writes in a non-native language, however, necessarily initiates or strengthens the formation of alliances that no longer depend on the mother tongue, thus contributing to the elaboration of alternative sites of belonging and a possible redefinition of the local.

What the early generations of authors of 'African literature' did share in common, if anything, was the experience of colonial domination and a determination to go beyond the role of native informant assigned to literate Africans, becoming as it were their own spokespersons. The ones who wrote in the languages of the colonizer were distinguished from those who wrote in mother tongues mainly in that they had traveled farther away from 'home' reaching the apex of what Anderson describes as 'academic pilgrimages' (1991: 121) in institutions of higher learning and locations where new relationships were formed and kinships constructed as part of the resistance against colonial rule. The critical locations for African literature in English were the universities of Ibadan in Nigeria and Makerere in Uganda. Many of the early East and West African authors in the Heinemann series met as students speaking different mother tongues at these universities and recognized each other as fellow companions on the same mission despite the diversity of their mother tongues. The critical locations for African literature in French were Paris, but also Gorée in Senegal, and Bingerville in Ivory Coast, both notable meeting places in the development of an 'African' literature in French. And those who were not graduates of those particular schools among others had almost all been contemporaries in Paris, and other major French cities.

By contrast, St Andrews College, Oyo, attended by early authors, like Fagunwa, who wrote in Yoruba, a mother tongue, did not represent the apex of the system, and most importantly, brought together a less diverse student body, speaking mostly Yoruba or languages closely related to Yoruba. Thus graduates of such schools drew upon a more restricted circle of associates linguistically speaking in their responses to the colonial experience. Often, these authors who wrote in mother tongues were also literate in English and could conceivably have produced their creative texts in this non-native language. Their decision to write in a mother tongue may be considered an indication of where the bounds of primary locality lay for them. It was a pointer to the fact that they envisioned the significant local community in their lives as defined by language rather than by geography and as comprising primarily speakers of a common mother tongue rather than simply residents of a given territorial unit.[37]

Identification with the site of Africa may be fairly young in comparison to some of the other forms of identification prevalent on the African continent today, yet it is a form of identification that has come to occupy a prominent position both within and beyond the continent at the present time. As I have suggested thus far, the logistics of constructing such expanded sites of belonging and networks of affiliation as 'African literature' and 'African culture' will require the use of languages of wider communication that will in some instances be non-native languages. What the recourse to non-native languages of wider communication therefore reveals above all is the latest scope, territorial and otherwise of the space of the local and the space of belonging. When the guard whom Hamilton encountered at the Mozambican border in the 1970s challenged his newly reclassified compatriot for not speaking Portuguese, he was in effect making a statement about the changing limits of locality from his own perspective. No longer was the interlocutor simply a fellow speaker of Ronga, he had become a fellow citizen of Mozambique, a territory whose borders extended beyond the ancestral lands of the Ronga-speaking peoples. Though unintended, the guard's statements offer some insight into what it means when members of any community begin to live parts of their life in someone else's language.[38] And as we track these varied interventions in non-native languages, including forms of imaginative expression identified by reference to territory rather than to language, we begin to get a sense of how spaces of belonging are being currently configured both in relation to native culture and in relation to those newer manifestations that I have described here as constituting local culture.

Notes

1. See for example the special issue of *Research in African Literatures*, volume 23, on the language of African literature in 1992, where most of the African contributors discussed the language situation from this angle. Later in this chapter (note 21), I provide a list of African authors and critics who have commented on the subject. With few exceptions, the majority of those African authors and critics writing about this question before the mid-1990s viewed the use of a non-native language in written African literature as singularly problematic. In textbooks and readers devoted to postcolonial theory (Williams & Chrisman, 1994; Ashcroft et al., 1995), Achebe and Ngugi were often seen as representing two poles in this debate: on the one hand, a reluctant coming to terms with the language of the former colonizer (Achebe), and on the other, a rejection of the language of the former colonizer (Ngugi).
2. And even among the Lagos Victorians, as Zachernuk (2000: 28–46) demonstrates, identification with the British was both fluid and variable.
3. Ali Mazrui (1975: 50) alludes to what he describes as a linguistic cosmopolitanism of many Francophone African leaders during the colonial period, motivated by their considerable attachment to the French language. There was no doubt a greater sense of loyalty to the imperial power among Francophone African politicians than was the case among Anglophone Africans at the same period. But I am not sure that one can argue that they were true cosmopolitans in the sense of being able to feel at home everywhere. They felt at home in France and among those who spoke French, but not in Britain and with those who did not share the French language in common with them. Furthermore, what I find remarkable is that these leaders began to think of themselves as forming some kind of confraternity with fellow politicians from other parts of the continent with whom they did not share a mother tongue, but who like them had mastered this language among other possible languages.
4. Most recently Gates (1990) and Appiah (1992).

5. See Crummell, *The Future of Africa*, (1862: 9–54).
6. In other words, the primary motivations are frequently instrumental (Edwards, 2001: 115). However, I am suggesting that there is also an integrative dimension to acquisition of non-native languages, one that pertains to an identity other than that of the native speakers of the language and which is particularly evident when these non-native languages begin to be used in cultural production.
7. Klíma, Růžička and Zima (1976: 156) refer to the levels of intelligibility between Fanti and Twi. Though the British Wesleyans taught in English rather than the vernacular, the first texts written in Fanti were produced by personnel of the Wesleyan mission.
8. Izevbaye (1997: 163) points out that Fagunwa was from Ondo, and was born in Okeigbo. Both locations are now considered part of Yoruba territory, but there is little doubt that before the coming of the missionaries, inhabitants of either place did not describe themselves as Yoruba.
9. For information on Bezoro, see Adejunmobi (1996). Ricard (1987) provides a useful introduction to Couchoro's work. After the majority of former French colonies in Africa had received their independence in the 1960s, Bakary Diallo's writing began to receive much more attention in discussions of Francophone African literature than it had in earlier decades.
10. See Adejunmobi (1996) for a further discussion of Rabearivelo's perception of his cultural identity.
11. Generally speaking, the earliest authors who wrote in the vernacular were not as well educated as succeeding generations who wrote in European languages, and they likely had fewer opportunities to interact with those who spoke other mother tongues. The absence of many vernacular language writers from discussions which developed around the category of 'African literature' may be attributed in part to this fact. But it is also true that there were writers for whom commitment to the mother tongue precluded involvement in alliances that did not involve speakers of the same mother tongue. An example would be the Zulu writer, John Dube (1870–1949) who, as he grew older tended to channel his political activities into customary Zulu political institutions while distancing himself from associations that cut across ethno-linguistic lines.
12. Ngugi (1981a: 82–4) implies this in his account of the sales of his Gikuyu-language novel, *Caitaani Mūtharabainī*. The specific question of an African audience's accessibility to written European-language texts is one that has preoccupied many African authors and critics who have lent their support to indigenous-language writing. I think here of critics and authors like Isola (1992), Mlama (1990), and Wali (1963). In Chapter 3 of this book, I consider the arguments made about African audiences and non-native languages in greater detail.
13. The politics of the individual writer, his or her style of writing, the infrastructure of publishing, the agenda of the literary establishment in place are all factors that will deter or encourage the emergence of an audience around a text. Thus Ricard (2000: 73) notes that Hussein's newer plays are not prescribed school texts in Tanzania, Hussein's country and many students are unaware of their existence. Again and again, he mentions texts by Hussein for which there are few or no reviews, and plays that are indeed written in the local language but not understood and rarely read.
14. Though institutional support does exist among interested scholars for litera-

tures in some indigenous languages in Africa, such support has thus far rarely attracted the kind of political urgency that would lead to a more widespread and consistent teaching of literatures in local languages since this obviously requires the support of the state. To reiterate a point made in the previous chapter, there are political and territorial implications for certain kinds of policies about language. An emphasis on diverse indigenous-language literatures makes sense in the educational system if a central government is willing to accord greater autonomy to administrative units constructed along ethnolinguistic lines. But where the territorial integrity of the multilingual state is itself far from secure and mutual suspicion is rife among different ethnolinguistic groups, it is unlikely that the dominant interests in control of a centralized educational system will make significant investment in the literature produced in the various languages spoken within the polity, though they may claim allegiance to the principle of education in the mother tongue. The tendency in such circumstances will be to teach literatures in mother tongues within circumscribed regions at the lower levels of the educational system as part of instruction in literacy, and to transition to an emphasis on languages of wider communication and literatures in those languages at the higher levels of the system as part of a program of nation-building.

15. Although I am not referring here only to printed matter, I have in mind the kind of network that Anderson (1991: 41) speaks of when he notes, for example, the role of 'print-languages' in establishing 'unified fields of exchange and communication' which were to play a major role in the development of European nationalisms.
16. See Werner Sollors (1998) for a discussion of some of America's literatures in other languages.
17. Sorensen (2000: 2) substantiates my point when she inquires 'Is Britain a nation? Or is it merely a state composed of four nations of Wales, England, Scotland, and Ireland?'
18. Gérard (1981: 311–12; 1990: 3–25) has frequently invoked the development of vernacular literatures in Europe as a model for educated Africans to consider. Ngugi (1981a: 29) too has made comments in a similar vein. So have Irele (1981: 54), Wali (1963: 14), Owomoyela (1992: 91), Kunene (1992: 33), and Sanneh (1993: 78–82). Although one could make a case for also examining the marginalization of writing in languages like Oromo and Tigrinya in relation to Amharic in Ethiopia, I have felt it important to address the European experience here since it has so often been proposed as a precedent worthy of emulation in discussions of vernacular language writing in Africa.
19. With respect to British literature, for example, Sorenson (2000: 29) alludes to 'recent moves towards understanding British literature as not simply the literature of England in English, but also as inclusive of the diverse languages and cultures of the British isles . . .'
20. I refer again to Sorensen's (2000: 19) recent and informative discussion of the dynamics involved in establishing official national culture by privileging one language at the expense of other languages spoken within the same domain with special reference to the case of Great Britain.
21. My survey of articles on the subject is far from complete, but just to give an idea of the spate of writing on the question of language and African literature since the 1940s, I provide the following as a partial list of articles and books written by African critics and creative writers: Chinua Achebe (1975, 1990); Kofi Anyidoho

(1992); B. I. Chukwuemeka (1969); David Diop (1956); Cyprian Ekwensi (1956); Kamini Gecau (1972); Akinwunmi Isola (1992); Abiola Irele (1981, 2000); Eldred Jones (1957); K. A. B. Jones-Quartey (1949); Mazisi Kunene (1992); Penina Mlama (1990); Ezekiel Mphahlele (1963); Ngugi wa Thiong'o (1981a, 1993); Ben Obumselu (1966); Gabriel Okara (1963); Isidore Okpewho (1978); Juliet Okonkwo (1976); Oyekan Owomoyela (1992); Ken Saro-Wiwa (1992); Obiajunwa Wali (1963); Edward Okwu (1966); O. K. Poku (1948); Wole Soyinka (1988).
22. A selection of papers from that meeting and from the 1992 issue of *Research in African Literatures* was recently published in a co-edited book by Smith and Kunene (2002).
23. Whether we refer to emerging local standards for these languages or to such creolized forms as Français Populaire Ivoirien and Nigerian Pidgin, there is no doubt that local forms of European languages are developing in many African urban settings. See Elugbe and Omamor (1991) for information on Nigerian Pidgin, and Gabriel Manessy (1994) on Français Populaire Ivoirien.
24. Friedrich Schleiermacher, a German philosopher, made the following observation about translators in the 19th century: 'Either the translator leaves the author in peace, as much as possible, and moves the reader towards him; or he leaves the reader in peace, as much as possible, and moves the author towards him' (cited in Venuti, 1995: 19–20).
25. And yet as McLaughlin (2001) has demonstrated in her essay on the language of cartoons in Dakar in the 1990s, the challenges of representing this mixed urban code can be overcome. However, such texts are fully intelligible only to those who are literate in *both* the languages used. Where authors offer representations of indigenous languages using a non-native language like English, monolingual readers of English need no proficiency in the indigenous language in order to follow the text.
26. And this fact is no doubt connected with his lengthy exile in France, but also and more importantly with his lifelong involvement with the Présence Africaine publishing house, journal and writers, historically one of the leading forces in the creation of a specifically 'African literature.'
27. Writing for example about Soyinka, Quayson (1997: 77) notes Soyinka's transfer of Yoruba ritual into an 'an Africanist cultural discourse' in his *Myth, Literature and the African world*, where Yoruba culture comes to somehow stand for African culture as a whole. Innes (1996: 138–9) makes a similar observation about both Soyinka and Achebe among other postcolonial writers: 'They narrate or dramatize events and stories which are local and specific to Igbo or Yoruba history, but which may be multiplied or enlarged to represent the stories of the colonial encounter in many other parts of Ireland, Australia, Nigeria, or Africa.'
28. Ngugi (1993: xiv) himself alludes to the difficulties involved in publishing critical and theoretical work in an indigenous African language.
29. Some of the articles on the subject of the universal and African literature include the following: Mahood (1977); Larson (1972); Armah (1976); Achebe (1975); Nwoga (1973-4); Awonoor (1973–4); Emenyonu (1972); Ngugi wa Thiong'o (1993).
30. Similar concerns continue to be expressed today, not so much in a discourse about language as in a discourse about the place of theory in African literature. The emergence of postcolonial theory as a major paradigm to be applied to

African literature did not help matters much, appearing as it did to privilege expatriate scholars and to undermine the specificity of location under its increasingly weighty analytical momentum. See Jeyifo (1990); Osundare (1993); Osofisan (2000).

31. On a somewhat different topic, Brennan comes to an identical conclusion about the possible tensions between theory and ethnography. He (1997: 270) writes about 'ethnography, whose late borrowings from literary criticism have provided compensatory capital for a discipline endangered by the extermination of its very object of study. What ethnography lost by giving up the primitive, it gained in theory.'

32. In several branches of the humanities, the work of African scholars consisted precisely in such acts of critical interpretation. Owusu himself engages in such an exercise of critical interpretation in this article as he corrects the translations and conclusions drawn by Dunn and Robertson (1974) in their work on a particular Ghanaian community.

33. 'J'ai pensé en malinké et écrit en français ... J'ai donc traduit le malinké en français en cassant le français pour trouver et restituer le rythme africain' (Cited in Koné, 1992: 83).

34. It is not surprising therefore that defenders of the vernacular legacy of missionary activity in Africa like Sanneh find the Pan-Africanist agenda that I have linked here to the use of non-native languages of wider communication guilty of 'overlooking linguistic and social particularity' (1993: 82).

35. See Law (1976, 1996) for information on what he describes as the activity of 'ethnogenesis' carried out by the educated Yoruba in the late 19th and early 20th centuries.

36. Brennan's remarks (1997: 45) are pertinent here: 'If the primary sense of place for many former residents of colonized countries is no longer the nation, it is often a local or ethnic culture packed off into exile, jumbled together with the official cultures of the metropolis (and the cultures of other immigrants), and where not carried on, remembered.'

37. Gérard (1981: 252), describes many early Yoruba-language writers as belonging to the 'school-teacher class', a class whose members, as I have suggested, mostly attended higher institutions where they shared the same mother tongue with many of their contemporaries. Later writers in Yoruba did not necessarily share a similar educational background, and indeed may have had considerable exposure to other languages and cultures. But no doubt, in choosing to write in a mother tongue they too drew the boundaries of significant locality mainly around speakers of the same mother tongue.

38. I am playing here with the question asked by Deleuze and Guattari (1986: 19) in their discussion of language and minor literature: 'How many people today live in a language that is not their own?' This chapter is intended to answer a related question: what does it mean when a people begin to live in a language that is not their own?

Chapter 3

Foreign Languages, Local Audiences: The Case of Nigerian Video Film in English

The relationship between 'foreign' languages, linguistic intelligibility and African popular culture has for long been the subject of significant misunderstanding. Founded on an extrapolation of principles first enunciated in respect of African literature to the realm of African popular culture, this misunderstanding has in time taken on the form of an unchallenged orthodoxy. According to the prevailing school of thought, cultural products in indigenous languages are often guaranteed acceptance among African popular audiences while activities in 'foreign,' especially European, languages hold little appeal for African audiences. A willingness to engage with activity in 'foreign' languages is presumed to depend on advanced proficiency, and thus on access to education, wealth and so on. Cultural products in 'foreign' languages are considered intelligible only to elite audiences, while European languages in particular are believed to operate in African cultural practice mainly as signifiers of the colonial experience. I am going to argue here that these assumptions embody the limitations of a framework for situating language in cultural production, largely predicated on the function of linguistic intelligibility. Activities in 'foreign' languages do not necessarily, and on account of language alone qualify as elite culture. But in order to extend our understanding of the multi-faceted ways in which Africans apprehend activities in non-native languages, we will need to address ourselves to questions other than those relating to proficiency and linguistic intelligibility alone.

The eclecticism and syncretism of urban-based African popular culture is now regularly acknowledged (Barber, 1987a; Hannerz, 1987). Interestingly, in at least some instances (Hannerz, 1987; Ben-Amos, 1977), categories borrowed from linguistics have provided the basic framework for understanding the growing 'creolization' of African urban cultures. Scholars of language, for their part, have been investigating the ramifications of this development for African language practices by, for example, studying code-switching in contemporary Africa and by describing African varieties of European languages.[1] My interest though, is not so much in the formal properties of language and cultural encounter as in the connection between language use and the constitution of audiences for particular cultural texts. I think it useful to separate such questions from descriptions of everyday language use because access to cultural activity in a given language does not consistently depend on everyday language practice. Where creativity and the imagination are at play, audiences engage with, but are not limited to features connected with comprehension in terms of language. We cannot assume therefore that those who are not proficient in a particular language will never take interest in the plays, songs, commercials and other cultural products available in that language, especially in urban settings where cultural activity is so often sought as a diversion from rather than as an extension of daily reality.

Objectively speaking and to start with, the English language in a country like Nigeria is undoubtedly the language of the former colonizing power. It is also the main language of higher education beyond the elementary level, the language used by the elite in its official transactions, one of the major languages of wider communication, and in these contexts an established second language. It is furthermore from the perspective of those Nigerians and Africans involved in promoting use of indigenous languages, non-native and subject to all the reservations expressed in respect of 'foreign' languages.[2] While most of the concern with the future of indigenous languages in Africa has emanated in connection with the growing use of such 'foreign' languages, several scholars have argued convincingly that indigenous lingua francas for the time being pose the greater threat to many minority vernaculars in Africa.[3] In the West African context for example, the shift to Wolof in Senegalese urban centers at the expense of other Senegalese languages like Serer, Pulaar, Mandinka, Dyula has received considerable attention.[4]

In other words, and with few exceptions, the use of European languages in select domains in Africa has rarely resulted in a complete language shift in favor of a European language. Rather, we are witnessing what seems destined to be a long-term cohabitation of European and other non-native languages side by side with diverse vernaculars. At the same time, indigenous lingua francas whose domain of utility is in constant expansion, are in contemporary Africa rarely perceived as 'foreign' in the way in which European languages remain marked by foreignness despite the fact that they have been present in places like the West African coast for several centuries now. Accordingly the upsurge of creative activity in indigenous lingua francas is not coded as 'foreign' even though such activity frequently signals growing detachment from other local vernaculars. Nonetheless, the fact that languages identified as 'foreign' flourish alongside both indigenous lingua francas and various vernaculars, means that at the level of cultural activity different languages can be used in different settings to generate different kinds of audiences.

My intention then is to propose and investigate additional ways of understanding the interaction between such 'foreign' languages and popular culture in Africa. By comparing Nigerian video film in English with other forms of Nigerian urban culture, I hope to further understanding of the principles underlying the deployment of English and other 'foreign' languages in some African popular cultures. This leads me to interrogate the category of the popular audience and the role of 'foreign' languages in the constitution of such audiences in contemporary Africa. I believe that within the realm of cultural activity, a non-native language will not have the same significance for all sectors of any society. Not only does local politics reconfigure the symbolic roles attributed to a 'global' language like English in each society, as suggested by Pennycook (1994: 225–6), the same language may acquire multiple meanings for diverse groups within the same society at any single point in time. It becomes critical then to determine what values appeal to specific groups and the role played by language in constituting these values for particular texts and contexts. I end this chapter by arguing for increased recognition of the multiplicity of responses engendered by disparate cultural activities using the same 'foreign' language within the same society.

Video Film in Nigeria

Nigerian video film makes for a productive reading of the varied functions of 'foreign' languages in African popular culture, especially since its emergence and scope of influence cannot be readily attributed to cultural imperialism.[5] On the one hand, the video film phenomenon in Nigeria is related to the upsurge of small-scale media technologies in many parts of the world at the end of the 20th century. At the same time, the global dimensions of these technologies are frequently moderated by the fact of their prominent intervention in constructions of 'locality.' Notwithstanding parallels outside of Nigeria and in other 'postcolonial' locales, each country and context therefore yields its own audio-visual narratives, its own appropriation of the technology towards local ends.[6] For one thing, local capitalism rather than foreign sponsorship has provided the financial incentive for the development of this vibrant field. In the words of Haynes (1997: 2), Nigerian films have from the onset been 'produced almost exclusively with Nigerian money.' But, not only do the films originate under the impetus of local market forces, they also pander to local tastes in very specific ways to be discussed shortly.[7] During the course of the 1990s, these films in languages like Yoruba, Igbo, Pidgin, Hausa, and English rapidly became a remarkable force on the Nigerian urban entertainment market. By the mid-1990s, annual production had risen to at least 250 (Adesanya, 2000: 43), while some observers now estimate that new films are being released on the market at the rate of one new film per day. And according to one of the leading producers of English and Igbo-language films in Nigeria, in the initial boom period of video film production, a successful film could sell as many as 50,000 copies per month (Ejiro, 1998: 19).

The origins of Nigerian video film are usually traced to the Yoruba-language traveling theater tradition. Frequently described as a 'popular theater' by reason of its audience and producers (Barber, 1982), traveling theater emerged among Yoruba-speaking communities in southwestern Nigeria during the colonial period. Although the itinerant troupes often performed live, some groups were already exploiting the medium of television on a regular basis by the 1960s. The most popular troupe directors began film production for their stage works in the late 1970s and early 1980s. Despite the success of the early Yoruba films, Nigeria entered into a period of significant economic decline at about the same time, making big screen production unfeasible for many smaller troupes. Discouraged by the increasingly low financial returns on television production, they turned to video technology, and by the late 1980s Yoruba video film had come into existence.[8] The producers of the first Igbo-language video films in the early 1990s soon discovered the potential of films in other languages, and pioneered English-language productions shortly afterwards. A Hausa-language video film tradition also began to emerge soon afterwards in northern Nigeria. As the earliest form of Nigerian video film, Yoruba-language film remains a significant force on the Nigerian video film market, nonetheless it was already evident by the end of the 1990s that English-language film had become the fastest growing sector of the Nigerian video film market.[9] And if the trend continues, English-language films will be one of the dominant forms of Nigerian video film even though production of Yoruba- and Hausa-language films in particular is likely to continue for reasons to be discussed later in the chapter.

Video film production has become a significant cultural and commercial presence within contemporary Nigeria and in the Nigerian diaspora abroad.[10] Nigerian video films are also widely available in markets across West Africa, particularly in Ghana, where a parallel video film tradition has also developed in recent years. In addition to generating envied incomes for the producers in particular, the Nigerian films animate attention around and visibility for all those involved in the production process. 'Stars' such as Richard Mofe-Damijo, Liz Benson, Zack Orji, or Ramsey Nouah, to name only a few, benefit from name recognition among English-language video film fans, as do major production companies like Mainframe, Nek Video Links, Mount Zion ministries, and the companies owned by emergent Nigerian 'film dynasties' like the Amata family, or by Zeb and Chico Ejiro.[11] Annual award ceremonies, including THEMA, Reel, and Afro Hollywood, further sustain and amplify interest in the films, actors and producers. Bigger production companies, in particular, have the means of packaging new films as commercial commodities to be marketed aggressively. Previews of coming films run in the first few minutes of many video films. Full-page and cover page advertisements appear in weekly tabloid magazines. Posters are plastered on public walls around town. Journalists are invited to the set while the films are being shot, and their reports serve to build up a sense of expectation around the films to be released. In addition to becoming the subject of orchestrated advertising in the available media, the films also function as conduits for advertising other locally produced goods and services. By focusing insistently on specific targets, many films ensure that special attention is directed towards identifying selected up-scale restaurants, private hospitals, and 'luxury' goods by name.

Given the sheer number of films already in circulation and the pace of production, it is difficult to describe the 'typical' Nigerian video film. However, some trends are beginning to become manifest. Increasingly, the industry is tending towards a diversification of style and content motivated by the emerging delineation of audiences for particular types of video film. Romances predominate in Hausa film, action dramas and tales of domestic intrigue in the Igbo and English films, while melodrama provides the characteristic format for many Yoruba films. Comedies in Yoruba, English, Pidgin, and Igbo account for a slim segment of the market, as do music video films, featuring mostly Yoruba popular music, while Christian dramas with an evangelical message, mainly in English or Yoruba constitute yet another sub-genre in the market.

At this point in time, the occult seems to exercise a considerable fascination on the minds of film viewers. Macabre rituals and diabolical figures endowed with supernatural powers occupy center stage in many Yoruba, Igbo, and English-language films. While Yoruba films frequently locate this negatively charged supernatural domain within a recognizable ethnic framework that relies on knowledge of traditional Yoruba deities, incantations, proverbs and the like, Igbo, English-language and Christian films envision an occultic sphere that is both the obverse of and antagonistic to Christianity. In general, the snakes, 'mammy-water' spirits and other creatures that make up the 'iconography of the occult' in these films owe more to the syncretic spirituality of urban Nigeria than to any form of indigenous religious practice. For example, in the enormously popular Igbo film from the early 1990s entitled *Living in Bondage*, Merit, the wife of the leading character, Andy, is sacrificed in a ritual constructed as a perversion of Christian communion, and performed not in the name of the Igbo deities, but to honor 'Lord Lucifer'.

The preoccupation with the occult intersects directly with what is perhaps the major concern of early Nigerian video films, particularly in English and Igbo, namely the quest for wealth. Indeed it is usually the pursuit of prosperity that motivates involvement with the occult on the part of many video film characters. Unlike the Yoruba plays of the 1960s and 1970s, which commended work to the audience as the ultimate source of enduring wealth (Barber, 1982: 444), contemporary video films suggest that prosperity is inconceivable without recourse to the occult.[12] The fixation with riches leads some characters to submit to these occult forces, but they inevitably come to an evil end, though they may enjoy the benefits of wealth for a season. This fact points to a contradiction which lies at the heart of many video films, and which takes the form of a latent tension between the high regard extended to the spectacle of wealth and excessive consumption, contrasted with the ultimate retribution visited upon the wealthy for their egregious moral lapses. Especially in the Igbo and English language films, the scale of opulence deployed is matched only by the degree of sacrilege and scandal implicated in the struggle for wealth and financial sufficiency. Becoming rich means engaging in betrayal of sacred trusts, aberrant sexual acts, prostitution, armed robbery, and inevitably manipulation of occult powers. In a very real sense, the expression of a certain excess becomes the fundamental imaginative currency of such films.

Released in 1994, the film *Glamour Girls* set the tone for many future productions in English. It is the story of five women, Doris, Thelma, Sandra, Jane, and Helen, all living in high style in Nigeria's commercial capital, Lagos. Though the women appear at various times to have jobs and businesses, relationships with wealthy men open the door to a level of almost unimaginable affluence. We see these women wearing designer clothes in a succession of lavishly furnished homes, driving expensive cars in upscale neighborhoods where Nigeria's often unreliable infrastructure becomes surprisingly functional: the phones work, and power outages never occur. The film takes us through a number of love triangles as the women seek to balance the quest for love with the lust for wealth. Doris decides to marry a younger man to satisfy social expectations while continuing her relationship with an older man who pays the bills for her life of luxury. Helen extorts money from an aspiring politician by threatening to sell compromising photographs he took with her. Sandra gives up her rich older boyfriend out of love for a younger man who jilts her and runs off with the money she had saved from her earlier relationship. The most tragic story is that of Jane who divorces successful Desmond, though he is hospitalized following an accident, in order to marry Alex who claims to be a wealthy businessman running for president in the coming elections. But Alex disappears immediately after Jane's divorce, taking with him money from Jane's joint accounts with Desmond, and Desmond's Mercedes Benz. The film ends with Sandra losing consciousness as the enormity of her financial and emotional loss sinks in, while an impoverished Jane is led handcuffed to jail after shooting Alex at pointblank range.

Though the different types of films may cater to specific constituencies to be described shortly, overall, the films do not significantly differ from other urban popular culture forms in Nigeria in terms of the ideological values promoted. That is to say, the films belong in orientation with other well-known forms of Nigerian popular culture such as Yoruba popular theater, Yoruba Juju music and Onitsha Market Literature. Military protagonists, for example, are almost completely absent from many early films though they rose to prominence at a time of unprecedented military repression in Nigeria.[13] Given the focus on money-making schemes, the unwillingness in the early films to depict the most obvious source of ill-gotten wealth – through patronage of the military – is nothing short of remarkable. Like contemporaneous and earlier urban popular culture forms in Nigeria therefore, video film remains largely favorable to ideologies that resist the idea of political analysis or a radical re-organization of society.[14] In this respect, the ideological orientation of Nigerian video film is strikingly 'popular'.[15]

English in Nigerian Popular Culture

If the existence of popular video films in indigenous languages like Igbo, Yoruba, Hausa and even Pidgin makes some sense, how do we explain the flourishing of locally produced English-language films on the Nigerian market? Can the films be assumed, at least on the basis of language, to cater to the inclinations and tastes of the wealthier segment of the Nigerian video film audience?[16] If advanced proficiency is considered essential for access to a leisure activity in a non-native language, then this must surely be the case. But the existence of another form of English-based popular culture in Nigeria a decade or more before the emergence of video film is at least one reason to question the usual correlations between use of English in cultural activity and elite audiences. I refer here to the popular literature associated with the Onitsha Market in southeastern Nigeria between approximately the 1940s and the mid-1970s.[17] Without expatiating, several observers (Adesanya, 2000: 47; Haynes & Okome, 2000: 71) have already drawn attention to the parallels between Igbo and English-language video films on the one hand, and Onitsha Market Literature on the other. The comparison is all the more apt since many English-language films are produced by the same companies that make Igbo films, and some of which operate out of offices based in the same part of the country where Onitsha Market Literature originated.

According to Obiechina (1973: 10) in his extensive study of Onitsha Market Literature, the authors belonged to the 'lower-income bracket' while the readers comprised 'grammar and elementary school boys and girls, lower-level office workers and journalists, primary school teachers, traders, mechanics, taxi-drivers, farmers and the new literates who attend adult education classes and evening schools.' For the most part, urban residents in the categories outlined by Obiechina were in the 1960s, and remain today the most likely to register some difficulty in writing or reading English. Given their minimal proficiency in English, why then did they spend precious money on texts in a language that they had barely mastered? Obiechina's study does not provide an explicit answer to this question, but he does enumerate the values that engaged the attention of this particular audience. They included a celebration of the creed of materialism, distrust of tradition, approval of Christianity and literacy. Above all, remarks Obiechina (1973: 118), '[w]e are confronted in the pamphlets with the aggressive assertion of individualism ... The bearers of old-fashioned ideas which impede individualist fulfilment are quickly dismissed.'

Obiechina then goes on to differentiate between the concerns of both authors and readers of Onitsha Market Literature and those he describes as serious or intellectual Nigerian authors. In Obiechina's opinion, the divergence in the interests of the two groups ultimately derives from the difference in their respective social standing and aspirations. The overt materialism of the Onitsha texts merely translates into an imaginative idiom the aspirations of low-income authors and readers to 'items of prestige' (Obiechina 1973: 25) which better-educated, intellectually-inclined authors could take for granted. Indeed, many Onitsha Market authors explicitly configured their texts as self-help literature designed to assist the readership in attaining the goal of social and especially material uplift. Within this context, mastery of English both prefigures and actualizes the project of material acquisition. It represented not just a means to an end, but among other things, the very end desired. I would further contend that English had such significance precisely because, like the other items of prestige desired, it lay somewhat beyond the scope and effective reach of this particular audience. Thus, while intellectual authors sought to incorporate oral tradition into their English-language texts, the Onitsha authors closely modeled Shakespeare, in their eyes the ultimate English writer, and a host of other profusely quoted and named European authors.[18] Regular readers of Onitsha Market Literature could likewise identify characters that subscribed to a 'backward' and disparaged worldview by their illiteracy, attachment to tradition, and especially by their exaggerated deficiencies in the area of English.

A parallel tradition of Onitsha Market Chapbooks did, however, exist in Igbo, the mother tongue of most of the authors and readers, and this tradition drew its subject matter largely from the traditional Igbo lifestyle that the English-language authors and readers found so unattractive. Interestingly though, the authors of the Igbo texts tended to be much better educated than those writing in English, while the Igbo texts were most often read as part of the curriculum for final examinations in local secondary schools (Obiechina, 1973:15–16). In other words, the Igbo-language texts did not form part of the same system of social validation as did the English-language texts. The Igbo texts were linked directly or indirectly to the formal school system and the real prospects to be secured by obtaining high school leaving certificates, admission to higher institutions and the like. English-language texts on the other hand served an ideational purpose in relation to particular goals, and represented a strategy of expedience for readers, excluded for whatever reasons, from further social advancement by way of the formal school system. In view of this fact, the audience for the Igbo texts probably constituted the most educated segment of the Onitsha Market readership (Obiechina, 1973: 16).

Defining the Audience

With this background in mind, it is now possible to investigate what kinds of audiences Nigerian video film in English produces, and to determine whether the use of English might have a similar significance the video film audience as it did for the readership of Onitsha Market Literature. By way of preliminary response, let me start by concurring with Barber (1987b: 110) when she rightly suggests that we pay closer attention to defining the publics of African popular culture, and indeed I might add, of African culture writ large. Too often, it is assumed that all English-language activities engender the same African audience, which always coincides with a single social class: the elite. But Obiechina's study of Onitsha Market Literature already suggests that this line of argumentation cannot be consistently sustained. The readerships for Onitsha Market Literature and much of Nigerian high literature did not largely coincide in regard of literacy levels and social class, even though both forms relied extensively on the English language. Similar conclusions can be drawn from M. Kropp Dakubu's work on the language practices of urban Ghanaians, for she notes with specific regard to radio audiences among residents of central Accra, that '[t]he practice of listening to English seems to bear little relation to claims of competence in the language or education' (1997: 61).

Like Erlmann (1991: 4) in his study of Black South African performance, I therefore find problematic attempts to establish one-to-one correspondences between individual cultural forms and particular social classes. Such correlations are perhaps useful when audiences appear to congregate along class lines and have been used in respect of the audiences of some forms of Nigerian popular culture. Scholars such as Barber (1982: 433; 1986: 5) with Yoruba traveling theater, and Obiechina (1973: 10) with Onitsha Market Literature characterized the respective audiences by referring to the class positioning of its members. Haynes and Okome's analysis (2000: 73) occasionally leans towards a class-based understanding of the video film audience. However, recent studies of other Nigerian popular culture forms indicate the emergence of audiences that cut across class lines. Marshall-Fratani (1998: 298) describes the congregation of a Pentecostal church located in a wealthy neighborhood of Lagos as both socially and ethnically mixed. Similarly, and according to Waterman, enthusiasts for Juju, one of the urban music styles of the contemporary Yoruba, include not only the well-to-do (Waterman, 1990: 171), but also less privileged Yoruba such as 'clerks, traders, policemen, soldiers, laborers, journalists, and their apprentices' (Waterman, 1990: 168). To insist, in the light of such examples, on class or even education as the sole or determinant principle for defining contemporary African audiences is to infer criteria for membership of a group convened solely in response to a given activity from parameters established independently of that activity.

In the case of Nigerian video film, the proliferation of video rental and sales outfits, occasionally operating out of mere shacks, not only in wealthier neighborhoods, but also in low-income neighborhoods in southern Nigeria, suggests the existence of a varied audience in terms of social class. Furthermore, in a society where those with direct access to power and significant wealth account for only a slim segment of the entire population, it has to be assumed that a product that is as widely distributed and as commercially successful as Nigerian video film reaches within, but also beyond the confines of that restricted group. But if the widespread distribution of video rental and video sales shops around Nigerian cities gives some indication of levels of interest among different social classes, this information does not in itself advance our understanding of the basis for the convergence of an audience around the video film phenomenon. Membership of a particular social class is not inevitably and permanently coterminous with belonging to an audience for a given activity. Certain kinds of data will reveal effective social positioning without, however, explaining the reasons for the enlistment of a range of individuals into occasional affiliations structured around shared experiences of viewership and consumption.

Instead of a model centered on determinations of class, I consider that my argument is better served by situating video audiences in relation to the concerns that engender them. For the purposes of this discussion, my interest lies more in understanding why particular groups of people have any interest in the films. This is also in keeping with the movement in media research towards defining audiences as 'organic and social groupings' rather than as numerical and statistical entities (Mosco & Kaye, 2000: 41). Identifying the considerations which prompt selective involvement with particular art forms will, I feel, produce a more nuanced sense of the audience as a responsive rather than autonomous entity, existing fully-formed and independently of diverse cultural activities. This in turn provides a framework for examining audiences as occasional mobilizations around specific interests and agenda. And if we think of interaction between particular producers, texts, and audiences as operating in relation to clearly understood guidelines or protocols, we cannot, when protocols diverge, presume that we are in fact dealing with the same audience, even if the activities share a common language.

The trend toward identifying audiences in relation to mobilization around issues of common interest is certainly evident in some descriptions of popular culture forms in contemporary Nigeria. Discussing, for example, the role of media technologies such as video film in the emergence of new Nigerian Pentecostal communities, Marshall-Fratani (1998: 292) differentiates them from other types of Nigerian associations, by representing them as 'a community of sentiment' or quoting Appadurai (1996: 8) as 'sodalities of worship'. For his part, Waterman (1990: 221) refers to the sense of 'a deep horizontal comradeship united by language, custom, political interests, and ethos' in speaking of the appeal to 'deep Yoruba traditions,' or *ijinlèe Yorùbá* in Juju music (Waterman, 1990: 14). Yoruba video film tends to exhibit a similar burden with the relevance of *ijinlèe Yorùbá* values to Yoruba experiences of modernity. In fact, Yoruba popular theater, Yoruba Juju music and Yoruba video film have all, at different points in time and using different media, contributed to the on-going configuration of designated Yoruba values as perennial and sufficient for every age, including the age of modernity.[19]

By contrast, Igbo and in particular English-language film can be associated, in terms of its audience, with what could be described as a sodality of social aspiration. The specific attraction of the films resides in their deployment of narratives of mobility that feed upon the anxieties and desires of disparate social groups seeking to rise beyond their present station in life.[20] Viewers of English-language film are loosely connected then, not by ethnic solidarity, nor even by class, but by shared interests in projects of individual enrichment. Much more than other types of video film, the English-language films are wholly invested in what Murdoch (2000: 56) describes as the 'cultural construction of demand and desire.' Thus, where Yoruba films appeal to 'ethnic' values, and religious films to evangelical conviction, English-language films substituted a blatant creed of consumerism linked to the audience's desire for narratives of social mobility. Advertising the film and advertising in the film has been at its most aggressive in English-language film. Consequently, the emergence of English-language film appears to signal a growing awareness of the potential for increased commodification of the video film industry, Nigerian entertainment in general, and its audience. Entertainment becomes not just a commodity to be sold, but a vehicle for developing new tastes and marketing other commodities. English is critical to this process of transformation to the extent that it enables producers to concentrate on values other than those tied to ethnicity, religious belief, and the like.

Compared to the earlier Onitsha Market Literature, English and Igbo language video film are much less focused on the acquisition of social skills and the practical details of procuring wealth. As explained earlier, perhaps the primary attribute of wealth as displayed in Nigerian video film is the mystery of its origin. It is easy to see how this perspective might be attractive to the well-placed who are therefore discouraged from further reflection on the sources of their wealth in a time of massive social corruption. At the same time, it offers hope to the underprivileged whose attention is likewise diverted from the real impediments to their prospects for social mobility. The state of being wealthy is also depicted in video film as precarious and unstable. Sudden reversals of fortune are commonplace as in *Glamour Girls* reminding the rich of the fragility of their position, and suggesting to the poor that their indigence may not be permanent. But perhaps most significantly, and unlike Onitsha Market Literature, the video films offer viewers direct and intimate access to the wealthy, vicarious participation in the lifestyle of excessive consumption. It is in this respect that the direct solicitation to consumption through aggressive advertising becomes important in the definition of the audience as prospective customers and consumers of various goods and services. The emphasis then is not on a program of predictable progression or a lengthy period of social apprenticeship that leads ultimately to success at some point in the future, but on the instant and gratuitous access of the audience to the lifestyle of the rich and famous.

Probably because they began to be produced at a time of extreme social instability created by the vagaries of military rule and the haphazard economic policies pursued by the government, video films do not then appear to fix the audience at a specific point on the social hierarchy. Highlighting the immediacy of wealth rather than the deferred prospect of its acquisition, the films sidestep the implied attribution of a specific class to the audience in the manner of Onitsha Market Literature. Instead, film viewers identify with characters seeking to come to terms with the unending fluctuations in personal social standing. In the films, wealth is lost just as easily as it is made through witchcraft, betrayal, unexpected deaths, and so on, while the supposedly true stories of shifting fortunes that fill the tabloid press complement the imaginary versions represented on screen.

Although Nigerian high literature has for the most part been produced in English, it is clear that these texts neither convene audiences around possibilities of social aspiration nor produce identical interactions with the audiences that they do generate. Nigerian high literature does share in common with video film in English the tendency to project characters, and by implication audiences as ethnically diverse. The newer narratives in particular frequently unfold in settings that are self-consciously Nigerian or even African rather than Hausa or Igbo. Where English-language video film however constructs its audience as a community of potential consumers destined for imminent prosperity, Nigerian high literature constitutes audiences around issues of political engagement. Political and social edification are the goals esteemed in the high literature texts, while the pleasure induced by the spectacle of wealth is the primary focus of English language films. Where producers of video film take for granted the subordination of all undertakings to the pursuit of wealth, high literature authors consider themselves and their readers willing to rise above commercial imperatives and the contingencies of social patronage. For video film directors, the value of any film is ultimately measured in sales. For high literature authors, however, the opinions of accredited readers, critics with the requisite qualifications, take precedence over sales. And generally, high literature texts achieve significant sales only by incorporation into school curricula. In other words, distribution of high literature texts often depends on the agencies of national and official culture, despite the frequent criticism of political authorities contained in the texts.

Video films, in contrast, do not rely on government agencies for distribution and are often treated as cultural trash by government representatives and educated film professionals.[21] Haynes (1997: 17) reports, for example, that during a workshop in 1992, there was antagonism between Yoruba filmmakers on the one hand, and intellectuals and bureaucrats linked to the Nigerian Film Corporation, on the other. While both traditional and elite arts can become symbolic capital in the hands of the ruling classes, as argued by Barber (1987a: 11), a phenomenon like video film falls somewhere in between, being neither elite nor traditional. As such, the films are frequently condemned on the art and culture pages of newspapers and 'serious' newsmagazines, as well as at religious events. They attract criticism for their lack of artistic content, their tendency towards stereotyping of actors, their suspect ideological positions, their immorality, their 'bad' portrayal of contemporary Nigerian culture. Interestingly, performers in the English-language films who are themselves often undergraduates or recent graduates of departments of drama in Nigerian universities, are equally vocal in their criticism of the Nigerian video film industry. Only in the tabloid press do the films benefit from positive commentary, but even there, the focus tends to be on the exceptional lifestyles of the stars rather than on the content and technique of the films.

Furthermore, the films are not packaged as products for the underprivileged that owe their existence to the burdensome generosity of sympathetic intellectuals, as is occasionally the case with high literature texts. Nor are they marketed to urban audiences as cultural artifacts for limited distribution, but as attainable commodities theoretically within the reach of everyone. Indeed, the publicity around the films projects a sense of democracy of access. Producers, marketers and reporters for the tabloid press will often describe the designated audience as 'lovers of Nigerian home videos', 'everyone', 'the people out there' and 'Nigerians.' High levels of piracy further counter the cost of new releases, making it possible to rent films at fairly cheap prices.[22] And underlying the appearance of unlimited availability to all is the suggestion that the lifestyle of ostentatious consumption associated with Igbo and English-language film in particular, is available to everyone, including precisely the economically disenfranchised and the socially disempowered. The ideology here bears considerable resemblance to the organizational premises of new Nigerian Pentecostalism as characterized by Marshall-Fratani (1998: 291), with its emphasis on the availability of spiritual powers and possibilities to all converts within the movement. Igbo and English-language film similarly profess faith in the principles of 'equal economic opportunity', and if they are to be believed, fabulous wealth is within reach for almost everyone.

In short, Nigerian video film in English does not appear to substantially overlap in orientation and audience with Nigerian high literature in English. Aside from language, little convergence exists between the commercially oriented and leisure driven activity of video film viewing and either the officially mandated reading of high literature texts within the school system or the elective reading of professional critics and the politically conscientious. Sodalities formed around an interest in individual enrichment will in all probability pursue agenda at ideological odds with those committed to radical re-organization of social structures. Cultural forms such as Nigerian high literature, Onitsha Market Literature, and English-language video film are to be understood, then, not simply as diversions from reality, even when, as is the case with video film, they rely heavily on fantasy and the supernatural for the representation of 'life.' For as Appadurai (1996: 7) reminds us, 'It is the imagination, in its collective forms that creates ideas of neighborhood and nationhood, of moral economies and unjust rule, of higher wages and foreign labor prospects. The imagination is today a staging ground for action, and not only for escape.'

Looking at the Nigerian video film phenomenon as a whole, there can be little doubt that a connection already exists between the audiences of some types of video film and formal coalitions in the Nigerian body politic. The religious films, for example, present a philosophical outlook acceptable to at least some, if not the majority, of those who consider themselves affiliated to groups like the Pentecostal Fellowship of Nigeria (PFN) and the Christian Association of Nigeria (CAN), that have become quite vocal in Nigeria's public sphere in recent time. Activities committed directly or indirectly to Yoruba cultural nationalism, including Yoruba film, Juju music, and traveling theater have long existed side-by-side with and overlapped in constituency with organized political movements claiming to defend the interests of the Yoruba people as a group. Thus far, the audiences for English-language film do not appear to have been transformed into a self-conscious social movement, but it is a transformation within the realm of possibility. Such audiences are, in the words of Appadurai (1996: 8), 'potentially communities for themselves capable of moving from shared imagination to collective action.'

'Foreign' Languages and African Audiences

If the fact of using the same 'foreign' language does not therefore imply that diverse cultural forms produce identical interactions with identical audiences, it becomes possible to envisage alternative paradigms for describing the role of acknowledged 'foreign' and other non-native languages in the convening of African audiences. To start with, and as has long been recognized by scholars of language, languages as intelligible means of communication can operate as mechanisms for the exclusion or inclusion of groups without proficiency in constituting audiences for particular cultural forms. In all likelihood, the majority of those who watch Yoruba video film in Nigeria are themselves Yoruba speaking. Similarly, according to Launay (1997: 442–3), some Dyula villagers in northern Ivory Coast, went to considerable effort to tune in to the brief radio broadcasts from the country's capital that were offered in their own language. Yet other villagers disregarded national boundaries and listened to the broadcasts of neighboring Mali which were more frequently in a language related to theirs. In these instances, audiences emerge in response to the fact of language and cultural intelligibility.

However, this is only one of several ways in which languages intervene in the convening of African audiences. On occasion, activities in 'foreign' and non-native languages will generate an audience in the absence of language intelligibility. Launay's research among Dyula Muslims in Ivory Coast also makes reference to the existence of yet other audiences in the same community that did not owe their existence to language intelligibility. For example, older Dyula males listened to North African broadcasts using a form of Arabic that was not intelligible to the Dyula. In the same villages, housewives with minimal proficiency in French appeared to constitute a significant proportion of the audience for American network shows dubbed into French that were being broadcast by Ivorian Television. To return to Nigerian examples, perhaps even more remarkable is the more than 30-year tradition of watching rarely sub-titled Indian films among the Hausa of northern Nigeria (Larkin, 1997; 2000). A similar practice of watching Indian films in Hindi has also been reported for Muslim women in Nairobi (Fredericksen, 1999: 57).[23]

Larkin (1997: 407) explains the attraction of Indian films in Hindi for the Hausa by invoking the concept of 'parallel modernities,' which he deploys to account for the multiple flows, cultural and otherwise, associated with the term modernity. Indian films in Hindi and Market Literature in the Hausa language apparently address issues of social change from identical perspectives, and have thus succeeded in engendering a significant following within largely the same constituencies. Although they rely on different languages, both forms articulate a particular vision of modernity that specific groups in urban Hausa society find meaningful. Ignorance of Hindi does not apparently detract from the popularity of Indian film in northern Nigeria since the audiences find the overall scheme of the films relevant to their personal experience. Indeed, Larkin (1997: 412) recalls being struck by how frequently Hausa informants claimed that the Indian culture depicted in the films was 'just like Hausa culture.'

The popular music scene in Africa provides further examples of this fascinating trend. While the most successful music hits have usually been in indigenous African languages, at least since the 1970s musicians who have the means to do so have sought to direct their productions at audiences larger than those of their own ethno-linguistic community. The popularity of Congolese Soukouss music with East and West African urban youth who speak no Lingala (the language most commonly used in Soukouss) provides another instance of an African audience congregating around a performance in an unintelligible language. Finally, there are cultural forms, whose appeal for specific audiences actually rests, at least in part, on the appearance of foreignness and thus on the absence of language intelligibility. Such is the case for the Western audiences of a new generation of African artistes like the Malian Salif Keita, the Béninoise, Angélique Kidjo, or the Senegalese Baaba Maal on the 'World music' scene who sing mostly in Malinke, Yoruba, Fon, Pulaar.[24] The popularity of performers in this mold derives from a skillful packaging of the unfamiliar for both Western and urban African audiences.[25] And thus we find that languages that are being marginalized as intelligible means of communication along the routes of global cultural flow retain value on the same circuits without having to be intelligible as sites of an opaque foreignness that almost dispenses with translation.

The African urban setting, we must keep in mind, differs significantly from the rural world. Where rural communities may be minimally multilingual and multi-ethnic, urban communities are highly multilingual and multi-ethnic. Some degree of interaction with non-native cultures and actual 'foreigners' is frequently unavoidable in most cities. Thus, given the heterogeneous composition of the population in major African cities and the increased knowledge about other cultures delivered via radio, television, film and other media, it would be a mistake in matters of language to envision African cities as contiguous islands of cultural homogeneity where local residents seek and encounter only sameness. Within the constraints posed by differentials in status, gender, religion and other social structures, the trend in most places, despite the occasional backlash, is towards greater creolization. In terms of language use, and particularly among young men in many cities, mixed languages have become a significant element in defining group identity.[26] The multilingualism of these cities is also made evident and formally recuperated in the development of new types of entertainment using several languages at once.[27] Even in the poorest neighborhoods and perhaps more so there than in wealthier localities, city residents do not imagine themselves as living in isolated and culturally bounded worlds. As Fredericksen (1999) has proposed with respect to urban youth in a Nairobi slum, real impediments to social and spatial mobility are not enough to prevent local aspirations from being articulated with special reference to foreign locations.[28] Indeed, the dimmer the prospects for real mobility, the greater the temptation to invest in imaginative trajectories and itineraries, both social and geographic, in pursuit of fantasy rather than the factual.[29]

In these urban settings, the indigenous has not lost its relevance, but the foreign, as in foreign texts, foreign styles, and foreign languages, is not without considerable appeal. Even for the most conservative city residents, the preferred repertoire of personal and larger imaginaries is worldly in composition, referring to diverse locations, diverse cultures, inclusive of, but not limited to the sites associated with indigenous ethno-linguistic units. These are people who rarely interpret their experience in the city in relation to primary ethno-linguistic affiliation alone. There is therefore little reason to presume with such city residents that the absence of full linguistic intelligibility would constitute a significant deterrent to interaction around cultural activity in non-native languages, or that audiences in these settings would respond only to texts in mother tongues, whether such languages function as indigenous lingua francas or 'foreign' languages of wider communication.

On this basis, I would like at this point to draw some preliminary conclusions: activities in 'foreign' languages are not consistently apprehended as inaccessible by urban African audiences in particular, and perhaps even for most audiences in Africa at this point in time. The tendency, though, has been to ground interpretation of the role of 'foreign' languages in the constitution of African audiences in discussions of intelligibility, as do authors like Barber (1987a: 25), Wali (1963: 13–14) or Ngugi wa Thiong'o (1981a: 22). My proposal is that we begin to envision the significance of 'foreign' languages for African audiences bearing in mind some of the following considerations. The protocols governing the interaction between author, text, and audience will in certain instances provide greater insight into the composition of the audience for a given activity than the singular fact of using a 'foreign' language. The absence of advanced proficiency does not by itself always suffice to prevent the emergence of an audience around an activity carried out in a 'foreign' language. Languages technically defined as non-native to particular communities can, depending on the circumstances, signify values other than those of foreignness and cultural extrinsicality when used in activities that generate local audiences. The language of cultural texts can, for example, also reference affective affiliations such as those manifested in shared aspirations and desires, in addition to marking inherited and chosen ethnic ties. Finally, foreignness and the absence of intelligibility may constitute a specific source of attraction for a new type of audience found not only in urban Africa but also in other parts of the world.

For the Dyula communities studied by Launay, North African Arabic was at once non-native, unintelligible, and yet connected to a religion that had been deeply implicated in Dyula definitions of ethnic identity over a period of several centuries. In Kenyan cities, Soukouss music in Lingala, a 'foreign' language, factors into contemporary elaborations of a Pan-African cultural ethos that depends on an acknowledgement of both the 'foreignness' and the 'familiarity' of the music style.[30] And to the extent that being 'African' now frequently takes precedence over primary ethno-linguistic and national affiliations for Kenyan urban youth (Fredericksen 1999: 60), listening to and creating Soukouss music provides an avenue for genuine self-expression, in addition to enabling the display of a cosmopolitanism much appreciated by these city residents. In the case of Nigerian video film, as a form of urban popular culture, a non-native language, English, has become implicated, not so much in the definition of ethnic identity, as in the construction of desire and social aspiration. In instances such as these where non-native languages no longer serve as one-dimensional signifiers of 'foreignness,' representation of the complex reality necessarily entails identification of the additional values that have accrued around their appropriation for local consumption in select activities. And if as Appadurai (1996: 7) has suggested, notions of neighborhood and community take shape in products of the imagination, then the growing significance of cultural forms that rely on 'foreign' languages extends understanding of the more recent configurations of community that may be developing in some African urban contexts.

While it is true that most people reside in one location on a more or less permanent basis, cassette technology among other technologies that have been widely disseminated around the world convene audiences in ways that transcend individual localities. South African Gospel music in Zulu, for example, is available in audio cassette form in Ghanaian markets, and is quite popular if local traders are to be believed. Yoruba video films are sold not only in the Yoruba heartland of southern Nigeria, but also in northern Nigeria, in major West African cities, in Europe and in the USA, wherever a significant Yoruba diaspora is to be found. The fact is, few audiences for activities realized primarily using media technologies in urban Africa remain entirely localized, and just as it is true that contemporary audiences are not always coterminous with class, so also it is true that they are frequently no longer coterminous with individual locations. Cultural entrepreneurs and other figures invested in the business of delivering and managing urban popular culture are sensitive to the changing configuration and locations of the entity of the audience. Some of these changes, as I have argued thus far, pertain to the language of cultural activity. Thus, while few people speak European languages as mother tongues anywhere in Africa, there is evidently an expanding audience all over urban Africa for activities in diverse languages of wider communication, whether these are indigenous lingua francas or other non-native languages. The emergence of such activities offers, in my opinion, a further signal of the growing awareness on the part of producers of African popular culture that the category of the audience in its on-going mutations need not necessarily coincide either with a single location or with an ethnic cluster, differentiated by its own vernacular language.

As such, it is perhaps overstating the case to speak of Igbo-language film productions mostly in terms of the politics of ethnicity, as does Ekwuazi (2000: 133), when he discusses several Igbo films in relation to their articulation of a cult of the individual emanating from what he calls a particular 'Igbo cultural matrix.' But Okome, another author in the same volume of essays on Nigerian video films, offers a slightly different viewpoint. Writing about the Igbo film, *Living in Bondage*, Okome (2000: 149) remarks, '*Living in Bondage*, even though it was seen as inaugurating Igbo video film production, also began loosening the ethnic affiliation of the videos ... It is not primarily about an Igbo society ...'

Unlike Yoruba films then, and very much in the tradition pioneered by Onitsha Market Literature, the Igbo films produced as from the early 1990s exhibited significant distrust for 'ethnic' values. Village life was portrayed as linked to ethnic tradition in its purest sense, but also correlated with customs that were irrelevant and even inimical to success in the contemporary world. Survival for characters in Igbo film often depended on willingness to embrace 'modernity' and on maintaining a physical and psychic distance from the values of the village. Already in the Igbo films, language had become detached from the project of ethnic identification and no longer appeared to have the kind of significance that the Yoruba language had for viewers of Yoruba film. In this context, the Igbo language served as the medium of communication rather than as linguistic embodiment of the ideological positions promoted by the films, as was the case in Yoruba film.

And so, when Haynes and Okome (2000: 86–7) attribute the emergence of English-language film from Igbo film to the supposed linguistic disloyalty of Igbo film viewers, they draw the kinds of conclusions about language and audiences that I find problematic. It is surely no coincidence that English-language film emerged from Igbo rather than Yoruba film, since modern Igbo configurations of an imagined ethnic community have generally relied less on linguistic nationalism than has been the case for some other Nigerian ethnic groups such as the Yoruba or Hausa. The Yoruba language is frequently essential to the construction of meaning in many Yoruba films, and one of the problems associated with selling Yoruba films to non-Yoruba audiences relates to the difficulty of successfully translating into another language proverbs and incantations that are so central to the narrative. However, the decisive factor in the emergence of English-language film appears to be not so much the disinterest of the Igbo in their own language, as the recognition by producers of Igbo film that the Igbo language was in fact incidental to the values being promoted in the films. In this connection, it is significant that, unlike early Yoruba or Hausa films, many early Igbo-language films actually had English-language titles, and were more consistently sub-titled in English than early Yoruba films. Linking the values portrayed to any one indigenous language was not crucial, especially since the films tended to de-emphasize the ethnic dimension of contemporary experience altogether. In relying on English, the producers thus recognized the existence of a potentially large audience of film viewers willing to de-emphasize ethnic identification in its leisure activities, an audience that was both ambivalent towards tradition and attracted to tales of instant wealth acquired by immoral and or supernatural means. This distancing from ethnicity was so successfully realized that critics at annual movie award ceremonies complained about the absence of identifiable cultural and geographic markers in the English-language video films (Haynes & Okome, 2000: 87).[31]

Another way of explaining the recourse to English here would be to simply highlight its neutrality as an international language. Pennycook, however, argues that such interpretations do not go far enough in recognizing how 'English is embedded in local political and economic relations' (1994: 16). While the reference to neutrality gestures at a dislocation from ethnicity that is rarely typical of indigenous languages that are not also languages of wider communication, it does not fully account for the significance of some 'foreign' languages. In other words, a language like English is envisaged in terms of what it does not do rather than from the perspective of what it actually signifies. Along the same lines, I would further suggest that to the extent that a 'foreign' language can be embedded in local political relations, it ultimately becomes a factor in the production of locality and local subjects, and this is clearly evident in Nigerian video films.

As such, the function of the films in extending the borders of a self-identifying 'modern' Nigerian culture is not to be overlooked.[32] In published interviews, directors, actors and viewers make consistent reference to 'our film industry' implying their awareness of other film traditions that are not 'theirs' to the same degree. The English-speaking characters of the English-language films are almost never represented as culturally estranged. The dialectical tension of the films is more frequently identified as unfolding at the dangerous crossroads between the perils of wealth and the ignominy of poverty, than as a confrontation between Western and Nigerian culture. In addition, wealth in these films emanates largely from 'local' sources rather than from the 'strategies of extraversion' or links with external economies described by Bayart (1993: 21–2). Consequently references to life 'abroad' or to consumption of imported items at home almost never signal a desire to disconnect with Nigerian culture, since physical displacement and expatriation are no longer synonymous with cultural alienation.

The magazine, *Nigerian Videos*, published in London, is a case in point. Adopting a tabloid format, the glossy, colorful magazine is available not only in London, but also in major Nigerian cities, and in other parts of the world connecting the Nigerian film viewing diaspora. Writing from Paris, on the 'Letters to the Editor' page, one Nigerian reveals: 'I live here with my wife and our four children . . . We watch lots of Nigerian Video films and I suggest that our film makers forward their films for the annual Canne [sic] Film Festival in France . . .'(July 1998: 12). Commenting on an event organized by the publishers of the magazine in London, a Nigerian in Johannesburg makes a request: 'I want you to know that there are so many Nigerians and others out there in South Africa who would want to be part of such a cultural event. Please extend invitations to us next time . . .' (March 1998: 6). Another reader from Enugu in Nigeria complains about the directors and their ethics: 'No doubt, 1997 was a year of boost for the Nigerian video industry. It is however surprising and disheartening that some producers still hold back on artistes' [sic] fees . . .' (March 1998: 6). Thus, while the audiences for Nigerian video film may be ethnically diverse and widely dispersed, it would seem that a desire on the part of expatriate Nigerians for reconnection with the localized reality of a place of origin supplies at least one of the primary motivations for watching the films. The films therefore contribute to an on-going construction of the local even as they cater to the desires and needs of some non-local audiences.

It is clear then that the films differ from the 'high literature' plays in English produced by Nigerian playwrights like Wole Soyinka, Ola Rotimi, or Femi Osofisan when it comes to matters of language. The English spoken by villagers and low-income urban residents in such plays is taken by general convention to represent indigenous languages. Indeed, several writers go out of their way to try and communicate the character of indigenous languages in the English-language dialogues of their plays. And where highly educated characters feature in these plays, a degree of tension often pervades their speech as authors seek to foreground its foreignness and incongruence in the setting. English-language video films, on the other hand, show minimal interest in either using indigenous languages or representing them through English. Furthermore, to the extent that the plot for most films unfolds in well-to-do urban settings, the ubiquitous English of the major characters represents precisely that: English.

In actual fact, few people speak English all of the time outside of formal occasions and particularly in the domestic situations which predominate in these films; consequently, the films do not depict reality as such even for affluent Nigerians. Nor do the films necessarily represent concrete aspirations in terms of language competence, since few Nigerians would want to speak English all the time. I have already described the projection of excess as the defining feature of English-language video films. The excessive use of English correlates well with the general hyperbole of the films, and signals affluence as surely as do the many cars, the extravagantly furnished homes, the rich meals and the abundant jewelry.

And it is this preoccupation with wealth that justifies the reliance on English in the films. If the producers had been merely seeking to communicate across ethnic and class lines, Pidgin would have sufficed for that purpose, as the most widely understood language for inter-ethnic communication in the cities of southern Nigeria. But as scholars interested in Nigerian Pidgin have often noted with dismay (Zabus, 1991: 64–76; Elugbe & Omamor, 1991: 143), within the Nigerian imaginary, Pidgin retains its associations with illiteracy, poverty, and sexual license.[33] English, on the other hand operates as linguistic signifier of affluence in the popular arts. While viewers might demonstrate minimal interest in the English language in and of itself, Nigerian video films in English are attractive because they are almost invariably films about modernity, cosmopolitanism, enrichment or domestic intrigues in high society. In the words of Bourdieu, linguistic exchanges truly function here as 'signs of wealth' (1991: 66).

Given the historical antecedents of English in Nigeria, the correlation between the use of English and the spectacle of wealth is hardly surprising. But there are conclusions to be drawn from this fact that have in the past been overlooked, especially with regards to audiences in Africa. The audience for a cultural activity in a particular 'foreign' or indigenous language is not always isomorphic with the community of those who are proficient in the language. As such, distinctions need to be drawn between the possession of proficiency in a 'foreign' language and willingness to engage with cultural activity in that language, between the deployment of a language in the project of ethnic identification and its implication in the formation of other affiliations. These are categories whose borders do not always coincide.

And if we think of ethnicity as pertaining primarily to perceptions of shared ancestry, then the use of languages of wider communication in texts about belonging, makes it possible in multilingual settings to expand the scope of these perceptions of shared ancestry by bypassing vernaculars and thus reconfiguring the geographic, cultural and other coordinates of new and older ethnic identities. But perhaps even more importantly, the use of languages of wider communication, which may or may not be perceived as 'foreign' facilitates the emergence of audiences around new types of sites of belonging, which because they transcend the borders of groups constituted around vernaculars and even nation-states, neither depend on nor even foster perceptions of shared ancestry.

Where both 'foreign' and indigenous languages of wider communication continue to flourish alongside diverse vernaculars, which retain their association with older ethno-linguistic identities, these languages of wider communication will on occasion play a significant role in convening audiences around issues unrelated to the affirmation of ethnic identities. As I have proposed in this chapter, audiences will engage with cultural activity in a non-native language, even given a lack of proficiency in the language of the activity. But the decision to interact with texts in intelligible non-native languages may be as much about *not* affiliating with sodalities of an ethnic character as it may be about constructing new configurations for ethnicity. In short, decisions about cultural activity in non-native languages are not always decisions in support of specifically ethnic agenda or associations constructed around the myth of shared ancestry.

Even where actual language shift has occurred, and a local population has gradually adopted a new language as mother tongue, evidence from African contexts suggests that in the absence of emigration to a new state, the underlying motivations for such language shifts do not initially and necessarily reflect a desire for change in ethnic identity.[34] When McLaughlin (1995: 164) asked Serer respondents in Senegal who spoke only Wolof whether they were still Serer since they no longer spoke the language of their forbears, she reports that '[s]everal interviewees were amazed by the proposition and even went so far as to ask what language had to do with their being Seereer.' And writing for example about the process of Wolofisation in Senegalese cities, O'Brien (1998: 27) remarks, 'Wolof identification is perhaps best seen as a process, one which relates to a range of subjects: urbanization, migration, religion, statehood.' That is to say, newcomers to Senegalese cities began speaking Wolof so as to fit into the city, so as to fit into a religious confraternity, so as to fit into a commercial network, rather than out of a desire to acquire a new ethnic identity or to disengage completely from a previous ethnic identity. Audiences constituted around activities in languages of wider communication may similarly and initially reference prospective investment in alternative (i.e. non-ethnic) sites of belonging and forms of association. I will investigate one such alternative site of belonging in the final chapter to this book.

Returning to Nigeria as I conclude this argument about 'foreign' languages and local audiences, I should make it clear that my intention has not been to suggest that all cultural forms in 'foreign' languages in contemporary Africa are potentially popular. Nor would I claim that English in Nigeria has become, as it were, the language of the urban 'masses.' However, it is clear that in particular circumstances, cultural texts in 'foreign' languages can and do engender socially diverse African audiences. And it is a pattern that with variations is becoming more significant in many other parts of the world. But we cannot become aware of this development unless we begin to take an interest in the ways in which different languages are apprehended in specific local contexts. The commercial success of forms such as English-language video film, the tabloid press, and Onitsha Market Literature with Nigerian sodalities of social aspiration, suggests that in conjunction with a focus on the prospects and spectacle of affluence, English, may in postcolonial contexts, factor into constructions of meaning for audiences excluded from acknowledged avenues for accumulating wealth.

If educational systems determine real access to discourse and privilege as argued by Foucault (1972: 227), then commercial ventures that traffic in hopes of prosperity become especially attractive for those permanently or temporarily positioned beyond the institutional frameworks of wealth and power. Thus, where some English-language cultural forms fail to generate popular audiences in Africa, the distance between the ideological positions identified with the activities in question and the audience may be more to blame than the sole fact of using a 'foreign' language.[35] Precisely because of its association with power and privilege, English plays a role in certain activities that substantiate the aspirations of Nigerian audiences constituted around concerns with social mobility. Though I have focused here on video film, it must be noted that there are a variety of other types of texts in English which are generating an equally varied range of audiences around other aspirations and concerns. In any case, cultural forms in 'foreign' and even unfamiliar languages do today generate popular African audiences and can acquire meaningfulness in ways that are not necessarily constrained by levels of language proficiency.

Notes
1. Abdulaziz and Osinde (1997), Myers-Scotton (1990), Bernsten and Myers-Scotton (1993), and Swigart (1994), among others, have focused on the incidence of code-switching involving European and indigenous African languages in African settings. Studies such as those undertaken by Bokamba (1982), Bamgbose (1995), Manessy (1994) among others provides useful information on African varieties of European languages.
2. And such reservations have been expressed not only in respect of the language of African literature, but also in relation to the language of instruction in Africa. There too, the debate pits supporters of instruction in 'foreign' languages against supporters of instruction in African languages, with minimal distinc-

tion being made between indigenous lingua francas, actual mother tongues and other non-native languages of wider communication.
3. See for example McLaughlin (1995) and Brenzinger et al. (1991).
4. See for example O'Brien (1999), McLaughlin (1995), Swigart (1994).
5. I have thought it useful to provide readers who may be unfamiliar with the phenomenon some background on the emergence of Nigerian video film in this section of the chapter. However, I would like to stress that my subject here pertains primarily to language rather than to film studies. I refer readers interested in a more detailed description of Nigerian video film from the perspective of film studies to the informative and comprehensive publications of Haynes (1997, 2000), Okome (2000), and Larkin (1997, 2000). I have summarized some of their findings in this section of the chapter.
6. Speaking for example about audio cassettes, Manuel (1993: xiv) notes that this kind of technology has enabled the emergence of small-scale producers targeting 'specialized, local, grassroots audiences...' The same observation could be made of video cassette technology in the Nigerian context.
7. Discussing television and video technologies in Africa, Barber (1997a: 4) contends that 'electronic media exist as vulnerable islands washed over by much bigger sea of live popular genres, produced by small-scale, localized artisanal methods, and disseminated on a face-to-face basis.' The point is that video technology has now and increasingly enabled small-scale groups using artisanal methods to appropriate media technology in ways that were inconceivable in the 1980s. And to that extent, certain types of electronic media in urban Africa no longer represent isolated sources of entertainment controlled by government monopolies.
8. Television drama is still being produced locally, though there is little doubt that where either the actors or producers have the means, they would probably prefer to work in video film production. With a successful film, producers and actors can make more money, in less time, and have greater control over their products than is the case on television. As an example, see Barber's (2000: 245–6) discussion of Yoruba-language drama and some of the problems of loss of control that have confronted drama groups seeking to make productions for television.
9. According to the figures provided by Balogun (1998: 41), there were 15 films produced in English in 1995 as against 161 produced in Yoruba. But just two years later, by 1997, there were 114 films produced in English compared to 89 in Yoruba.
10. Nigerian video films are frequently available in stores that cater to the needs of Nigerian communities in the United Kingdom and the United States. In places where the concentration of Nigerians is significant, there are even video rental stores that specialize in Nigerian films.
11. I have borrowed the term 'dynasty' from Ibagere's (2001) article on Nigerian video film where he describes the Amata family as an 'Acting Dynasty.'
12. Onitsha Market Literature, to be discussed later in this chapter, similarly commended the value of wealth acquired through honest labor (Obiechina, 1973: 13).
13. The 1990s when the video film industry took off coincided with the last years of the military rule of Ibrahim Babangida, the cancellation of election results in 1993 and the extremely repressive regime of Sani Abacha.
14. Barber (1986: 5–6) notes for example the 'radical conservatism' of Yoruba travel-

ing theater. In Waterman's opinion (1990: 227–8), Juju music minimizes the impact of economic transformations that have benefited the elite. And for their part, Onitsha Market authors embrace the creed of materialism without reservations (Obiechina, 1973: 25).
15. However, unlike Onitsha Market Literature and Yoruba traveling theater, the video film industry does not represent the kind of African popular culture in which the social class of the producers of the activity exactly overlaps with that of the consumers (Barber, 1997a: 4). Nor do the films correspond to the kind of foreign material for local consumption that Barber (1987a: 24–5) envisages in talking about art consumed by the people, but not produced by them. Producers and marketers of the films are increasingly successful local businessmen who are able to invest considerable fortunes in film production and advertisement. The differences between the wealthiest Juju band owners like King Sunny Ade and scores of less privileged Juju music fans may provide a better model for understanding current trends in video film production. It is not surprising that the disparity in class between consumers and producers is most marked in the case of English and Igbo films which are described as being more 'highly capitalized' (Haynes & Okome, 2000: 64). This fact should not exclude video film from consideration as popular culture, for as Fiske (1989: 170) has observed, '[p]opular cultures, unlike folk culture, is made out of cultural resources that are not produced by the social formation that is using them.' Although Barber (1987a: 6) warns that models derived from Western artistic traditions are not always applicable in Africa, the functioning of the video film industry in Nigeria might point to the emergence of a new, more capital dependent, orientation in some African popular cultures. As Nigerian video film becomes more commodified, requiring larger infusions of capital, and ironically better able to cater to popular tastes at affordable prices, the gap in terms of class between producers and consumers is likely to become ever wider.
16. Lawuyi (1997: 483) contends in his discussion of video marketing in Ogbomoso, a Nigerian town, that English-language films appeal mostly to children of the elite. However, Lawuyi makes no mention of locally produced English-language films in his enumeration of types of films available in Ogbomoso (Lawuyi, 1997: 482), even though such films represented the fastest growing sector of the Nigerian market. In other words, the English-language films to which he refers are actually foreign films, and these foreign films in English do have a greater appeal for the well-educated and affluent. At the same time, Lawuyi acknowledges that the spectacle of consumption by 'big men' portrayed in many Nigerian films is the factor that young viewers find most attractive. Given that this spectacle of consumption is more pronounced in English and Igbo language films rather than in Yoruba films, it seems likely that in Ogbomoso, a Yoruba urban community, as elsewhere in urban Nigeria, an audience will also exist for locally produced English-language films.
17. The comparisons I am making here would also be valid for Ghana where popular writing in English emerged by the 1940s and where video film production in English has also taken off in recent years. Newell (2000) and Priebe (1978) among others have written on Ghanaian popular writing. Newell (2000: 89) reports print runs of up to 60,000 copies and more for both Ghanaian and Nigerian popular writing in English between the 1950s and 1970s. Compare this to print runs of between 750 and 1000 for high literature texts in many places in Africa since the 1980s (Rathgeber, 1992).

18. As Newell (2000) has pointed out, the quoting of Western authors was a significant feature of both Onitsha Market Literature and Ghanaian popular writing in English.
19. And probably for this reason, Yoruba-language video films have remained very popular among those who self-identify as Yoruba both within and beyond the Yoruba homeland in southwestern Nigeria. Nonetheless, English-language films are also widely available in both major and smaller Yoruba cities, and make up anywhere from a third to at least half of the films available on display in many video stores.
20. See Haynes and Okome (2000: 79). Somewhat similar aspirations are also expressed in Yoruba Juju music (Waterman, 1990: 227), however in Juju music, the prospects for becoming wealthy reside in an awareness and manipulation of specifically Yoruba networks of power rather than in ethnically-neutral occultic activities.
21. It is interesting to note that official response to video film in Nigeria offers striking parallels with public responses to Indian film in South India as reported by Dickey (1995: 131).
22. In order to try to recoup their investment before the bootleggers move in, video film producers try to produce and sell as many films as possible when a new film is first released. Ironically, foreign films, which are almost always bootlegged, are generally cheaper than locally-made films, especially in the early weeks when a local film has just arrived on the market.
23. Interestingly, both in northern Nigeria (Larkin, 1997: 412), and in Kenya (Fredericksen, 1999: 57), regular viewers of Indian film claimed that they had become so familiar with the Hindi language by watching the films that they could now understand or even speak it.
24. 'African music' abroad in the 1990s thus clearly differs from the kind envisaged by Barber (1987a: 27) in the 1980s where she speaks of '[a] simplified disco-like beat, English language lyrics and short dance format' as the defining characteristics of the music marketed to Westerners as 'African'.
25. As explained by Hannerz (1990: 250), the unfamiliar and the 'local' hold special appeal for those he describes as 'cosmopolitans' in a global world. Paradoxically, cosmopolitans have opportunity to reveal their cultural ecumenism because others ensure the survival of cultural diversity by remaining narrowly committed to their culture of origin. However, a number of African musicians are increasingly resentful of the restrictions placed on their creativity by the expectation that they be purveyors of a musical style that is recognizably 'African' or 'localized' for the satisfaction of Western cosmopolitans. Musicians like Youssou N'dour and Angélique Kidjo have recently defended their right to behave like cosmopolitans in embracing non-African cultures and by representing their music as a deliberate experiment in cultural blending rather as a continuation of some traditional African style (Durán, 2000: 55).
26. Abdulaziz and Osinde (1997) and Githiora (2002) have written about 'Sheng,' a mixed English/Swahili code among Nairobi youth. Swigart (1996) discusses what she calls 'Urban Wolof' integrating French and even English in Dakar. With respect to Accra, Ghana, M. Kropp Dakubu (1997: 164) talks about an urban register of Ga that 'appropriates foreign-language material via the speech styles of a wide range of domains and speakers.' May and Stapleton (1987: 175) refer to the use of Hindubill, a mixture of French and indigenous languages in Kinshasa.

27. Kuria (2001: 92) describes multilingual street comedies in Nairobi, noting that 'oral literature researchers, who would be expected to have given this mode of literary activity some attention, operate under the assumption that orature is collectively owned by their respective communities and they therefore only investigate monolinguistically constructed orature'. Both the Ivorian singer Alpha Blondy and the Nigerian Lagbaja! frequently alternate between a number of different languages within the same song.
28. One of Fredericksen's informants in the slum where she carried out her research thus describes his dreams for the future: 'Me, I see myself somewhere in the US – somewhere like Michigan State . . . (1999: 49)
29. Slum dwellers in African cities are in this respect not unlike marginalized immigrants in the Western world who compensate for their disempowerment by cultivating imaginaries of the old homeland, cultural styles, texts and languages associated with the place of origin even as they seek to advance their assimilation into a new society using whatever social structures are available to them.
30. The fondness of some Kenyans for music in a 'foreign' language is apparently not a new development. As far back as the 1970s, Kenyan urban middle classes preferred music in Lingala to music in Kiswahili, a language widely spoken in Kenyan cities (Manuel, 1993: 265). Fredericksen (1999) now identifies the phenomenon with poor urban youth in Kenya. And in some instances, Kenyan youth who produce Soukouss music for the Kenyan audience will go so far as to try to learn Lingala or to pretend to speak it.
31. And though I have been mostly concerned in discussing video film in English with what I have described as a sodality of social aspiration, as it continues to expand in scope, it is interesting to remark that the English-language video film phenomenon seems to be undergoing even greater diversification in subject matter and style, and generating an even greater variety of audiences along the way.
32. The films are therefore not apprehended as 'foreign' or 'Western'. I had the following experience while waiting to be served at a Nigerian video rental store in London. A customer could not find the Nigerian video film of his choice but declined to follow the advice of the storeowner and rent an American movie. Instead the customer complained: 'Ah! Foreign films, who wants those!'
33. There are actually a few films that have used Pidgin extensively, but which continue to exploit the negative connotations of Pidgin use. *Domitilla*, for example, focuses on prostitution in Nigerian cities, while *Lagos na wah* is a comedy about low-income workers in Lagos. In my opinion, a film about the well-to-do made entirely in Pidgin would be a contradiction in terms that failed to recognize the cultural codes I have been discussing here. When the rich are represented in Nigerian texts, they are almost never imagined as speaking Pidgin.
34. Eastman (1984: 261) argues forcefully for this position, stating: 'When we stop using the language of our ethnic group, only the language use aspect of our ethnic identity changes; the primordial sense of who we are and what group we think we belong to for the reminder remains intact.' She adds in the same essay: 'Language is changed for instrumental reasons – we use language to communicate and we communicate to survive' (1984: 267).
35. Barber (1987a: 20–1) argues that Soyinka's use of Western dramatic conventions, and a high style of English explains why his plays do not have a popular audience in Nigeria. In addition to these reasons, I would add that the positions

embraced in Soyinka's plays are not necessarily those most appreciated by urban popular audiences. As Barber herself points out (1987a: 64), popular culture in Africa and elsewhere is often (though not inevitably) concerned with upholding the economic status quo, while Soyinka's plays for the most part, tend to be critical of the existing political and economic order. Given Nigeria's recent experience with military regimes, his political views are reasonably attractive to popular audiences, his mockery of the wealthy much less so. The popularity of English-language video film suggests that popular Nigerian audiences can relate to some Western dramatic conventions and to a type of English that is not heavily infused with all kinds of literary allusions, when all of these are mobilized in the service of a cause which interests them.

Chapter 4

Romance Without Borders: Narrating Love, Femininity, and the Local in Contemporary Ivory Coast

In one of his best known songs, entitled 'Lady,' released in 1972, the popular Nigerian musician, Fela (1938–1997), contraposes two images of African femininity, embodied in the rhetorical figures of 'Lady' on the one hand, and 'African woman' on the other. The 'Lady' in Fela's song claims equality with men, expects men to do her bidding, and seeks to establish herself in a position of authority over men. The 'African woman' by contrast, acknowledges man's right to headship, accepts her subordination to man, and in the words of the song will, 'do anything he says.' By describing the submissive female figure as 'African,' the song implies that authentic African femininity is best represented by figures like 'African woman' while those who emulate the 'Lady' are like ships without a mooring, that have lost a sense of origins and direction somewhere on the high seas. There are two additional observations to be made about the song: one is the fact that Fela did not compose it in Yoruba, his mother tongue, but in Nigerian Pidgin, which was undoubtedly for him, like most residents of Lagos where his band was based, a second, or even third language. Secondly, the female figure who receives approval in this song is described not as Yoruba woman, or Zulu woman, or Wolof woman, but as 'African Woman,' a fact that is surely significant in view of the arguments made thus far in this book. Both the song 'Lady,' and 'Mattress' another title released by Fela in the 1970s, are often cited as illustrations of the enduring sexism that was an integral part of his sometimes radical, and sometimes reactionary, but always intensely personal political philosophy.

In itself, the recurrent denunciation of certain kinds of women is unexceptional in the urban cultures of postcolonial Africa.[1] What I find interesting in Fela's 'Lady' is not so much its expression of male chauvinism as the specific transmutation of an envisaged conflict between the sexes into a conflict between cultures. This too is a fairly familiar stance in contemporary African culture. We find echoes of it in Okot p'Bitek's *Song of Lawino*, which pits the traditional Lawino against the Westernized Clementine, and as I hope to demonstrate shortly, we encounter similar oppositions in recent Ivorian romance fiction. Texts like these, I would suggest, are to be distinguished from those that merely affirm or imply the normative character of male domination and female subordination in human society. In a song like 'Lady,' Fela makes patriarchy the exclusive preserve of a particular culture, identified here as 'African' culture. My intention in this chapter is to examine other West African examples of this conflation between conceptions of ideal femininity and cultural distinctiveness, as a basis for explicating the settings in which patriarchy begins to be explicitly represented as cultural, peculiar to a people, as that which differentiates one community from another.

I have chosen to start this discussion of West African romance narratives by referring to Fela since the incongruence of his invocation of African custom and culture in his songs and other statements about women is perhaps more obvious than for most.[2] As several scholars of African music have emphasized, far from being a paragon of African 'tradition' as he himself claimed, Fela's conscious choices in his life and music were almost consistently at variance with the traditions of the community in which he lived.[3] I am not concerned at this point, with further documenting the veracity or falsity of Fela's claims in respect of African tradition, as in ascertaining the circumstances in which interactions between cultures begin to engender the associations of particular models of femininity with tradition that have tended to acquire even greater salience in many expressions of local culture around the world in recent times, despite the reality of broader exposure to alternative and often 'foreign' values.

Fela's decision to justify many of his own novel artistic and lifestyle choices by appealing to the court of tradition will serve to highlight a number of critical questions for which I will seek answers in this chapter, namely: why did he consistently appeal to custom and tradition rather than to modernity in rationalizing personal conduct and a musical style that were considered fairly unusual and unconventional in his own time? While patriarchy unquestionably has indigenous roots in Yorubaland and southern Nigeria, there was frequently in Fela's life a disconnect between his statements which appeared to have some basis in tradition, and both his public actions which were more often than not in conflict with social convention, and his musical style which was clearly innovative.[4] Given the multiple levels of disconnect between Fela's activities and Yoruba tradition, it is important to come to a more precise understanding of his very selective alignments with customary practices in his music and his statements. Where the art form being produced is itself patently new to the community in question, we can safely assume that the producer/artist hardly represents a fully devoted advocate of 'tradition.'

Discussing the role of 'tradition' in Fela's life and work offers an opportunity for defining precisely what connections exist between the 'local' and the 'traditional' as categories for processing cultural encounters. As we study the works of Fela and other more recent artists, we may wonder whether the 'local' is always 'traditional.' We may also seek to determine what exactly the motivations are for invoking the category of 'tradition' in contemporary productions of the local. Some cultural practices are clearly viewed as 'traditional' whether or not they are of distant ancestry. Others are merely considered as local, which usually means that they are identified as emanating from inhabitants of a circumscribed space, who also claim legitimate belonging to that space. However, cultural practices identified as local are not always envisioned as also 'traditional.' In fact, very often, they may be perceived as 'modern.' In order to further our understanding of the strategies through which practices in non-native languages become embodiments of local culture, I intend in this chapter to address a number of questions. As categories of interpretation, what kinds of interactions exist between the local and the traditional? How is it that practices which may have been identified as foreign at one point in time begin to be described as local? Since my broader interests in this book pertain to the use of non-native languages, I would also like to examine how the categories of the local, the modern, and the traditional are deployed in respect of popular texts realized in non-native languages.

Because texts in non-native languages provide some of the best examples in urban Africa of an acknowledged fracture between 'traditional' and 'modern' creative practice, the orchestrated intersections between constructions of the foreign, the local, and the traditional can often be more easily made legible with these types of texts. And though the debate has continued to ebb and flow since the 1960s on the appropriateness of writing in European languages, it is generally true today that the fact of being produced in a European language no longer suffices to preclude a play or a song by an African from being considered 'African' or 'Ghanaian' or 'Malian' as the case may be. Foreignness, therefore, is not consistently and automatically imputed to all contemporary African texts in non-native languages. Yet the need to explicitly affirm local identity by adopting particular strategies has persisted for some African texts in European languages. The goal of this chapter is to specify some of the contexts which necessitate this on-going engagement with issues of localization for texts in non-native languages, and to identify some of the responses that arise out of this need for localization. In the interests of space, my discussion here cannot be exhaustive, and as such, I will be focusing on a single context, that of competition with identical foreign forms and on responses manifested in the dissemination of conservative discourses on femininity, among other strategies, as peculiarly emblematic of the local.[5]

My main argument is the following: in the contemporary African setting and given the frequent associations of non-native languages of wider communication with the experience of modernity, imaginative texts in non-native languages play an increasingly important role in the deployment of tradition as a strategy for endowing modernity with local character. That is to say, for African communities invested in the pursuit of modernity, the concept of tradition remains relevant, precisely because it furnishes a framework for localizing cultural practices identified as modern, particularly when the modern becomes indistinguishable from the foreign for a variety of reasons, including the possibility that it is formulated in a non-native language. From this perspective, there is, for example, no contradiction in terms in proclaiming one's commitment to the vernacular in a language that is not one's own vernacular, as does another Nigerian musician, Lagbaja! when he sings a song in Pidgin in an emergent transnational style about the importance of the 'vernacular,' interspersed with comments by his compatriot, Fela, made entirely in English.[6] Without such expressions of commitment to real and metaphoric vernaculars, what is constructed as modern culture in postcolonial locales runs the risk of being construed as a foreign production divested of local attachment. Given these kinds of interactions, it is clear that non-native languages do not consistently stand in antipodal relationship to a concern for and with tradition and the local. Rather both entities frequently function as complexly interrelated dimensions in the African production of modernity.

This chapter then will seek to demonstrate how images of ideal femininity linked to ideas about tradition are manipulated in contemporary Ivorian romance narratives as a means of distinguishing foreign culture from modern local culture. My intention here is to move us away from the tendency to see the local and the foreign as fixed categories, exemplified, inter alia, in choices to be made between using indigenous and non-native languages. On the contrary, these are classifications whose scope of application is in constant flux and always subject to revision. Through the successive placements and displacements of terms like the foreign and the local, texts in non-native languages operate as at least one of many significant arenas for the elaboration of new and acceptable standards of localness. We see the role of such texts in the dissemination of certain images of ideal femininity and in the ready assumptions made about the significance of the images. Wherever they appear, these models of ideal femininity are construed as pointing to the persistence of and continued attachment to a pre-existing and apparently ineradicable substratum of tradition that confers legitimacy on a cultural project whose identity might otherwise be subject to question.

For the purposes of my discussion here, the intention is not so much to determine whether such models of femininity formed part of an earlier cultural patrimony in particular African locations. There is little doubt that some of the values recycled in these models of femininity do have roots in 'traditional' culture. The question to be asked is why artists largely committed to the pursuit of modernity and to the use of non-native languages should feel any need for identification with templates so clearly associated with the idea of 'tradition.' By way of response to this question, let me start by suggesting that the artists who make such identifications are as preoccupied with the production of the local as they are with the production of the modern. Now the modern does not by definition have to be foreign, but the condition of being unapologetically modern is not one that is easily appropriated in the postcolonial world. On the African continent in particular, the tendency to represent African culture as the ultimate repository of tradition has outlasted the colonial period with the result that contemporary cultural practices, even when produced by Africans, cannot be viewed as local until they are subjected to specific processes of localization, including among others, the invocation of conservative models of femininity.

Depictions of such models of femininity in African and other postcolonial societies are perhaps better interpreted, then, not so much as figurations of a continuing commitment to tradition, but as signs of a growing need to invest representations of the modern with the distinctive attributes of locality. And far from representing only the advancing encroachment of foreign cultural practices upon African societies, popular texts in non-native languages have increasingly provided a stage for re-inscribing the category of tradition into the construction of African modernity at this point in time. Not only do such cultural practices in non-native and foreign languages constitute an integral part of contemporary local culture, they are in some respects essential to the very dissemination of selected traditional values associated with individual cultures over larger spaces and among more diverse audiences, notwithstanding the considerable preoccupation of those audiences with experiences of modernity.

Visions of Femininity in the Romance Narratives of Ivory Coast

Speaking about representation of women in African male writing between the 1950s and 1980s, Stratton identifies one of its defining features as what she calls the 'mother Africa' trope. In its various manifestations, Africa and its distinctive culture is represented as female, and is either a 'nubile, erotic' maiden for the male author's gaze or 'fecund, nurturing mother' (Stratton, 1994: 41). As will become clear shortly, both manifestations are directly relevant to conservative African discourses about women, whether they occur in literary texts, in religious texts, or in music lyrics. While she acknowledges the extensive exploitation of the Africa as female trope in colonial literature, Stratton remarks that the emphasis on 'mother Africa' is present in at least some indigenous African art forms and calls for studies that relate its functioning in contemporary male writing to its function in oral art forms. The logic implicit in Stratton's suggestion is already evident in Schipper's 1987 essay on African male writers. In that essay, Schipper appears to find a continuity of gender bias extending from an eclectic collection of African proverbs and creation myths to the works of contemporary African male writers, thereby implying that the male writers in question have apparently transposed the contents of an older discourse into the format of a newer idiom. In my opinion, this reading of the texts written by modern African male writers, though understandable, does not adequately problematize the authors' deployment of particular models of femininity, suggesting as it does that a current discourse is inevitably the prolongation of a prior discourse, or that a contemporary artist necessarily operates within the same conditions of possibility as a previous generation of artists.

Although reading the present as a perpetuation of the past is common practice in both popular and scholarly interpretations of contemporary African experience, it is precisely this approach that I have chosen to avoid in my discussion of West African romances in general and of those discourses of distinctiveness constructed around conceptions of ideal femininity. In contrast to Schipper, Stratton, and many other scholars, I hope to explain the emergence of these discourses by foregrounding the deep implication of writers and sundry artists in their own times, in a period characterized by the increasing prominence of non-native cultural forms in the delimitation of the cultural space of the local and the distinctive. I therefore do not seek to approach these 'conservative' African discourses about women as either corruptions of pre-colonial African discourses on gender,[7] or as prolongations of pre-colonial African discourses on gender.[8] Rather, I prefer to draw upon events and texts that are contemporaneous with my object of study, because the factors at work in the conjoining of certain representations of women with particular expressions of distinctiveness appear to my mind to be largely located in the present even when they involve as strategy appropriations of the past.

The contraposition of the Lady with the African woman that we find in

Fela's well-known song features regularly in recent Ivorian romance writing in French, making the Ivorian market for romance narratives an ideal context in which to study the production of certain types of conservative discourses about women in African urban culture. These romance narratives also offer considerable opportunity for disentangling some of the connections between local and global culture in the West African setting. A thriving readership clearly exists for Western romance fiction in major West African cities, including those located in Ivory Coast. In Abidjan, the commercial capital, French romances published by the Editions J'ai lu, American Harlequin romances translated into French, and novels of well-known romance authors writing in English such as Barbara Cartland, Danielle Steel, are all available in French translation. Locally published romance narratives are also available in most other West African major cities. Narratives published by small independent presses constitute one category of locally published narratives. Larger African publishing houses and local subsidiaries of multinationals like Macmillan in Nigeria and Ghana, or Nouvelles éditions ivoiriennes in Ivory Coast have also been active in romance narrative publishing in West Africa.

The largest publisher in Ivory Coast, the Nouvelles éditions ivoiriennes (NEI), began publishing romance fiction as part of what it called the Adoras collection in 1998. According to the editor of the series, Méliane Boguifo, an Ivorian audience already addicted to the foreign romances sold in bookstores, the Latin American telenovelas, and American soap operas shown regularly on television, provided a ready market for the new series.[9] Within two months, over 36,000 copies of the first six novels in the series had been sold,[10] notwithstanding an increasingly difficult economic situation in Ivory Coast and in the West African sub-region. The managing director of NEI, Guy Lamblin, was so pleased with the performance of the Adoras novels on the market that he qualified it enthusiastically as 'le phénomène Adoras' (the Adoras phenomenon).[11] At least 19 titles had been published under the series by the end of 2000, and plans were underway to add new titles, while extending sales and publication to other Francophone West African countries.[12]

At first glance, the Adoras novels would appear to amply merit the accusations of imitativeness sometimes made in regard of African popular writing (Newell, 2000: 4–7). For one thing, they appear to replicate the format and narrative patterns of Western romances almost without modification. In fact, an Ivorian critic who asked not to be named, refused to consider them as original literature, describing them as nothing more than 'les Harlequins sous un autre nom' (Harlequins under another name). Practically all of the elements characteristic of the Western romance as described by Radway (1984) are present in the Adoras novels: the extensive use of dialogue and descriptions of decor, the exceptionally beautiful and unconventional heroine, the exceedingly wealthy and masculine hero, who can be both brutal and gentle with women, the manipulative female rival interested only in material gains, or the male rival seeking only sexual favors, are all stock features of the Adoras novels. As in the Western romances, the novels express complete confidence in the benefits of 'love' for the heroine as manifested in verbal declarations, the giving of gifts, and above all, in the marriage proposal leading to the wedding ceremony which usually concludes the narrative.

Furthermore, and no doubt in recognition of the fact that some of the most popular foreign romance writers available on the Ivorian market are English or American writers whose works have been translated into French, most of the first crop of Adoras authors published chose to use pseudonyms, and specifically English sounding pseudonyms rather than their own real names. So we have novels by B. Williams, by Christopher Hill, Eva Stone, Gladys Pemberton-Nash among others, and even one author with a Spanish name: Carmen Lopez. The covers of the novels, too, are not without resemblance to the Harlequin novels. As with the Harlequin novels, the covers of all Adoras novels are identical in format, including a horizontal division prominently featuring the name of the series and author in the upper half, and in the lower half of the cover a picture of a man and a woman who seem to share some degree of familiarity with each other, and are clearly dressed in Western style.

I find it interesting though, that those involved in the production, writing, and sales of the Adoras novels have frequently insisted on the specifically local dimension of these narratives. Most persons connected with the Adoras series seemed to share an awareness of the cultural politics at stake in their particular location, and consciously set out to construct an image for the series as being in some way distinct from Western romances. Far from accentuating the narratives' closeness to Western romances, those who stood to benefit from the sales of Adoras novels repeatedly stressed its local identity. When asked, for example, about the popularity of the series with Ivorian audiences, workers in bookstores in Abidjan frequently mentioned two factors: the affordable prices and the local relevance of the narratives. In many bookstores, the Adoras novels were set apart from other romance fiction, or removed completely from the romance section and displayed next to other African literature texts. It is fair to say that more than anything else the cultural politics of location determined the interpretation that NEI officials, authors and other cultural brokers chose to give to the kind of cultural appropriation represented by the appearance of the Adroas novels on the Ivorian market.

Fibla Koné, a graduate student at the University of Abidjan, and author of *Cache-cache d'amour*, described as an Adoras best-seller by Méliane Boguifo, emphasized the importance of providing cultural information in the Adoras novels. She stated in an interview: 'Dans Adoras, en plus de l'histoire sentimentale, la lectrice doit pouvoir découvrir des éléments culturels en plus de 70% de dialogue. Imaginons une histoire sentimentale qui se passerait à Bamako. Le roman doit contenir des informations sur la ville de Bamako, l'art culinaire et artistique au Mali . . .' (In addition to the romantic story and 70% of dialogue, the reader of the Adoras novels should be able to find cultural elements. Imagine a story set in Bamako. The novel should contain information about Bamako, about art and cuisine in Mali . . .).[13] Méliane Boguifo made a similar point in her discussion with me. The authors of the Adoras novels were to treat themes of local relevance: arranged marriages, polygamy, local beauty pageants, local music hits, infertility in contemporary African society, inter-racial marriages in the African context, sexual harassment, AIDS, widowhood in Africa, and a host of other topics that featured in discussions in popular Ivorian magazines, and on radio and television talk shows. Another Adoras author, Isaïe Biton Koulibaly, who writes under the pseudonym B. Williams, echoed both Koné and Boguifo stating: 'nous sommes très implantés dans le décor africain, nous évoquons les problèmes qu'on ne trouve pas dans les Harlequins' (we are very rooted in the African context, we raise issues that don't appear in the Harlequin novels).[14]

The commitment to representing the distinctiveness of place and culture expressed by Koné, Koulibaly and Boguifo is exemplified in most of the Adoras novels published thus far. Indeed, one of the most fascinating qualities of the Adoras novels is the extent to which they put local identity and place on display. Many Adoras novels make it a point to mention local foods by name, *Attiéké* for novels set in Ivory Coast, and *Thiof* and *Mafé* for novels set in Senegal. Koulibaly goes further in the novel, *Tu seras mon épouse*, written under the pseudonym B. Williams, mentioning local musicians Youssou N'Dour, Amy Koïta and the titles of their hit songs. The agenda of the authors and publishers is rendered all the more visible in the representation of place. Thus while the characters in the novels are entirely fictitious, the location is as close as possible to a specific reality, relying on an almost obsessive naming of known places – major avenues, neighborhoods, restaurants, stores – in order to anchor the narrative in a space identifiable by readers and clearly differentiated from the setting of the Harlequin novels. The plot in the Adoras novels typically unfolds in a capital city, Abidjan, Dakar, or Brazzaville, but a significant turning point in the narrative often occurs during a trip outside the city, providing the setting in which the hero and heroine first verbalize and acknowledge their attraction to each other.

As Radway's (1984: 110) work has shown in respect of the United States, there are romance readers who specifically prefer foreign settings and read the texts as a substitute for unaffordable foreign travel. Using the trip outside the city, the Adoras novels are able to cater to a similar desire for the unaffordable unfamiliar without renouncing the commitment to portraying non-Western sites. Significantly enough, if the journey is to a rural destination, it almost never takes the protagonists back to a familiar village. Rather, by a fortuitous turn of affairs, the protagonists run into each other at luxurious hotels in well-known tourist locations where the most frequent guests are usually foreigners. Thus for example, in the novel *Premiers Frissons*, Aïda, the heroine meets Claude, the hero at a guesthouse in the beach town of San Pedro, several miles away from Abidjan. Still later in the story, Aïda and Claude have further encounters at the well-known Hotel Sarakawa in Lomé, Togo, while the protagonists of *Nuit fatale*, Noëlla and Roger get together at a hotel in Pretoria, even though they live in the Congo. The intrusion and elaborate description of the tourist site in narratives whose local identity is so insistently advertised encourages the West African reader to approach the African setting from the perspective of an outsider discovering for the first time the exceptional attributes of an unknown place.

In no regard is the concern with localness more explicitly articulated than in the contrast set up between the heroine as an ideal embodiment of African femininity and a rival female also seeking the attention of the male protagonist. In updated form, it is the classic duel between Lawino and Clementine in p'Bitek's *Song of Lawino*, and between the African Woman and Lady in Fela's song. The heroine of the Adoras novels is beautiful but unaffected, and in some cases has just moved to the city from a smaller town or village. The rival, by contrast, is elegant, sophisticated, and very much at home with the ways of the city. The heroine's connection with non-urban setting and values is all the more important as all Adoras narratives are set in a city, a place of possible moral degradation and cultural loss. In *Nuit fatale* (2000: 61), Noëlla, the heroine is described as 'une fille typique du pays' (typical of the country), while her rival, Barbara, who is bi-racial is portrayed as dripping with modernity and lacking in personality, which is another way of saying that she is deficient in local culture. Barbara spends her time reading foreign magazines while Noëlla, who works as a governess, reads African history books to Barbara's son. Noëlla's concern for the education of the young boy is typical of Adoras heroines who almost invariably reveal a predisposition towards motherhood, and a great affection for young children. Though most Adoras heroines do not yet have children of their own, they are portrayed at some point in the narrative, showing great care and tenderness with the children of other characters.

The Adoras heroine thus combines both dimensions of Stratton's 'Africa as female trope,' the nubile erotic beauty, and the nurturing mother. Finally, Noëlla is courteous and obedient to the mother of the hero, Roger, while Barbara disregards the wishes of her own parents. Noëlla works hard in the kitchen to cook the special dishes of the country, while Barbara spends her spare time being unfaithful to her fiancé.

In *Tu seras mon épouse*, the heroine, N'Dèye Ramata, is crowned winner of the title at a local beauty pageant, Miss Jongoma, where women are ranked on the basis of their faithfulness to what are described as traditional African criteria for beauty. Her rival, Fatou Niang, prefers the Miss Senegal pageant where the contestants must show familiarity with Western conventions of beauty. Justin Gnala, the hero, complains that Abidjan has become too Westernized, and this seems to explain why he seeks a bride in Senegal, where it is implied the women have remained more traditional rather than in his own country. Indeed, he has a girlfriend in Abidjan, a highly educated woman, and teacher of English, who is portrayed as overly aggressive and possessive. Meanwhile N'Dèye Ramata, the heroine, waits patiently in Senegal, allowing herself to be courted in the most traditional manner, requiring the services of a griot as a go-between, and the distribution of numerous gifts to her parents and other members of her extended family.

At the same time, the quest for love by the female characters in the Adoras novels clearly parallels the pursuit of modernity. The male protagonists all live in a fashion that definitely locates them in the realm of modernity. They are highly educated, having spent several years schooling somewhere in the Western world. They have acquired considerable wealth through the resources of the contemporary global economy, and their very attractiveness to the female characters resides in their familiarity with the diverse trappings of modernity, whether they be the high tech furnishings of homes and offices, cars, trips abroad, foreign hotels or tourist locations. The point, however, in these novels, and in this chapter is that modernity is experienced as foreign except it is tempered by a selective and appropriate appreciation of the values of tradition, embodied here in the equal familiarity of the female characters with the trappings of tradition.

Biton Koulibaly and Ivorian Popular Writing

Notwithstanding the growing popularity of the Adoras collection, any examination of popular fiction in contemporary Ivory Coast that does not highlight the role of Isaïe Biton Koulibaly must be considered incomplete. Long before Adoras appeared on the market in 1998, Koulibaly was already publishing short romance stories in French in local newspapers and magazines. Perhaps more than any other Ivorian writer, he is responsible for developing an Ivorian audience for popular literature, and was recently described by an Ivorian newspaper as the most popular writer in Ivory Coast.[15] So popular is Koulibaly that an Isaïe Biton Koulibably Fan Club now exists in Abidjan, and has even set up an annual short story competition in his name. Koulibaly is pivotal to the argument I am developing here, because not only has he published stories under his own name, he has also contributed to the Adoras collection using a pseudonym. In addition, he seems to represent a more active presence for a cross-section of Ivorian readers than authors like Ahmadou Kourouma, Bernard Dadié or Amadou Koné who are well-known to scholars of Ivorian literature located inside and outside Ivory Coast.[16]

Koulibaly's first short story was published by a local newspaper in the 1970s. By the 1980s, he had become a local correspondent with the Paris-based African women's magazine, *Amina*, which also provided a forum for the publication of his short stories on a regular basis.[17] At the same time he worked for one of the major publishers of African literature based in Abidjan, and he recalls being astounded at the insignificant quantities of these African classics being ordered by local bookstores and institutions. Armed with his experience in the publishing industry, he consciously set out to produce narratives that would reach a wider audience than was the case for the texts that had up till that point in time furnished the model for acceptable Francophone African writing in Ivory Coast. Considering the volume of mail that his stories in *Amina* and local newspapers have frequently generated, there seems to be little doubt that he succeeded in attaining this objective.[18]

Although Koulibaly has described his three major themes as God, Women, and Politics, he has concentrated in most of his short stories on the urban West African woman and her quest for fulfilling relationships. His exceptional popularity can be attributed to his reputation for being an insightful interpreter of the female experience in contemporary West Africa. But the stories that Koulibaly has written under his own name differ significantly from those he has authored, using a pseudonym as part of the Adoras series.[19] For one thing, in Koulibaly's independently written stories, the couple almost never live happily ever after. Indeed, one might say that Koulibaly's stories depict both the modern African woman's longing for love and the impossibility of finding love.

In one of his short stories, for example, a young schoolteacher who has been assigned to a distant village school discovers that her boyfriend left in the city has betrayed her and married another woman. Despite the opposition of her family, friends and acquaintances, she subsequently falls in love with and becomes engaged to an uneducated fisherman in the village where she now works. Unlike her former boyfriend in the city, the fisherman is caring, considerate and gentle. A wedding day is set, but the night before the wedding, the fisherman goes out on the high seas and is killed in an accident, thus the promise of love remains unfulfilled. In another Koulibaly story, a wife discovers that her husband is having an affair despite her complete devotion to him. Her best friend advises her to retaliate by also having an affair. Initially things seem to work out well when the wife follows this advice, she finds satisfaction in her affair with another man, and her husband even becomes nicer once she stops worrying about him. However, on a weekend away with her lover at a hotel outside town, she runs into another couple: her husband and her best friend, and discovers that she has been twice deceived, first by her husband, and secondly by her best friend. These are typical Koulibaly stories, which end as they begin with the characters unsuccessful in their pursuit of love and emotional satisfaction.

It is interesting to note that unlike the Adoras novels, Koulibaly's stories do not generally develop a discourse about local identity within the narrative. Indeed, the narratives appear to take questions of ethnic and national identity for granted. More often than not, the narrator plunges directly into a sequence of events, giving very little attention to description of sites or to locating the story in a particular place. Nor do Koulibaly's stories set up the kind of opposition between the Westernized and the more traditional African woman that we find in Adoras. In Koulibaly's narrative universe, there are no inherently good or bad types. Both men and women are equally capable of duplicity in matters of the heart, the educated and the illiterate are equally untrustworthy, the Christian priest and the practitioner of indigenous religion are equally susceptible to the lure of money and the wiles of women. Neither conformity to social convention, nor rebellion against it is able to guarantee success in love. Both devoted and unfaithful wives, 'honest' single women and high-class prostitutes are equally unlucky in their quest for satisfying relationships. If the quest for love in African popular writing is often a metaphor for the pursuit of modernity, one can only conclude that Koulibaly is as ambivalent about the gains of modernity as he is about the benefits of tradition. Whether Koulibaly's narratives should even be called romances is a matter for debate, though they are unquestionably stories about courtship and love. Certainly, his stories bear only the most fleeting resemblance to Western formulaic romances. And while Koulibaly has written as many stories from the male perspective as from the female perspective, on the whole, his stories appear slanted to generate sympathy for the urban African woman, probably because many of them were originally written for publication in women's magazines.[20]

Some of the differences between Adoras and Koulibaly's independently written stories begin to make sense once we consider the contexts of production, and how this informs representation of place and engagement with questions of identity. Because Koulibaly sought to connect with the widest possible Ivorian and West African audience, he chose to publish in magazines and newspapers, which are more affordable, and where, of necessity, the narratives had to be brief. Though most of his stories are non-sequential, the absence of closure in the quest for love in many of his stories was probably impelled by the need to keep the audience for these periodicals on the lookout for new stories, and new twists on old stories, to be published in subsequent editions. It is also evident that the short story format provided less opportunity for extensive descriptions of place. But perhaps more importantly, the author had no need to localize narrative events through descriptions of place because the implicit location of the narrative had already been circumscribed by the scope of this periodical publication's primary readership. Only when authors writing for African periodical publications were producing texts designed to appeal through constructions of the exotic, or constructions of places foreign to the primary readership, did detailed descriptions of place and identity become imperative.

The absence of an emphasis on the construction of place in Koulibaly's works can also be traced back to the fact that he has tended, in his desire to create a more accessible kind of literature, to position himself in contrast to earlier generations of African authors who wrote in French, rather than in competition with metropolitan French authors. The localness of African writing in French had already been established by these earlier writers, and Koulibaly felt no obligation to further justify either the language or the format of his writing. Nor did he share the preoccupation with challenging metropolitan models of writing which led earlier African authors to invest significantly in strategies for distinguishing their writing in European languages from the literatures of the Western world. In short, the specific attention to constructing particular and often conservative models of ideal femininity became superfluous for this African artist because he was not primarily concerned with establishing cultural distinctiveness and locality as a means of distinguishing his narratives from or competing with works in a similar format produced by cultural outsiders.

The contrast between Koulibaly's independent writing and the Adoras novels is instructive and appears to point to a larger pattern of engagement with Western formulaic romances replicated in several other types of West African romance narratives. The novelty of a new literary genre may go unnoticed where resolution of the adopted plot requires conformity to social convention, but if resolution of the plot is configured around rebellion against social convention, the strangeness and thus the 'foreignness' of the new literary genre is accentuated to the local readership. Thus, in the realm of African popular culture, a re-affirmation of tradition in thematic matter is often the corollary of conscious stylistic innovation. And the closer the stylistic innovations are to patterns previously or contemporaneously identified as foreign, the greater the inclination to moderate the trace of foreignness by appealing to tradition writ large, and especially to conservative discourses on gender.

Koulibaly's stories may be taken to represent one trend in popular West African creative writing on courtship where resolution of the plot reveals the author's ambivalence towards traditional gender relations.[21] However, because his stories do not resemble Western formulaic romances where love always triumphs over all, and most importantly do not actively privilege rebellion against convention over conformity to convention, they have not been targeted as 'foreign' or as imitations even though respectable members of the society like to show disdain for his style of writing. Based on the different kinds of narratives that Koulibaly has produced, it is possible, I think, to make some observations with regard to popular narratives in the West African context. When the foreignness of a text is highlighted by factors such as the use of a non-native language, by a significant degree of novelty in style, by a certain distance in thematic matters from the topical and provincial, authors are more likely to mediate this appearance of foreignness through a variety of strategies of localization. In the specific case of popular romance narratives, such strategies have often included the projection of an opposition between Westernized and traditional figures of femininity as well as the subordination of the romantic plot to the demands of tradition and local convention in gender attributes.

Nigeria's Market Literatures on the whole go further than Koulibaly's texts on questions of love and further exemplify these principles. Unlike Koulibaly's stories, the Soyayya booklets and the Onitsha Market chapbooks mentioned in the previous chapter, express greater confidence about the possibility of finding true 'love,' and thus of securing personal fulfillment by embracing modernity. For example, the Hausa-language Soyayya booklets more clearly reward heroines rebelling against tradition and social convention in order to satisfy the demands of love.[22] While some of the themes in the Soyayya booklets certainly represent a recently developed orientation in Hausa literature, creative writing in Hausa has a fairly long history dating back to pre-colonial times, and prose writing in particular has been cultivated at least since the colonial period. The unquestionably local character of creative writing in an indigenous language, Hausa, probably accounts for the relative disinterest of the Hausa Market literature authors in plots woven around systematic respect for social convention and traditional gender roles. Where the local identity of the creative text is not in doubt for the reasons suggested earlier, the tendency to underscore the conventional and to conflate representations of femininity with tradition loses its *raison d'être*, for it is primarily and frequently a means of localizing that which would otherwise be perceived as foreign.

While the possibility of finding true love does not systematically appear to be contingent upon respect for customary beliefs and practices in the Hausa-language Soyayya narratives, the Onitsha Market chapbooks written in English are, like the Adoras novels, ambivalent on this point. Though the Onitsha Market authors do present heroines who rebel against fathers seeking to impose marriage partners in sympathetic light, it is not surprising that the authors of these texts in non-native languages resort in the end to the criticism of a certain kind of woman, characterized by a surfeit of independence from sexual partners, and presented as excessively urbanized and Westernized.

Romance narratives produced by larger publishing concerns such as the Adoras novels, published by Nouvelles éditions ivoiriennes in Ivory Coast, or the Sunshine romances, Heart to Heart series, Eagle romances published in Nigeria by either multinationals or major Nigerian publishers, represent another trend in West African romance writing. In this context of publication, the narratives adhered more closely to the formulaic structure of Western romances and their emphasis on the ultimate victory of love, while at the same time the authors were less likely to depict heroines successfully contravening the dictates of 'tradition' and social convention without encountering disappointments and setbacks in their relationships. They differed in this regard from the various Market literatures and Koulibaly's stories where the authors have been more concerned with recreating immediate concerns emanating from within specific communities than with simply replicating the formulaic structure of Western romances.[23] These trends in narratives published by larger publishing houses may have as much to do with editorial preferences on the part of the publishers as with a conscious orientation on the part of the writers themselves, but such factors do in any case contribute to a particular configuration of what I am describing here as the conditions of possibility for certain productions of the local.

Authors, on the other hand, who were subject to the immediate sanction of the reading public either because they self-published their texts and were dependent on quick sales for continued involvement in the 'business' of literature, or because their work appeared in publications with shorter life spans like magazines, were of necessity obligated to be more responsive to the topical and the controversial within their communities.[24] In such instances, the topical is itself a sign of localness, and when the topical involves transgression of local convention, high levels of interest can probably be sustained among local audiences over a considerable stretch of time. As tabloids rely on the publicizing of the latest transgressions of local convention to sustain interest week after week, so also narratives constrained by the politics of quick turnovers within localized audiences must embrace non-political deviations from the norm and fractures within dominant gender ideologies to keep the unbroken interest of an easily detachable audience. It would seem then, comparing several types of romance narratives marketed over the past few decades in urban West Africa that a growing preoccupation with the representation of tradition and with respect for social convention is among other things also an indication of a growing detachment from the topical and thus from versions of the local that are legible to and mainly significant for circumscribed audiences in a select location.

At one end of the literary spectrum then, we have authors of Market literatures, and writers like Koulibaly producing works that may be described as literatures of immediacy grounded in the specificities of the here and the now, of a specific place and a specific age. The desire of such writers is not so much for works that endure but for the ability to recreate with speed the potential story buried in the day's news. Like Koulibaly, authors working in these contexts often plunge directly into the story and do not engage in an elaborate display of local identity and place. Locality, however, must be minutely and carefully reconstituted where narratives diverge significantly from the most recent concerns and debates to animate a spatially circumscribed and localized readership, whether this activity is carried out on behalf of foreign readerships seeking the exotic, or for an expanded local readership seeking relevance. Because authors of the literatures of immediacy can take time and place for granted in their stories, they frequently exhibit only minimal interest in strategies of contextualization that involve differentiating one place from another place, and one culture from other cultures. For similar reasons, such authors derive no real benefit from representing woman as metaphor for place. While these popular texts are not without their own gender biases (Newell, 1996), they frequently represent women as gendered beings in their own right and not as figurations of the land, of its culture, of its people.[25] Finally, given the evident commercial value of scandal, it is hardly surprising that the authors of these short-lived and market-driven publications depict wherever possible, women who cross the line and transgress social convention in respect of traditional gender expectations.

At the other end of the literary spectrum, we have the works of major African authors, literatures of the longue durée, eschewing the transient and topical, focusing instead on the systemic, the characteristic, the conventional, that which typifies a place and an age. It is not fortuitous that these texts are printed and distributed by major multinational companies with audiences spread around the globe. The very distance of these dispersed audiences from each other and from the events and places depicted, makes a significant investment in the representation of place, of custom, and of convention all the more necessary, particularly where the selling point of the text is its claim to cultural distinctiveness. Thus, the more dispersed the potential readership, the more likely it is that authors constrained by editorial boards with clearly defined marketing goals will invest in the representation of place and in the display of acts of ethnic signification which may rely on the figure of woman as a possible metaphor for place and tradition.

African popular series like Adoras, Sunshine romances and Heart to Heart romances represent a kind of intermediate type between these two extremes. Unlike the literatures of immediacy, they do not draw their thematic matter from the well of the ephemeral that feeds other Market literatures and tabloid publications; rather the story draws its outline from a set of formulae, mostly derived from Western romance fiction, to be replicated at will. Localization of the narrative through extensive descriptions of place and or convention is important here, but not only for the reasons that govern reception of literatures of the longue durée, since collections like Adoras and Sunshine romances are often sold to audiences within relatively circumscribed geographic areas. If these audiences do not have the impression of reading the same story with the purchase of every next romance, and a story with minimal relevance to the challenges of their own lives, it is partly as a result of the variations introduced with changes in décor, setting, location and in social custom. In other words, the distinctiveness of the customs presented, and the diversity of places encountered in each formulaic romance account in no small measure for the continuing appeal of successive romances to the same audiences. One of the main attractions of this narrative type may even be its introduction of readers to supposedly local sites and places which they could otherwise not visit. But perhaps most importantly, the association between the representation of traditional gender roles, and the construction of place and cultural distinctiveness remains important because it is this specific element that localizes a narrative with little connection to the local and the topical.

All of the narrative forms discussed thus far were perceived in their various locations as examples of a modern African culture. And they all likewise emerged in a context where similarly organized foreign narratives were already available and evidently accepted, whether it was in the shape of Indian film for the Hausa-language Soyayya booklets, or American Harlequins translated into French for the Adoras novels. Notwithstanding their foreignness, these non-native cultural forms enjoyed some degree of acceptance among specific audiences probably because they offered a haven for processing sensitive materials and questions that could otherwise not be discussed within the local frameworks of the community.[26] However, to recognize an activity as foreign is not only to acknowledge that it is produced outside the boundaries of local culture, but also to signal the presence in its configuration of elements that are potentially disruptive to and subversive of the constituted social order. Explicit strategies of localization such as we see in the Adoras novels and in contemporary Nigerian English-language romances, that is in local texts that closely resemble foreign texts, are both an acknowledgement of this subversive potential and an effort to contain it. Ironically the development of such appropriately localized forms ensures even greater acceptance for the foreign genres themselves, which cannot after all be that dangerous, if they are so amenable to domestication.

If the adopted foreign cultural genre is not modified using explicit strategies of localization, it runs the risk of being viewed as an inauthentic deviation from the values of the local community even when it is produced and consumed exclusively by members of the local community. It is not surprising that in the end, the use of an indigenous language did not suffice to protect the Hausa-language Soyayya narratives from all accusations of foreignness by detractors, no doubt because the narratives so openly challenged traditional gender roles.[27] At the same time, the acceptance formerly extended to the foreign genre itself may be withdrawn because its subversive potential is now being realized within the framework of local artistic production, and in a manner which makes it difficult to deny the possibilities of local application for the ideology of the foreign genre. This principle is amply illustrated in the relationship between Soyayya booklets in northern Nigeria and Indian film where Larkin (1997) identifies the emergence of a local reworking of the types of conflicts found in Indian film in the Hausa-language Soyayya narratives as being at least partly responsible for generating a new wave of censure of a foreign cultural genre, Indian film, that had hitherto been accepted in spite of its foreignness, and whose potential for corruption of community values had not been recognized.

As possible qualifiers and evaluative barometer of creative work, references to both foreignness and localness are rarely intrinsic to a cultural practice in terms of the actual place of origin of the practice or the artists involved. Artistic forms are not foreign or local by sole virtue of the nationality of an artist or of the artist's audience. Rather these are characteristics to be imputed on the basis of criteria that more frequently relate to domestic political agendas than to a verifiable place of origin. They are purposive in intent and function mainly as a means towards a specific end. Foreignness can be invoked with respect to an art form by and for locals, just as foreignness can be denied when it is in the interest of both local and foreign cultural brokers to do so. Thus a narrative form written in an indigenous language like Hausa by native Hausa can be criticized for being too 'foreign' because of its overt confrontation with dominant gender ideologies, while the foreignness and novelty of Fagunwa's discursive strategies in Yoruba goes unrecognized by the Yoruba-reading public. Some texts in non-native languages are more local than others while some texts in indigenous languages are more foreign than others.

With the exception of the Soyayya market literatures, all the different types of West African urban popular writing discussed here have been written in English or French, one of many possible indicators of an involvement with modernity which may or may not generate accusations of foreignness, and which may or may not be associated with the adoption of unambiguous strategies of localization. Authors and artists tend to resort to these strategies when they are conscious of not extending earlier indigenous styles or versions of the local. Koulibaly, who took for granted the location of his texts within a growing body of African periodical writing in French, felt no need to use such strategies, and has not generally attracted criticism for the foreignness of his writing style. The authors of the Hausa-language Market literatures, situated in a place where creative writing in an indigenous language had a long and well-established ancestry, also appeared more willing at least in an initial stage, to forgo localizing strategies and to challenge dominant ideologies in terms of gender roles.

Where the local producers of various art forms already have an awareness of transgressing cultural boundaries in the very form and style of their creative activity, and furthermore must compete on the local market with identical foreign forms, they become more sensitive to the fact that their work may be perceived as a mere variant of a foreign prototype, and seek to obviate this eventuality by investing in specific gestures of localization which in the urban African setting have often included conservative discourses on gender. The awareness on the part of both authors and producers of the contiguity of the Adoras novels to Western romances probably led them to forestall possible criticism by adopting explicit localizing techniques, while the localness of Onitsha Market Literatures which certainly represented a novel form of narrative in early 20th century Nigeria was enhanced, not only by the integration of strategies reminiscent of indigenous quoting techniques, as suggested by Newell (2000), but also by the recurrent criticisms of a particular kind of female figure associated with excessive Westernization. One thing is certain, whether the strategies of localization are overt or latent, authors of popular texts writing in non-native languages remain in variety of ways deeply implicated in the politics and production of the local.

In their discussion of Nigerian literature, Griswold and Bastian (1987: 340–4) point out some departures from the Western model in contemporary Nigerian romances. The departures in question are, I would suggest, typical of those found in texts produced by major West African publishers and where resolution of a crisis often depends on conformity to traditional expectations in respect of gender roles: there are unimpressive male protagonists whom the heroines eventually accept in order to fulfil social expectations of marriage, there are problems with infertility that must be overcome in order for the relationship to thrive, there are antagonistic parents who must give their consent if 'love' is to flourish. As in the Western romances, love finally triumphs over all, but only to the extent that Nigerian traditions and social conventions in respect of female gender roles are not violated.

Although Griswold and Bastian (1987: 349) maintain that Nigerian romance authors 'have no need to compete with imported romances by offering something different,' I think that this precisely is the problem, that they cannot compete unless they offer something different. Both authors and publishers of popular writing have at the very least financial grounds for imputing local identity to the works they put on sale, even if such works are completely identical with works considered to be foreign. And since the Western romances continue to be readily available and popular in larger West African cities, there is really no reason to buy the locally-authored romances except they present themselves to readers accustomed to different types of romance as a significant variation on the master text and formula. Like other cultural commodities in an age of mass production, most published literary texts succeed in generating curiosity and attention by virtue of establishing a distinct identity, and belonging to a distinct genre, whether the genre is 'serious' literature, science fiction, or formulaic romance, among other possibilities. For most authors working in European languages from the former European colonies of the 19th and early 20th centuries, this distinct identity has been 'ethnic' whether or not they themselves approve of this classification. And so, though the Nigerian-born author, Buchi Emecheta could boast that her paperback publisher had 'now stopped putting [her] books in the Africa section' in British bookstores (James, 1990: 39), it is likely that most readers of Emecheta's work in Britain or elsewhere continue to buy the books mainly in order to see the world from the perspective of a Black and African Third World woman writer. In any case, the elaboration of distinctive identities for cultural texts as a method for circumscribing target audiences and facilitating sales will depend as much on the discursive strategies used by the author as on the marketing techniques adopted by both publishers and bookstores.

In the instance of the Adoras novels, where the organization of the narrative and even the packaging marked the series as almost completely identical with locally available foreign romances, detaching a readership from the audience already constituted around the Western romances depended on the elaboration of an explicit and conservative discourse of local identity represented essentially in contrasting visions of true African femininity. As Méliane Boguifo herself pointed out, the inspiration for Adoras came principally from the Latin American telenovelas on Ivorian television and the Western romances available in Ivorian bookstores rather than from the model provided by Koulibaly's almost 20-year experience in writing romances for magazines and newspapers. While there is surely some overlap between readers of Koulibaly's stories and readers of Adoras, it seems evident that in starting the Adoras collection, the intention of the Nouvelles éditions ivoiriennes was to tap into the already existing and vibrant market for foreign romances. The similarities in the formatting of book covers, the adoption of foreign pseudonyms by the authors, the strict adherence to the structure of the Western formulaic romance in many Adoras novels, served to mark the novels as 'romance narrative' following a generic Western model while the localizing techniques in and around the texts helped to identify Western romances as the 'other' against which the Adoras collection was to compete.

Cultural Outsiders and the Politics of the Local

There are interesting convergences between the context of production of the Adoras novels and the circumstances surrounding the development of Fela's conservative views on gender. Fela is widely recognized as the initiator of the musical style that is now known as Afro-beat in West African popular music. But as late as the mid-1960s, when he formed his first musical bands on his return from England, local publications in Nigeria were still describing him as a Jazz musician. That is to say, his musical style was recognized at best as innovative and new, at worst as completely foreign, despite the fact of being produced by a local musician.[28] In any case, and by his own admission, Fela's performances attracted only minimal interest from Nigerian audiences at the time. Fela himself attributed the disinterest of local audiences in his music to the competition he had to endure from 'authentic' performances of foreign musical styles, in particular, the soul music of personalities like James Brown and Otis Redding being produced by local artists who were commonly described as 'copyright' musicians.

The turning point in Fela's musical and political development came during a trip to the United States in 1969, where he became friends with an African American lady, Sandra Smith, who introduced him to the ideology and political writings associated with the Black Nationalist movement. On his return to Nigeria from the trip, he gave his band a new name to highlight its new local identity: first Nigeria 70, then Africa 70, and later still Egypt 80. These names, by their references to political locations rather than to ethno-linguistic sub-divisions, all reflect the territorialism implicit in African nationalist ideologies, while encompassing units other and larger than West African pre-colonial entities, or designating spaces like Egypt with a symbolic importance for diverse Black Nationalist movements in the world. He also made another crucial decision: to begin singing mostly in Nigerian Pidgin rather than in Yoruba, his mother tongue, so as to reach wider audiences in West African urban settings. Meanwhile, his musical orientation continued to diverge from older musical styles known locally, and incorporated an original mix of influences from a variety of Black diasporan sources.

However, Fela's growing public investment in nativist discourses tended to neutralize the appearance of foreignness for a musical style that was truly innovative. Music performances became increasingly a forum through which Fela castigated the Nigerian military, the Nigerian middle class, 'foreign' imperialists, and also a forum for advancing a particular model of ideal femininity which he always characterized as truly African. This, then was the crucible in which a song like 'Lady' was forged. In other words, the defining context of Fela's career was the competition posed by foreign musical styles, and the challenge of remaining local while integrating elements of these same styles into his own music. Similarly, the defining moment in Fela's ideological and musical development was not a re-acquaintance with indigenous musical traditions, but a trip to the United States which equipped him to compete with foreign musical styles at home by providing him with a template of nativist discourses and rhetorics of localization which he then deployed on his return in acclimatizing the Nigerian and other West African audiences to what continued to be an essentially novel and non-native musical style.

In what circumstances then do some imaginative texts become in contemporary times vehicles for conservative discourses on femininity? These discourses develop where author/producer/artists who are creating new orientations for local culture enter into direct competition with cultural outsiders within the borders of their own home territory, which is why such notions of femininity must be presented not only as distinctive, but also as deriving from the past or from a time without cultural contamination.[29] The preoccupation with conservative representations of ideal femininity further acquires significance in instances where contact can no longer be avoided with alternative forms of a practice once envisioned as monolithic in character and distinctive to a single community. In such circumstances, conservative representations of ideal femininity serve as strategies of accreditation and authentication to be invoked in confronting discourses of the same type in their variable formulations around the globe. Such representations enable cultural spokespersons in specific locations to affirm when confronted with alternative versions of the same practice: 'our version is distinctive to our society and represents the purest form.'

It is clear that discourses around human bodies have a special appeal for groups unable to claim sole proprietorship of a practice, and who also do not generate their own heritage industries, their own memorials and pilgrimage sites, because such discourses literally enable embodiments of the past, and provide visual markers for audiences and constituents to hold on to.[30] The fact that men are perceived in societies with relatively recent memories of foreign domination, as being more deeply scarred by experiences of acculturation through their greater interaction with and exposure to the agents of domination makes the prospect of preserving cultural purity in and through women's bodies all the more attractive and imperative.[31] Thus, a discourse foregrounding women as sites of cultural purity becomes the means through which a perceived decline in masculinity blamed on excessive contact with cultural outsiders can be reversed and counteracted.

Speaking about nationalist discourses, Anderson (1991: xiv) inquires: 'Supposing "antiquity" were, at a certain historical juncture, the *necessary consequence* of "novelty?"' Anderson's intuition finds validation in those conservative African discourses around identity that turn up in cultural compositions where there is a consciousness on the part of the producer/ author/artist of a novelty of form, a novelty that always runs the risk of being apprehended as foreign particularly because the authors are to some extent pioneers, inaugurating a new cultural practice, more closely linked to and or influenced by cultural outsiders. Both Fela's music and the Adoras novels drew upon styles and narrative strategies that were certainly considered novel and non-native when produced by individuals who were not foreigners to the society. As Appiah (1992: 58–9) has remarked, speaking about Fela's music, 'the sounds of Fela Kuti would have astonished the musicians of the last generation of court musicians in Yorubaland.' Nonetheless we encounter with both Fela and the Adoras novels discursive repudiations of novelty and newness. In both cases, the author/producers appear to express implicit faith in the old ways, so that distinct value is vested in figurations of the traditional. It is this specific feature that I consider emblematic of conservative productions of the local.

Given this background, it is easy to understand why some of the most vituperative denunciations of assertive womanhood, often portrayed as 'Western' in urban Africa, have actually been produced in texts in various non-native languages and diverse languages of wider communication by those using the most novel media, who for this reason among others, also have a more highly developed consciousness of the erosion of cultural distinctiveness to which they themselves contribute by assimilating foreign cultural styles and deploying new means of communication.[32] The critical element of course, is not language alone, though recourse to non-native languages will often heighten an awareness of possible foreignness and therefore of the need for bolder demonstrations of localization, especially when the discursive strategies in use appear in every other respect to reference a foreign prototype. Unflattering representations of women are no doubt as present in contemporary indigenous-language texts as they are in works in non-native languages, but, and this is my argument, the tendency to portray these models of femininity as specifically non-African, and Western, is especially typical of works that incarnate in some way a clear modification of or even departure from older cultural forms and which must compete with identical foreign forms for the attention of the local audience. And although all cultural forms are local in the sense of originating somewhere and engendering separate groups of spatially circumscribed audiences whose reception and interpretation of an event, a performance, a text is mediated through and colored by locality, conservative discourses of femininity among other explicit affirmations of cultural specificity and attachment to place are deployed in these cultural forms only under specific conditions. That is to say, local cultures do not consistently advertise an awareness of their own localness and parochialness. In fact, it would seem that most flagrant manifestations of and preoccupations with specificity and place owe their existence more to interaction with novel, dynamic conditions than to the unchanging traditions of any one place.

As such, clearly formulated expressions of attachment to 'tradition' which involve legitimizing a contemporary activity by appealing to past custom take on even greater urgency where cultural boundaries are becoming blurred by such processes as appropriation of ideologies and cultural forms considered disruptive of established social order or the widespread adoption of non-native languages. In a sense, every generation re-imagines the local to suits its purposes for a particular age. By claiming the Adoras novels for local Ivorian and West African culture, for example, the publishers of the series were engaged in precisely such an act of re-invention. However, to be truly local is to possess a genealogy, so that the continual novelty of the local in its successive embodiments dictates the appeal to tradition and a fictitious genealogy, as a mechanism for justifying the affirmation of localness and moderating the appearance of newness. In recently introduced cultural practices therefore, the invocation of tradition is hardly a sign of a desire for the perpetuation of the customary and the ancestral in pure form even if such an undertaking were possible.

Bearing this in mind, the questions we ought to be asking are the following: what constitutes the local at a given point in time, and how exactly is localness being conceptualized and exemplified in a specific place? To which I would respond in the case of the Adoras novels and several other new cultural forms realized in non-native languages, the local is defined in these novel literary forms by reference to custom and in particular by reference to conservative models of ideal femininity and their presumed associations with traditional practice. The local owes its distinctiveness to tradition, and at the same time, tradition finds continued relevance thanks to the unceasing interactions of the local with non-native practices, which require constant justification. Thus, the critical element in the recourse to these conservative discourses seems to be an awareness on the part of the producers of their proximity to the battle lines of cultural encounter, manifested in the increasing remoteness of artists from a single spatially circumscribed home audience, and the impossibility of avoiding cultural outsiders on home ground forcing local artists to compete at home with non-native models by offering alternative versions of the foreign, recreated as the local. In this respect, the incidence of conservative discourses about women in texts in non-native languages serves as further confirmation of the fact that adoption of diverse 'foreign' languages in cultural texts need not foreshadow a diminished role for the idea of the local, of the indigenous and of the traditional. On the contrary, strategies for localizing texts, which may include conservative discourses about women, take on increased importance where the cultural particularity of a text, and its relevance to a designated locality have been obscured by a range of factors, including the use of a non-native language.

The increased contiguity with foreign culture on home soil impacts both the new forms of local culture and the old forms of indigenous culture. In fact one of the most fascinating developments in West African urban cultures is the extent to which expressions of the indigenous (identified with the most limited geographic and cultural scope) have become detached from home-bound audiences in places of origin and increasingly dependent on transnational circuits for performative realization of their distinctiveness. The 'web of interdependencies' as Featherstone (1993: 176) describes it, has become ever tighter for productions of local culture even and especially in its most indigenous forms and styles. Klein (2000) discusses in her work, for example, a West African musical genre that is in decline on home ground and with home-bound audiences due to the greater attraction offered by foreign-inspired cultural forms, with the consequence that this indigenous musical genre now thrives mainly in relation to the value it has acquired on foreign stages and beyond home territory. Balogun (1998: 42) evokes a related phenomenon in discussing the role of French institutions in the development of an 'African' film tradition, whose content, and I might add, penchant for quintessential images of the rural Third World Other, are dictated by the tastes of 'art house circuits in Europe.'

At the same time, the local in its hybrid and composite formulation is in many postcolonial urban settings tending to overshadow the indigenous as a preferred site of identification. By this, I mean that people in postcolonial settings retain a commitment to cultural forms associated with territorially circumscribed spaces of belonging. However, such cultural forms are not necessarily perceived as wholly indigenous or as unmediated productions of the traditional practices of any given ethno-linguistic group. Home-bound audiences in urban West Africa are no exception to the trend. For example, West African fans of Fela's musical style, Afro-beat, would certainly consider the style to be African; however, few would describe it as traditional or specifically Yoruba music. The significance of this growing involvement with forms of local culture that are recognized as not being traditional derives in part from the fact that home-bound audiences in postcolonial contexts have come to rely more and more on deliberate consumption of foreign cultural forms, offering imaginations, and as such, vicarious experiences of displacement and travel. These forms are particularly meaningful for populations aware of the possibilities of social mobility offered by travel, but whose limited resources make actual experiences of expatriation unlikely. Through their consumption of the foreign, these audiences signal their willingness to interpret experiences accumulated in one place (home) by reference to experiences generated in other places. Their actions indicate how integral foreign culture has become to the way home-bound audiences now interpret the realities of lives lived at home.

Consumption of foreign culture also enables such audiences to access the perceived attributes of foreignness: novelty, modernity, exoticism, but also subversion, corruption, moral decay without succumbing to the dissolution of cultural boundaries. Indeed, for the most part, the appeal of the foreign lies precisely in the fact that it remains foreign, that is distinct from that which is acknowledged to be either indigenous or local culture. This quality of being considered separate from the local and indigenous accounts for the willingness of some communities to tolerate in foreign cultural forms the evocation of issues and subjects that would in any other context be taboo within the community. But this tolerance for 'social deviance' in entities recognized as foreign also explains why they make convenient targets for community anger and can serve as proxies to be blamed in the event of calamities and mishaps for which a local community would otherwise have to accept sole responsibility.

These developments, however, put local entertainers and artists in the unusual position of having to create foreign-inspired styles and forms in order to secure the attention of contemporary home-bound audiences. Occasionally, local artists introduce new styles that are almost completely identical with foreign forms, and still manage to generate enthusiastic responses from home-bound audiences, despite dissolving the boundary between the foreign and the local. It is more often the case though, that once the local becomes in public perception coterminous with the foreign, such forms of local culture begin to be considered problematic imitations. We should keep in mind here, that most societies require visible sites and objects of foreignness, because the foreign that is distinct from local culture plays a significant role in the community's elaboration of its own identity. Those local artists who create forms of local culture that are completely identical with the foreign occupy a precarious social position because they essentially obliterate the very concept of foreignness by making new forms of local culture isomorphic with foreign culture. What then are home-bound audiences to do for vicarious experiences of travel? Where then are communities to find surrogates to blame for social evil if the foreign no longer exists as something distinct from the local within their own community?

It is precisely this eventuality that gives rise to the kind of discursive techniques I have been discussing in this chapter. To preserve a space for foreignness, which remains a vital necessity in most communities, while allowing for local artists to draw upon the appeal of the foreign for contemporary home-bound audiences, it then frequently becomes necessary for local artists to resort to explicit strategies of appropriation. In speaking of appropriation here, I do not mean that local artists simply generate forms patterned on foreign cultural models; by appropriation, I refer to the subjection of the new art form to flagrant processes of domestication, specifically intended to divest the cultural form of its foreign identity while endowing it with local identity.[33] It is in this setting among others that many conservative discourses of femininity take shape in postcolonial societies and not in unmediated revivals of customary expressions of sexism and misogyny, real as these may be in any one society or community. Local formulaic literature written in non-native languages is particularly susceptible to such pressures for localization to the extent that it is virtually indistinguishable from foreign formulaic writing.

At the same time it is true that there are many texts in non-native languages that no longer resort to such methods. The fact that authors using non-native languages do not engage in explicit strategies of localization in such cases indicates once again that every appropriation of a non-native language is not perceived as a deployment of a foreign language. It also suggests that the audiences, sodalities and affiliations whose very existence depends on a given non-native language have by this stage become so normalized as to render superfluous any further attentiveness to the foreignness of the language in question. Thus, the dispersed, urban, young, and largely female audience of the works of authors like Koulibaly had certainly come to the point of taking its own existence for granted as a 'community of interpretation' (Fredericksen, 1999: 54) with shared interests, whose interactions are transacted with no self-consciousness in a non-native language, namely French. In this regard, the readers see themselves as modern, young, cosmopolitan, 'Black,' Ivorian, West African, rather than as Dyula, Bété, or Senufo readers.

But whether or not the texts requiring localization have been produced in non-native languages, we need to acknowledge these texts for what they truly are: that is, the latest incarnation of the local in a given place. We also need to recognize the presence of these gender discourses in art forms considered 'new' for what they really are: that is, as authenticating devices and strategies for localizing that which might otherwise be perceived as foreign. They have more to do with the need to create order in contemporary delimitings of the local by effacing irregularities and inconsistencies than with preserving the indigenous in its supposedly uncontaminated character. And thus, conservative discourses on femininity rarely signal a comprehensive persistence of the convictions linked to an earlier age in a contemporary period, as much as they indicate a need to mitigate the association of some appropriations of modernity with foreignness through a selective return to the past, enacted in, and through discourses about women's bodies.

Notes

1. To consider only a few examples, Stapleton and May (1987: 147–8) comment on songs about women in Congolese (Zairean) Soukouss; Asante-Darko and Van Der Geest (1983) present similar material with respect to Ghanaian highlife; Newell's (1996) work considers the gender politics of Onitsha Market Literature; Adeleye-Fayemi (1997) writes on problematic representations of women on Nigerian television.
2. Certainly, there was little in Fela's background to explain his later commitment to what he described as African tradition. He grew up in Abeokuta, the Yoruba town with perhaps the largest contingent of the most Westernized Yoruba, in the early 20th century, namely the Sierra Leonan receptives. Both Fela's parents

and even his grandparents were Christians at a time when Christian Yoruba were decidedly a minority, and their lifestyle clearly diverged from the norm of the wider society in which they lived. By his own accounts, both his parents were dismissive of indigenous practices (Veal, 2000: 14) and Fela undoubtedly received greater exposure to Western culture than many of his contemporaries in the same place. Fela also spent a number of years in England studying classical music and trumpet. Both Fela's father, an Anglican clergyman and his mother, Funmilayo Kuti were social activists, and his mother is credited with having founded and led one of the earliest organized women's movements in 20th-century Nigeria. Indeed, Fela's mother, with her radical politics and willingness to confront men in positions of authority, was the very antithesis of the 'African woman' as defined by Fela in his famous song. Nonetheless, he maintained a close relationship with her, and she even lived in his residence in her later years and until her death in 1978.

3. The point has been most recently made in Veal's (2000) comprehensive study of Fela's life and music.
4. For example, Fela organized a ceremony on February 20 1978, in which he 'married' 27 of the women who had been associated with him as dancers, back-up vocalists, workers, etc. Although polygamy is respected and widely practiced by wealthier Yoruba men, Fela's wedding provoked angry reactions from many in the community, who saw the wedding as an example of deviation from and not conformity to tradition. The women were viewed either as prostitutes or ignorant females being exploited by Fela. It was noted that the usual rites associated with marriage had not been observed, and that traditional polygamy in any case, never occurred in such mass ceremonies. Veal (2000: 159) quotes a letter written by a Nigerian to a major Nigerian newspaper in response to the wedding and which reflects the mood of Fela's critics. The writer remarked, 'Fela has openly defied the tradition he purports to uphold . . . Fela has merely used the cloak of tradition to grab cheap apples to munch, washing his hands of the customary demands that would have been too costly for his insatiable tastes . . .'
5. I should point out here that my use of the term 'conservative' does not necessarily reference the political affiliation of the artists and authors in question, since those involved in the production of these forms of local culture will frequently find themselves on opposing sides of a political divide. Rather, I describe as conservative those articulations of localness that confer value on and establish sanction for particular practices and activities by invoking the trope of the traditional.
6. The song titled 'Vernacular' appears on Lagbaja!'s compact disc *WebeforeMe* released in 2001. Lagbaja! an Afro-beat singer may have drawn inspiration for his song from the father of Afro-beat himself, Fela who in the 1970s had already composed a song in Pidgin, 'Mr Grammartology-lisationalism is the boss' criticizing the African elite's use of English.
7. See Oyewumi (1997) and Amadiume (1987: 136) for arguments constructed along these lines.
8. See Ogundipe-Leslie (1987: 130) for this kind of approach.
9. Méliane Boguifo disclosed this in an interview with me on 13 September 2000.
10. See 'Romance African style' *Courrier*, 1998.
11. Cited by Vauguy in an Ivorian newspaper, *Notre Voie* (19 January 2000).
12. To my surprise, in August 2003, I even came across several Adoras titles in the

French-language section of an E. P. Bookstore in Accra, Ghana, right next to school textbooks. When I inquired from the sales clerk why they would be selling French-language novels in an English-speaking country, she responded that the novels were popular with the French-speaking community in Accra, and that sales were quite brisk.
13. Interview with Biton Koulibaly (1999b: 69).
14. Isaïe Biton Koulibaly mentioned this to me in an interview held 11 September 2000.
15. Cited in an article by N'koumo, in an Ivorian newspaper, *Ivoir' Soir* (12 September 2000).
16. For example, I did not come across a single trader in the second-hand book trade in Abidjan, popularly called the 'libraries par terre' who did not know of Koulibaly, and the profits to be made by selling his books. These traders apparently liked to stock both the Adoras novels and the Koulibaly short stories because in both cases, sales were quick.
17. Though it is published in Paris, *Amina* caters almost exclusively to African audiences based in Africa, and functions like a local magazine in Ivory Coast and much of Francophone West Africa where it is widely available.
18. For example, according to Koulibaly, there was such a massive response from interested suitors to his story 'J'ai trente-quatre ans et je suis encore célibataire' (I'm 34 years and still single) when it was first published in *Amina*, that eventually the magazine had to publish a rejoinder to convince readers of the magazine that it was only a story, and that a heroine in need of a husband did not really exist (Koulibaly, interview with Adejunmobi 2000).
19. It should be mentioned here in passing that Koulibaly is not only an author for the Adoras series. By the late 1990s, he was once again working in the Ivorian publishing industry as an editor for literary texts with NEI, the publisher of Adoras. In fact, he was by his own account one of the prime movers in the decision made by NEI to establish a popular romance series (Koulibaly, interview with Adejunmobi 2000). The differences in style between his writing under his own name and those carried out for Adoras thus point to a conscious strategy and an awareness of the cultural politics at work in the desire to present Adoras as a genre specifically rooted in Ivorian and West African reality.
20. Koulibaly has noted though that male readers more often write letters to the editor in response to the stories written, whether or not the stories are written from the male perspective. Newell (2000: 140) has made similar observations for stories published in Ghanaian women's magazines.
21. I emphasize the word popular here; in other words, the sale of Koulibaly's stories in periodical publications depends on a reception among audiences that is not mediated by educated critics who are more likely to be tolerant of attacks on social convention.
22. See Larkin (1997), Furniss (1996), Johnson (2000) for material on Soyayya, and Obiechina (1973) and Newell (1996) in particular for material on Onitsha Market Literatures. Both Furniss (1996: 37–51) and Larkin (1997) note the relative independence of the female characters and the openness towards cultures and values identified as foreign in recent Hausa popular fiction.
23. Many of Koulibaly's stories refer for example to the very real tensions and conflicts generated by post-independence Ivorian legislation on marriage, such as the formal prohibition of polygyny, and the provisions linked to the community of property within registered marriages. The legislation was apparently

intended to offer greater protection for women than 'traditional law,' but far from promoting the consistent practice of monogamy, or offering most women relationships protected by the law, 'the unique regime of the community, with its insistence on monogamy, has encouraged a proliferation of concubines whose relationships are controlled neither by the state nor by tradition' (Toungara, 1997: 69). The advantages and disadvantages of different types of relationships between Ivorian men and women are a recurrent theme in Koulibaly's writing. Indeed, he pays particular attention to the emotional insecurity confronting most women within and especially outside relationships that are defined as marriage by contemporary Ivorian legislation.

24. For example, the conflict between arranged and love marriages, which is a major theme of the Soyayya booklets of northern Nigeria, would generate much less interest as a scandalous issue in southern Nigerian cities where marriages are hardly ever arranged now. In contrast, the duplicity of husbands, wives, girlfriends and lovers remains topical both in southern Nigerian popular narratives (in film and in magazines) and in the kinds of stories produced by Koulibaly for Ivorian audiences.

25. Thus Koulibaly's stories are really about Ivorian women and not about Ivory Coast.

26. That is why Hausa respondents could describe Indian film as being 'just like Hausa culture' (Larkin, 1997: 412), since the very foreignness of the genre made comparisons between supposedly dissimilar entities possible. Larkin (1997: 433) observed that once the differences between Hausa and Indian narratives began to be dissolved, there was much less tolerance for Indian film itself.

27. For example, one critic of the Soyayya booklets described them as 'copying shamelessly from other cultures' (Larkin, 1997: 431). Perhaps in order to forestall such criticisms, some of the female authors associated with this literary movement have lately developed what Whitsitt (2003: 150–2) describes as a conservative, Islamic feminism.

28. Writing about the use of the term 'jazz' in West Africa from the 1940s onwards, Veal (2000: 40) remarks: 'From this time, the term 'jazz' tended to be used to [sic] throughout sub-Saharan Africa to denote two things. First, it often referred to any large dance music ensemble with Western instruments – especially a horn section – an association derived from American big-band jazz ensembles . . . Second, 'jazz' was also often applied to any ensemble or genre in which improvisation played a major role . . .'

29. Y. F. Tuan (1977: 198) has written, 'a truly rooted community may have shrines and monuments, but it is unlikely to have museums and societies for the preservation of the past.' Fela's imaginative reconstructions of traditional African femininity were necessitated precisely by the fact that he no longer formed part of a rooted generation.

30. Fela's troupes always included a large number of women who were not simply part of the background of his performances. They were prominently featured on the cover jackets of many of his albums, and clearly served on stage, in their singing, in their dancing, and attire, as a visual anchor for the message of his songs. See Veal (2000: 109, 111) for further discussion of how Fela used photographs of women in his troupe to project his own vision of African culture and 'tradition.'

31. Obbo's (1980: 143) contention that in African societies, women are expected to 'act as mediators between the past and the present' and men as 'mediators

between the present and the future' is relevant here not only for contemporary African discourses, but for conservative discourses on gender around the world.

32. By way of illustration, Fela's early songs in Yoruba addressed women as the objects of male love and flattery. It was when he started singing in Nigerian Pidgin that these highly charged images of Westernized African women began appearing in his songs. Given my argument here, I find it helpful therefore to distinguish within the broad spectrum of diverse manifestations of sexism that one may find in many more or less popular West African cultural forms, those particular expressions of sexism that involve an explicit opposition between a denigrated model of femininity linked to Westernization and an ideal model of femininity attributed to tradition. I would like to suggest that these oppositions will most often surface in circumstances where the novelty of a new cultural style is still fresh, and will be most often though not always expressed in non-native languages.

33. It is usually the case that adoptions of new cultural styles that do not incorporate these discourses of localization are the most likely to be described as imitations by both local and expatriate cultural brokers, as has often happened with most forms of African popular writing. In any society there are manifestly many practices inspired by foreign cultures, but only a few of these foreign adoptions are labeled as imitations, which in effect makes them open to various kinds of censure. The difference lies then not so much between imitations and original works, but between those novel styles that incorporate discourses of localization, and those novel styles that do not engage in this practice.

Chapter 5

Languages of Wider Communication and Alternative Sites of Belonging

The main question I have been considering in this book is the following: what is the significance of the fact that people learn and begin to use a language that is not a mother tongue? If the German Romantic Johann von Herder was right, these changes to language repertoires would be signs of shifting national allegiances, and evidence of the fact that commitment to one nation is (forcibly and tragically) in the process of being replaced by commitment to another nation.[1] When, in postcolonial contexts, the additional languages being acquired are the languages of former colonizers, such changes might also be read as a perpetuation of the structures of colonial society.[2] As I have argued thus far, four decades and more after the formal end of colonial rule in most parts of Africa, neither perspective adequately explains how and why people in contemporary Africa have a growing interaction with activities conducted in languages that are not their mother tongues.

For one thing, the nation, envisaged as a territorially-fixed community, with claims to common origins, a common history and cultural specificity, is only one of many possible types of community to which people may want to belong and that can be constructed with reference to a discourse about language. Furthermore, supporters of individual nations tend to develop very specific kinds of positions with respect to the role of language in human community. Here exclusive attachment to territory is justified by professions of cultural specificity purportedly exemplified for example in diverse ritual practices, religious beliefs, distinctive dress, and frequently language. The nation, we are told, belongs in this place and exists as a distinct community because it is already united by an ancestral language, or because it will shortly be unified by a suitable language. To this end, nationalists in postcolonial territories deploy discourses of the lingua franca that may in due course be transformed into discourses of the vernacular, and which always serve to distinguish citizens of this polity, members of this nation and legitimate residents of this place from citizens of other nations in other places.

But what happens when an increasing number of people are polyglot, and begin to join formal associations that require quasi-exclusive loyalties from members, but do not locate their specificity in a mother tongue, and do not foreground this kind of connection between language, territory, and cultural specificity? What happens when people choose to become members of an organized community that elects to use a language that is potentially common to groups in many places because precisely it is no longer peculiar to groups from only one place? Are these developments too to be read from the perspective of changing national affiliations? I do not think so, because as I have suggested in earlier chapters, statements about the specificity of a group's language are also ultimately statements about the territorial scope and limits of the space of the local for members of that group; to identify an individual by their vernacular language is also to affirm the individual's connections with and claims over a circumscribed territory. References to languages as vernaculars are also then references to significant locations for those who experience the languages in question as vernaculars.

Against this background, I would like to suggest in my final chapter that the willingness of a certain type of formal association to use a language recognized by most members as something other than a vernacular often points to a larger pattern of dislocation from the space of the local, and a loss of faith in the ability of acknowledged spaces of locality to provide the kind of security normally attributed to the space of home and the space of the local. In other words, commitment to and involvement with associations using non-native languages that are also languages of wider communication should be interpreted not as a resolution to replace one space of locality with another space previously considered foreign, but as an expression of doubt in the complete adequacy of the space of the local as a framework for survival in the contemporary world. Given these premises, my intention in this chapter is to consider possible responses to the following questions: what kinds of community are being constituted in the contemporary world? What is the significance of the fact that people become members of sodalities that do not establish any kind of correlation between language, particular territorial units, and group identity? What does the fact that such sodalities use languages that are no longer specific to people in only one place tell us about how newer types of community are responding to the space of the local and expressing their own specificity?

In the African context, languages which are potentially common to members of groups from many places because they are no longer peculiar to groups from only one place are almost always second or third languages;

or to use the terminology I have most consistently employed in this book, they are non-native languages. They are in addition, languages of wider communication, and here I return to the definition proposed earlier for such languages. The language of wider communication is one that enables the formation of sodalities whose members do not necessarily share in common the same mother tongue or primary site of belonging, and where therefore imaginations of the local are subject to reformulation. In other words, the language of wider communication as I have defined it here, is often for a significant proportion of those involved in a specific communication circuit, a non-native language, a secondary language enabling those who have acquired this language to form networks that do not rely on residence in the same location and or communication in a shared mother tongue. Because the language of wider communication is used by individuals who do not necessarily share the same mother tongue, it is frequently also familiar to at least some individuals in a multiplicity of sovereign territorial units, where it may either enable members of particular sodalities to expand their conception of the space of the local, or in other instances, to position themselves beyond the space and allegiances of the local.

In defining the language of wider communication, I am not thinking solely in terms of the number of speakers involved, though any language of wider communication will attract a large number of speakers. Rather, I am more interested in the fact that speakers of a language of wider communication can form sodalities that are not as territorially circumscribed as those sodalities where communication occurs in a mother tongue that is not at the same time a language of wider communication. All human beings have membership in a multiplicity of sodalities and communities with more often than not a territorially circumscribed sphere of operation. In other words, most communities or associations to which we belong are envisaged as local. As I see it, the specific attribute of the language of wider communication is to facilitate the emergence of communities that are no longer necessarily envisioned as localized in character and operation.

Language, the State, and the Nation

Before proceeding any further, I do wish to recognize that the transformation of a language into a language of wider communication does not derive from any inherent qualities in the language itself. Languages are neither naturally endowed nor destined to become languages of wider communication. They attain to that status by being associated with particular trading networks and or by virtue of an association with institutional powers, and especially with the forces of domination, colonization, occupation and so on. My interest here is not in the often violent processes which lay the groundwork for the emergence of languages of wider communication at particular moments in time – these are questions that have already been adequately addressed by a number of other scholars – my concerns have to do with determining how those who do use contemporary languages of wider communication respond to the space of the local.

Some readers might object to my suggestion that languages of wider communication have a fundamentally different impact from mother tongues on perceptions of the local; after all, all languages of wider communication start out as someone's mother tongue. Anderson (1991: 133–4) seemed to be making just such a point when he declared that, 'imperial languages are still *vernaculars*, and thus particular vernaculars among many.' Anderson is not entirely wrong in this observation; imperial languages do start out as and remain vernaculars for large sections of the population in metropolitan centers who use these languages as mother tongues. However, those who learn the imperial language in former colonies and outside the metropolitan centers do not experience the same languages as vernaculars, very simply because they already have other languages as their mother tongues. For these people, the imperial language is not a vernacular, but a non-native language that can occupy a range of functions: it may simply be a foreign language, it may be identified principally as the language of the colonizer, or possibly as in some of the instances considered thus far, it may begin to function as a language of wider communication. As such, it is important to determine what the function of a given language is for an individual speaker in a given context of communication since the same language can be used by the same speaker to establish different kinds of communication networks.

The purpose of this chapter is to suggest that associations which emerge out of networks where communication occurs in languages functioning for involved speakers as languages of wider communication, will frequently tend to develop a different kind of understanding of the connection between the practice of belonging to a community and the idea of the local. By this, I do not simply mean that such associations reformulate the territorial coordinates of the space of the local, which is certainly one possibility as explored in Chapter 2. Rather, I am referring in this instance to cases where membership is no longer solely defined in terms of circumscribed localities. As I understand it, a language becomes a language of wider communication at the specific point when the majority of those who speak the language have acquired it as a non-native language. In other words, the majority of those who use the language already have membership in a variety of localities.

To take the best-known case in our own time, English has not become a global language mainly due to a significant increase in the number of mother-tongue speakers. If English today is a global language, it is because non-native speakers of the language now outnumber native speakers of the language many times over (Kachru, 1986: 20; Strevens, 1992: 28). Though the position of English is unparalleled in world history, what is true for English is equally applicable to several other languages around the world, such as Arabic and French, which are also acquiring an increasing number of non-native speakers. On a somewhat smaller scale, indigenous languages of wider communication on the African continent like Kiswahili and Hausa are also developing in a similar fashion. I consider the fact that these languages remain second or third languages for large groups of people to be highly significant in relation to the kinds of functions that they can have for these non-native speakers of the language.

Now, it can and does happen that the language of wider communication ultimately becomes over a few generations a mother tongue. Even then, to the extent that the language is not peculiar to residents of territorial units that are perceived to be sovereign entities and which provide the framework for particular visions of the local, it still functions as language of wider communication and can enable residents of a particular place to expand the scope of their imagination of the local. In any case, whether people speak the language of wider communication as a mother tongue following a shift in language practices, or because it has always been the first language of their community, it is essential to differentiate between instances where the language is being invoked as part of a discourse of the vernacular and where it is being used to establish communication across recognized boundaries. It should also be noted that for individuals whose mother tongue is also a language of wider communication, the language in question will not always provide a basis for the formation of the kinds of sodalities that I will be examining in this chapter.

For the most part, I do not anticipate major changes in the language policies pursued by the majority of African governments in the foreseeable future. Even in those parts of the world where the system of government is relatively secure and the territorial integrity of the state is not under attack, debates over language policy are often contentious and perceived as an assault on the hallowed principle of national identity. In places where the legitimacy of the government is being constantly questioned, and debates over the composition and organization of the nation-state are far from settled, few governments will be willing to stoke the already raging fires of dissent by initiating major changes in language policy and thus provoking what is likely to become a violent discussion over the character of national identity. We can probably expect then that in the majority of African countries, European languages will remain official languages, and many people will learn a regional lingua franca in addition to their mother tongue, except their mother tongue is a language of wider communication spoken across considerable distances.[3] At the same time, government officials will continue to invoke the importance of the mother tongue, though actual policy may tend to favor the emergence of national and regional lingua francas.

Nonetheless, and though most African governments are unlikely to introduce significant modifications in language policy any time soon, there are changes taking place in language practices, and these changes are best apprehended not by looking at the nation-state and its unchanging discourses about language but at the new forms of community, the new alliances and sodalities that are being formed and founded in various African locations. As I argued in Chapter 2, from my point of view, the main significance of the adoption of non-native languages in the area of cultural production lies in the indications that it provides regarding the gradual modification of the spatial coordinates of belonging and the character of belonging among the individuals involved in producing, disseminating, and receiving these cultural products. For much of the 20th century, for example, narrative production in European languages on the African continent referenced identification with the space of Africa, with the emergent nation-states following the end of colonial rule, and with a global Black culture. These were newer spaces of belonging, constructed in fields of interaction and communication based almost entirely on former colonial languages. Therefore, one of the questions to be asked in connection with the use of non-native languages is the following: what kinds of fields of interaction and spaces of belonging are now being constituted through recourse to these languages?

While I do not share the opinion of those who predict the imminent demise of the nation-state as a form of human community and polity, it is not a distortion of recent developments to remark that the hold of the state became increasingly less secure in many parts of Africa in the last decades of the 20th century. Armed militia groups, diverse rebels, opposition parties, and religious entities regularly challenge the authority of a state whose effective control over the full territory allotted to it on internationally recognized maps is often tenuous. Entire villages and districts depend on a continuing basis on NGOs and other non-state actors to provide the services usually dispensed by a state. Systems for circumventing the provisions and decrees of the state to which one is theoretically committed as a citizen are widely circulated and publicly advertised.

Although a similar degree of decline in the powers of the state has not necessarily been observed elsewhere in the world, it is perhaps a mistake to assume that the nation-state will always remain the most significant type of community in which individuals will want to claim membership. People want to belong to some form of community. For this reason, they take out membership in all kinds of associations. But, there is no reason to assume that the nation as currently understood, will always represent the ideal form of community in which people may seek to affirm membership. And this is where changing language practices become important, for they alert us to the emergence of new types of community which may begin to play a more prominent role in the lives of people, especially in the contemporary period. Given these developments, we might consider interpreting changing language practices specifically in relation to the constitution and emergence of types of sodalities and associations that may have at least an equal if not a greater hold on people's allegiances than any one nation-state and primary ethno-linguistic unit. In this respect I find particularly interesting the growing importance and visibility of certain types of interests groups around the world.

Some of these groups function as new expressions of civil society within the state while a growing number might conform to the model of transnational civil society as described by Rudolph (1997: 2) 'whose commonality depends less on coresidence in 'sovereign' territorial space and more on common worldviews, purposes, interests, and praxis.' Yet others might be categorized with the kinds of associations that Appadurai (1996: 167) has described as 'complex, postnational social formations. These formations are now organized around principles of finance, recruitment, coordination, communication, and reproduction that are fundamentally postnational and not just multinational or international.' The Sufi orders and networks discussed by both Kane (1997) and Simone (2001) might serve as examples of these transnational civil societies, while Charismatic churches in urban Africa at times seem to be evolving in the kind of postnational direction envisaged by Appadurai. The fact that such sodalities may play a more important role in the lives of people in parts of the world than other types of political and ethnic entities is no also longer in doubt (Marshall-Fratani, 1998: 282; Rudolph, 1997: 5; Simone, 2001: 17). And though religious affiliation is only one of many possible affiliations that any individual might invoke, such affiliations are becoming increasingly prominent in the postcolonial world and in the many places around the globe where the state has become particularly ineffective or ceased to operate as a significant source of security and inspiration for many of its citizens.

Moreover, paying greater attention to broad social trends can only enhance the kinds of inferences we as literary scholars draw about language practices. This is the reason why I have chosen to extend my discussion of non-native languages and contemporary African culture beyond the usual literary suspects. By looking at institutions and practices, other than those linked to Literature, we begin to realize that what is sometimes presented as a solitary exception, that is activity, and specifically, the production of written creative texts in non-native languages, is in fact neither solitary nor exceptional. On the contrary, it represents a major current in the cultural practices that we now observe in contemporary African society. Instead, therefore, of using qualifiers like 'foreign' and 'local' as if they referred to static realities and making all manner of inferences based on prior determinations that particular languages are foreign or local, we might also consider the role that various languages play in redefining the border between the foreign and the local, and even in some instances in suppressing the category of foreignness as a significant variable in self-definition. My objective, then, in this chapter is to move us away from the ready classification of languages as foreign and native languages and to a point where instead we take note of how certain languages enable the formation of certain kinds of networks, whether the languages in question are indigenous to the population or additional non-native languages, and the purposes for which these networks are being constituted.

The activity and reach of religious sodalities is especially intriguing since such sodalities often require voluntary financial expenditure and are not bound by government directives in terms of their language practices. As sites of belonging which may command the kind of allegiance from members that many states are unable to muster from so-called citizens, one only needs look at the renewed interest in religious groupings among government agencies around the world following the events of September 2001 in New York. When we encounter in the context of some religious sodalities, languages that are for a significant proportion of members, non-native languages, we must begin to wonder whether this practice merely represents further evidence of the subordination of indigenous cultures to 'foreign' values or whether there is something else afoot in this willingness to engage in activities in non-native languages. Referring to English in particular, Kachru (1986: 14) has already called attention to the formation of what he described as a caste of English-speaking fellowships around the world. The West African Charismatic church represents precisely this type of fellowship, though the language in question is not always or necessarily English. In any case, it is important that we consider what the rise of these types of fellowships means for the way in which we speak about language and identity. That is what I intend to do in the rest of this chapter, by focusing specifically on the West African Charismatic church.[4]

Language and the Charismatic Church

In mid August of 2000 I walked into a prayer meeting at the Accra headquarters of one of the largest Charismatic churches in Ghana – the Christian

Action Faith Ministries International. Though it was a weekday, Thursday, and in the morning, a huge crowd of probably up to a thousand people had gathered for the meeting. I was surprised that there were so many people present at the service on a weekday. There was enthusiastic singing, often in Twi, prayers from the audience in a variety of languages, as well as 'confessions,' exhortations, testimonies led from the podium in English. One of the testimonies recounted by the leader of the prayer service concerned a church member who was giving thanks because a relative had received a desired professional posting to Washington DC. Another testimony was from a lady who had finally succeeded in obtaining a German visa and who was intending to travel abroad shortly to join her husband. There were many children present at the meeting, evidently accompanying their parents. And the leaders of the service called up some children to the front to pray for them. They also led parents to make 'confessions' aloud along the following lines for their children: 'Our children will become directors of banks, they will work in the United Nations. They will go to schools abroad, they will be number one at Oxford, Cambridge, and Harvard. Our daughters will marry great men . . .'

A year later, I attended a service at another Charismatic church, this time, a smaller Nigerian-led church in Sacramento, California called Livingspring Christian Center. The guest speaker who had pastored churches in Nigeria and Kenya before moving to the northwest United States spoke at length on the importance of being willing to leave home. 'It is Satan's strategy,' he explained, 'to keep us local.' A true Christian, he suggested, should be prepared to leave home, to break with the past and with history in order to embrace destiny probably abroad. To support his argument, he recounted his own personal experience of moving to a new country, Kenya, and surviving with nothing more at the onset than a conviction that he was led of God. Here too, the sermon was in English, while the audience included Nigerians, but also Ghanaians, Congolese, Batswana, Ugandans, some Europeans, and a few Americans. And no doubt this sermon had a special resonance for an audience made up of fairly recent immigrants trying to survive in a new environment.

The events described here shared a number of things in common. In both instances, the services were conducted in the English language alone or in tandem with another language of wider communication. What is important to me here is not so much the fact that the language used was English rather than say, French, after all many American Charismatic churches also conduct services in English as the mother tongue of most of their members. To my mind, the noteworthy element is the fact that the services were being conducted in a language that was for the majority of those present a non-native language and a language of wider communication according to the definition proposed in this book. Furthermore, the Charismatic church was one of the most important associations to which those attending in Accra and Sacramento belonged. In this respect, the fact that so many people were willing to attend a service on a weekday morning in Accra is significant. Indeed identification with the church often seemed to take precedence over identification with a nation-state and with a primary ethnolinguistic unit among church members. Finally, the opportunity of traveling away from 'home' seemed to represent a central and important aspiration in both of the instances described above. The mainly African members of the Sacramento church were evidently already away from home. Judging from the prayers at the podium, the members of the Accra church apparently also had aspirations of moving away from home. To that extent, the African Charismatic church offered for its mostly African members in and outside Africa a community and space of belonging parallel to, and in several respects, different from the nation-state and their primary ethnolinguistic unit as defined either by themselves or the state

Ideas about belonging often tend to overlap with conceptions of the local. The communities in respect of which we claim a sense of belonging and legal rights have historically been envisaged as local in character. That is to say, the community is not only envisioned as a distinct group of people; it is also a distinct group of people occupying a particular space that is circumscribed in scope, and differentiated from other spaces by virtue of the special claims the community has in regard to that place. The spaces inhabited and controlled by the community to which we belong also coincide with our imagination of the extent and dimensions of the local. Even though the concept of the 'world citizen' has its attractions for cosmopolitans, there exist as of yet, no legal avenues for attaining to that state. Perhaps more importantly, human beings cannot for the most part visualize the entire world as local. This does not however mean that our interactions with the concept of the local remain static. It is clear that growing numbers of people in the contemporary world no longer find membership in communities whose jurisdiction and area of activity is only local sufficient for their needs. Thus, they aspire to membership in as many organizations as possible, each with its own area of jurisdiction, or better still they join organizations that claim to be international in scope and universal in application, that is, they join sodalities that are perceived as transcending the constraints of the local. West African Charismatic churches and their language practices hopefully focus attention on the role that language plays in the emergence of these kinds of sodalities and the changes that are occurring in the way such associations now respond to the concept of the local.

Although a number of scholars refer to the type of churches I will be discussing here as Pentecostal,[5] I prefer to use the term 'Charismatic' as the term most often employed by members to distinguish themselves from older movements which shared in common some of the same core beliefs and practices. According to Gifford (1994: 241), the term 'Charismatic' is used to distinguish these churches 'from the churches of established Pentecostal denominations like the Assemblies of God.' The churches share in common with the older Pentecostal churches a belief in the importance of speaking in tongues and the continuing operation of miraculous spiritual gifts among contemporary Christians. However, the Charismatics differ from the older churches in being largely autonomous from missionary bodies located in the Western world, in being a more recent phenomenon, and in not observing some of the strict rules governing individual conduct that were enforced in the Pentecostal churches. Many Charismatic churches are located in urban centers and the most successful have become mega-churches with thousands of members in individual branches. The largest of the Charismatic churches in West Africa are located in Ghana and Nigeria, though Charismatic churches, small and large, are now present in every West African country with the possible exception of Mauritania. The best known of the mega-churches in the West African sub-region include: the International Central Gospel Church of Otabil Mensa in Ghana, the Christian Action Faith Ministries International of Bishop Duncan Williams in Ghana, the Church of God International associated with the late Archbishop Benson Idahosa of Nigeria, the Winner's Chapel founded by Bishop David Oyedepo of Nigeria, the Redeemed Christian Church of God, led by the Reverend Adeboye of Nigeria, and the Deeper Life Christian Church led by Pastor W. Kumuyi of Nigeria.

In their theology and frequently also in their language practices, these Charismatic churches are unlike other types of churches that can still be found in West Africa. They differ in the first place from the missionary-founded Protestant denominations present in the former British colonies of West Africa like the Baptist, Methodist, Anglican, and the Presbyterian denominations, to name the best known ones. For the rest of this chapter, I will describe these missionary-founded churches as the historic mission churches. Though they have come under increasing influence from the Charismatics in different ways, many members and leaders of the historic mission churches do not believe in the continuing operation of miraculous spiritual gifts and do not see church membership as incompatible with membership with other types of sodalities formed on the basis of the mother tongue. Furthermore, they frequently consider themselves members of their respective denominations by birth and see no need for the dramatic conversion experiences that Charismatics and other evangelicals equate with being 'born again.' Nor are the Charismatic churches to be confused with the churches often described as 'spiritual' or independent in the West African context, such as the Aladura and the Celestial Church of Christ. Although the 'spiritual' churches do believe in miraculous powers, they do not subscribe to a literalist interpretation of the Bible, and frequently use objects as conduits for spiritual power in a manner reminiscent of practices in indigenous religion. The 'spiritual' churches are also often characterized as syncretist in practice and belief.

Though citizens of a particular state may predominate in any West African Charismatic church in major cities, these churches are often more ethnically and nationally diverse in membership than other types of West African church congregations such as those connected with the historic mission churches or the 'spiritual' churches. Members of the Charismatic churches have almost always been earlier members of the historic mission churches or the 'spiritual' churches, and the decision to join the Charismatic church often represents a conscious choice to distance oneself from the kind of affiliations established in the historic mission or 'spiritual' churches. Most Charismatic churches are also autonomous in organization and finances.[6] In fact, these churches have often been criticized for taking independence to such extremes that church leadership revolves entirely around a single individual, usually the founder.

Though they do maintain extensive links with churches and pastors within and beyond Africa, these churches do not generally have the kind of relationship that the historic mission churches and even older Pentecostal churches once had with Western missionaries. West African Charismatic churches today receive visiting American evangelists, but also visiting evangelists from around Africa: Kenyan preachers in Nigeria, Nigerian preachers in South Africa and so on. And many of the bigger Ghanaian and Nigerian churches are now founding their own missionary churches outside the state in which they originated: the Christian Action Faith Ministries International, the Deeper Life Church, the Redeemed Christian Church of God, the Winner's Chapel all have branches in West Africa outside their state of origin as well as in Europe and North America. Some are even beginning to establish branches among African immigrants in Asia. Like the video films examined in Chapter 3, Charismatic churches are strikingly open to trends emanating from beyond the state where they originate, yet they are almost entirely of local organization.

In my discussion of Charismatic churches as examples of a new type of sodality, I will draw many of my illustrations from Charismatic churches in Accra, Ghana, and specifically from one neighborhood, Sakumono. However, I do not intend in this chapter to undertake the kind of comprehensive survey of religious institutions carried out by Peil and Opoku (1994) in their study of churches in Madina, another Accra neighborhood.

For the sake of convenience, I refer mostly to Ghanaian examples, but I should make it clear that I am more interested in the general features and language practices of these churches as we see them around West Africa.[7] Thus, I will also refer to churches in Nigeria and Ivory Coast in particular to illustrate my arguments. In my experience, Charismatic churches in major West African cities are identical in the way they organize services so that the neighborhood church does not have the kind of specificity that makes it remarkably different from churches in other locations. The comments I make in respect of these churches are valid for many churches elsewhere in Ghanaian cities and across West Africa. Each church is distinct and independent, yet there is a certain uniformity to Christian life and practice in these churches which is not merely incidental. The fact that the basic structures can be recreated at will, and with minimal investment in a variety of places, is part of the attraction that Charismatic Christianity holds for growing numbers of adherents in urban West Africa.

The perception among workers and officials in Christian bookstores, music stores and Ghanaian Christian organizations such as the Ghana Evangelization Committee, the Ghana Institute of Linguistics Literacy and Bible Translation, and the Bible Society of Ghana is that the majority of Charismatic churches in Ghana use mostly English in their services.[8] Gifford (1994) confirms the accuracy of the perception for some of the best known Charismatic churches in the major cities, noting that most of them used English in their services. The Charismatic churches that I visited in Sakumono also conducted their services in English.[9] Songs were sung in a mixture of English, Twi, and other Ghanaian languages. This pattern is typical of Charismatic churches in major cities across West Africa: sermons tend to be in a European language and or an indigenous lingua franca while many of the songs are sung in a European language and diverse indigenous languages. To accommodate those who might not understand English, leaders in some churches indicated that they planned to introduce translation to and from an indigenous language during the major services. Even though the pastors I spoke to all recognized Ga as the language of the original inhabitants of Accra, none of them anticipated introducing translation into Ga. Rather they expressed a preference for translation into Twi, because as Pastor Joseph Ekuban of Springs of Life International told me, it was the most widely understood language in Ghana.[10] Why not simply use Twi instead of English, I inquired of another pastor, if so many people understood the language? Pastor Emily Buabasah of the Christ Family Foundation Church responded that that would not work because their congregation was international and also comprised non-Ghanaians who did not speak Twi.[11]

As further confirmation of the transnational vocation that Charismatics tended to attribute to their activity, it is interesting to note that one of the best known private universities in Ghana, the Central University College, founded by the International Central Gospel Church, a major Charismatic church in Ghana as one of the first private universities in Ghana, offers courses in French to its students, but not in any of the indigenous Ghanaian languages. This is despite the fact that the Central University College has a Department of Black Studies and that the statement of mission of the University states that one of its goals is '[t]o develop in students a deeper understanding of traditional and modern African culture and to equip [students] . . . to effectively provide Christian approaches to socio-economic and political development of the African continent.'[12] The Vice Chancellor of the Central University College, Dr Kingsley Larbi, further explained to me that French was in fact fully integrated into instruction at all levels in the college so that all students were required to take classes in French, no matter their major because, as he put it, 'we now live in a global village' and 'people should not be limited to only one context.'[13]

Other Ghanaian evangelicals who were critical of the Charismatic reliance on English often pointed to the Church of the Pentecost, a much older church in the Pentecostal tradition, as a model for the newer Charismatic churches in Ghana to emulate. The Church of the Pentecost, I was told over and over again, used indigenous languages in their services and were thus open to a wider cross-section of the population than the newer Charismatic churches which might be viewed as elitist. A number of leaders in the Church of the Pentecost confirmed this to me, but also indicated that though the Church of the Pentecost was successful in reaching a wide base of people around the country, they had become increasingly worried about losing a particular segment of the Ghanaian population. Though it was not explicitly stated in those terms, it seemed that the segment in question comprised the kind of young urban residents who patronized the newer Charismatic churches in the cities. To counter this trend, Alfred Langdon, an elder in the denomination, explained to me that the Church of the Pentecost had recently begun setting up new kinds of churches called 'Worship Centers' where services were entirely in English with occasional translation into French, and where many of the restrictions associated with the typical churches of that denomination were relaxed. Not surprisingly, these 'Worships Centers' had been set up mainly in the larger cities like Accra, Tema, Kumasi, and Cape Coast.

It is certainly true that the Charismatic churches were not alone in using English in their services. Peil and Opoku (1994: 216) found, for example, that most churches in Madina were multi-ethnic in membership and larger churches in particular often resorted to English as a language most likely to be understood by the majority of members.[14] However, the Charismatic churches have been the most likely to have services in English alone or to start off new churches entirely in English and to continue using English alone as the main language of communication during the services. Interestingly, Peil and Opoku (1994: 216) encountered only one major church in the Madina neighborhood they studied where the sole language used was an indigenous language, Ewe, which though the language of a major ethnic group, cannot really be described as a language of wider communication as I have defined it here. This was the practice at the Madina branch of the Evangelical Presbyterian Church, one of the historic mission churches. Presumably, most members were Ewe-speaking migrants who had settled in Accra.

Given their origins in missionary linguistic activity, it is not surprising that the historic mission churches have continued even in multi-ethnic urban centers to build up congregations catering to groups of people who share the same mother tongue, and have more consistently than the Charismatic churches offered services in vernacular languages or in a combination of English and particular vernacular languages. The Calvary Baptist church in Accra, for example, offered services in a combination of any two of the following languages: Ewe, Ga, Twi, English. The pastor of the church, Dr Osei Bonsu, also informed me that the Baptists in Accra still maintained one Yoruba-language church and a Frafra-language church in Accra.[15] Like the historic mission churches, 'spiritual' churches too tend to carry out their activities in the mother tongue of the members since the membership of individual churches comprises mainly those who speak the same mother tongue, whether the church is located at home or abroad. And here, the functioning of the church often overlaps in at least some areas with the functioning of 'home town associations' and the like.

It is tempting to correlate the use of English in the Charismatic churches solely with the level of education of their members and to treat this phenomenon only as evidence of diglossia. Gifford (1994: 248), for example, describes the members of one of the largest Charismatic churches, the International Gospel Central church, as largely educated, English-speaking, and upwardly mobile youth. No doubt such people make up an important proportion of the membership of many Charismatic churches in urban West Africa but, as reported by Marshall-Fratani (1998) in her study of a Nigerian Charismatic church, a wide range of groups and classes are also represented in these churches. Furthermore, one also finds educated, upwardly-mobile members in the urban branches of the historic mission churches as well, and yet they tend to use particular vernaculars in their services rather than English or even emergent lingua francas. In the Mount Zion Methodist church in Sakumono, for example, services were conducted mainly in Fanti, probably due to the fact that many initial members spoke Fanti as their mother tongue and that some of the first Methodist missionaries in Ghana established their base in Fanti-speaking areas. Here, the services were not in Ga, the true vernacular of the original inhabitants of Accra, or in English, widely spoken and understood by the mostly middle class members of this church, or in Twi, the most widely understood language in many Ghanaian cities. This was a clear illustration of the historic mission church's policy of envisioning congregations as consonant with particular language groups and as fully congruent with recognized ethno-linguistic units. In the Charismatic churches, on the other hand, congregations were envisioned as international (comprising citizens of many states), multilingual (with members speaking different languages) and polyglot (with each member speaking more than one language). In other words, this was an entity whose membership extended beyond that of the other purportedly 'natural' communities to which members may have belonged, whether it was the nation-state or ethno-linguistic unit.

Charismatic churches obviously do not have at their disposal the resources of a state. They cannot enforce particular language practices in the way a state can. However, by using only certain languages and providing instruction in the same languages in their own private educational institutions, churches certainly have a lot of leeway to strengthen or weaken particular languages in any given location. As Rudolph (1997: 11) has pointed out, these groups may not have sovereignty, but they certainly have authority, and they bring considerable legitimacy to certain languages by making them languages of the group, and especially by providing instruction in those languages. Furthermore, churches have in the past been quite adept at fostering group consciousness quite apart from any efforts taken in a similar direction by a state. To that extent, the language practices of these and other associations within a society provide an opportunity for understanding the characteristics of communities that are under construction in different places.

Languages of Wider Communication and the Community

Since English is the official language of a country like Ghana and taught in the schools for those who have access to formal education, there are any number of organizations in the country that use English as a language of communication. There are political associations, professional organizations, recreational associations and so on. In using English, I would suggest that the majority of these associations are already envisioned as 'Ghanaian' and that they do not present membership of the group in competition with or in opposition to membership of 'natural' communities such as the ethno-linguistic unit and the nation-state. Rather membership of the group frequently complements and overlaps with membership of existing and recognized 'natural' communities.

However, there are sodalities that appear to reconstruct 'natural' communities or seek to supersede 'natural' communities in terms of the allegiance they demand from members. When such movements develop out of networks using languages of wider communication, they can evolve in one of two directions in their responses to the idea of the local. Where the local retains its appeal as an adequate framework within which to resolve the personal, political, and economic challenges facing members, the recourse to a language of wider communication will be associated with an expansion of the space of the local for those who identify themselves with this sodality. In instances, however, where the space of the local in all its configurations begins to be viewed as problematic and offering limited options, the decision to join a movement using a language of wider communication can be interpreted as a rejection of more localized attachments. Thus, the first characteristic of movements of this type is a projection of the organization as one whose reach transcends the local, however the local may be defined, and one whose foundational doctrines have universal application.

In Sakumono, the Accra neighborhood that I visited, for example, Charismatic churches bore such names as Grace Chapel International, Springs of Life International, Radiant Life International, Lion of Judah Ministries International, International Christian Worship Chapel, Christian Action Faith International, International Central Gospel Church, Lighthouse Chapel International.[16] Peil and Opoku (1994: 204) specifically interpret the use of such titles as an indication of the church leaders' 'aspirations to be more than a local church.' To justify the use of the adjective 'international' in the name of a church that had as yet only one branch, Pastor Ekuban of the Springs of Life Chapel International, showed me photographs of individuals who had worked with him in the brochure advertising the church. The individuals were from Nigeria, Greece, India, the Philippines and Singapore. He also explained that it was possible that members of the church would one day travel abroad and take the vision of the church with them, and begin planting branches of the church wherever life took them. The concern with becoming international is a pattern that is replicated with Charismatic churches virtually everywhere in West Africa.[17] Charismatic churches are always from the very beginning envisioned as potentially international in their locations and membership. It is their very vocation to become international so that expressions of specificity in the group are never mobilized with intentions of justifying exclusive attachment to only one place above all other places. There is a strong belief in the members' potential to find a foothold anywhere in the world. Deuteronomy 11.24

'Every place where you set your foot will be yours . . .'[18] is a popular verse with West African Charismatics.

In the many books and pamphlets authored by Charismatic pastors around West Africa, specific attention is frequently directed at the travels of the author around the world and his or her contacts with Charismatic pastors in other parts of the world. The invocation of these non-local references legitimates the author's claim to be taken seriously. On the blurb of a book by the Ghanaian couple, Kwame and Bea Owusu-Ansah (1997), we read for example: 'Kwame and Beatrice Owusu-Ansah are founders of the Great Expectations Ministries International. They are seasoned international preachers. They have traveled extensively in the United States and have ministered in many cities there.' On the cover of the book by the Béninois Megnanou Bienvenu (2000), we read 'Megnanou teaches missionary students in Bible schools in Ivory Coast, in Togo and teaches correspondence courses for schools in France and Belgium on witchcraft, the occult and fetishes.'[19] The Nigerian, Emeka Nwankpa (1998) has an even more impressive résumé. The section on the author in the blurb indicates that '[h]e has ministered in over thirty countries and four continents.'

And in the branches and or related Charismatic churches located outside Africa, visiting pastors from Africa are a regular feature of the services, just as African pastors working in North America and Europe are frequent guest speakers at churches in West Africa. At the Livingspring Church in Sacramento, there have been between the year 2000 and 2002 guest speakers visiting from Malawi, from Nigeria, from Botswana, from Kenya. In both services I attended at the Christ Foundation Family Chapel in Sakumono, an outgrowth of Action Faith International in 2000, guest ministers from abroad were present, one a Ghanaian evangelist living in London, but also active in South Africa, and the other a Ghanaian minister working in the United Kingdom. At the headquarters of the Christian Action Faith Ministries International, photographs on the walls leading to the office of the founder, the Bishop Duncan Williams testified to his travels around the world and encounters with religious and political leaders in various places while also providing visual evidence of his translocal credentials.

The second characteristic of these movements using what are for most members a non-native language of wider communication, is a clearly expressed antipathy towards selected manifestations of local culture viewed as both disabling and detrimental to the well-being of members. Alongside this antipathy, one also finds a tendency to frame perceived problems in the lives of members as signs of the continuing power of more localized allegiances, which have not yet been consciously and formally renounced. In the case of the West African Charismatic churches, ethnic and extended family ties are considered particularly suspect and much of the ritualized activity during public prayer sessions is especially directed at severing such ties, supposedly represented in and associated with practices that van Dijk (1997: 153) describes as affirming the 'locality of cosmology.' Significantly, these dangerous spiritual forces with which Charismatic Christians must occasionally contend are often referred to as 'territorial spirits' or spirits presiding over a particular locality (Nwankpa, 1999: 145). Thus, Francis Akwaboah (1994: 57–88), a Ghanaian evangelist based in London, condemns as demonic several practices that mark membership of individual ethno-linguistic units and localized communities, including bodily scarification, participation in traditional festivals and customs, the wearing of locally-manufactured beads, the pouring of libations, the observance of traditional puberty and funeral rites. The Nigerian evangelist, Adewale Adekoya (1997: 26) working out of Ivory Coast likewise holds sexual perversions, occult practices, but also ancestral ties, responsible for bringing on demonic possession. At the same time, involvement with the Charismatic church is credited with enabling members to break free from the hold of diverse 'territorial spirits.'

Starting from the late 1990s, the city of Accra witnessed what was surely one of the most ironic consequences of this opposition to selected expressions of local culture. As is well known, early Western missionaries who chose Africa as their mission field of choice were often opposed to the use of indigenous musical instruments and in particular drums among Christian converts. Attitudes gradually changed towards the use of these instruments starting from the 1960s in both the historic mission churches and in the Pentecostal and Charismatic churches. During the 1990s, a number of Christian churches in Accra began to come into conflict with traditional Ga authorities over a month-long ban on drumming pronounced by traditional Ga councils preceding the annual celebrations marking the Homowo festival of the Ga people, who consider themselves the indigenous inhabitants of the Accra area. The majority of churches that were willing to defy the ban were apparently Charismatic and Pentecostal churches attracting occasional attacks from young men who claimed to be defending Ga culture.[20] Interestingly and not surprisingly, members of Charismatic churches in Accra maintained that they were not bound by the dictates of the traditional rulers of the Ga people even if they resided in Accra. Their allegiances were to the constitution of the state of Ghana and to the presumably worldwide church of God.[21] The historic mission churches, which in any case made less frequent use of drums were apparently willing to compromise and to forgo the use of drums during the period of the bans for the sake of peace. And an editorial in a Ghanaian evangelical publication noted the appearance of a rift between the leaders of some historic mission churches and the Charismatics on this matter, complaining: 'Unfortunately, some members of some main-line, so-called 'noise free' churches and even some leaders use the opportunity to attack Pentecostals...'[22]

Eventually leaders in the Charismatic community and of the historic mission churches were able to come to an agreement with the Ghanaian government and Ga authorities in the year 2000 to allow churches to continue to practice drumming if they wished to. The entire incident provided a telling illustration of the kind of shifts that had occurred over a period of 100 years and alert us to the danger of assuming unbroken continuity between the positions of the missionaries and those of the historic mission churches on the one hand, or between the positions of the Charismatic churches and those of the historic mission churches on the other. The historic mission churches whose founders had once opposed drumming appeared to have come to terms with indigenous culture and specifically with bans on drumming by the late 20th century and were thus able to accommodate the Ga traditional authorities. Members of the Charismatic churches, meanwhile, whose disdain for local culture might have been read as a sign of excessive Westernization, strongly defended their right to drum in a complete reversal of the position once taken by Western missionaries.

The response of the historic mission churches in Ghana to this crisis is entirely in character especially when one considers that in West Africa these churches have since the 1970s been at the forefront of consciously undertaken efforts to indigenize Christianity, to endow Christian practice in West Africa with a more localized identity.[23] As examples, one might note the efforts made by the late Reverend Bolaji Idowu of the Methodist church in Nigeria and reforms undertaken by Professor Noah Nzobo, Moderator of the Evangelical Presbyterian Church of Ghana.[24] In some instances, as Meyer (1999: 126–37) notes with the Evangelical Presbyterian Church in the Volta region of Ghana, these attempts at indigenization actually prompted the formation of secessionist groups that eventually became Charismatic in orientation.[25]

Given the general hostility to what one might describe as ritualized practices of locality in West African Charismatic churches, it is not surprising that the desire to travel abroad is a popular subject of prayer in these churches. For many of those who become members of the West African Charismatic churches, traveling away from home apparently represents one of the main paths to self-sufficiency and a personal experience of Christian prosperity. Among the older generation of Pentecostal churches, van Dijk (1997: 145) found prayer requests for 'travel,' 'passport,' 'visa' at the prayer camps run by such churches in Ghana. In the newer Charismatic churches, as my experience at the Christian Action Faith Ministries International in Accra indicates, the preoccupation with traveling abroad was just as vivid and according to van Dijk (1997: 148), the Charismatic churches actually seemed to provide a clearly organized infrastructure facilitating emigration outside the state of origin on the one hand and support groups offering practical assistance to West African immigrants once they arrived abroad on the other.

Yet another characteristic of the West African Charismatic church and of sodalities that use languages of wider communication is the tendency to elevate associations where membership is a personal choice over inherited affiliations. Vernacular languages are associated with communities perceived to be natural, even organic. Such communities are inevitably constructed as native, national, and emblematic of the local. Languages of wider communication are often associated with chosen affiliations, conscious choices rather than inherited relationships. Although Rudolph (1997: 5) has suggested that the distinction between inherited and voluntary affiliations may no longer be entirely useful in describing the new types of civil society emerging around the world today, I would argue that this remains a helpful element for understanding perceptions of the local in Charismatic churches and other organizations where most members communicate using what is for them a language of wider communication. In such cases, the decision to join this kind of movement does represent a deliberately undertaken disengagement from other ongoing productions of locality and local subjects, defined by Appadurai (1996: 179) as 'actors who properly belong to a situated community of kin, neighbors, friends, and enemies.' After all, the point of establishing ancestry is to provide proof of legitimate connections not only to a designated group of people, but also to a designated place. Inherited affiliations thus form part of the larger body of practices through which the scope and the limits of the local are defined. By contrast, Charismatic churches, like the Sufi tariqa described by Kane (1997: 58), form what he has termed a 'community of affinities,' a bond constructed around common convictions rather than around a common place of origin. From this perspective, the hostility of Charismatics towards blood ties and other markers of ancestry makes perfect sense. These are all signs of localized attachments viewed as potential hindrances to those for whom migration on some scale has become a necessity.

One can argue that this privileging of chosen affiliations is typical of all churches, even those that rely mainly on vernacular tongues and bears little correlation with the fact of seeking membership in organizations using non-native languages of wider communication. There is certainly an abundance of information confirming that early missionaries required

African converts to make a break with their families and with what were considered the pagan practices of their birth community. In these circumstances, conversion clearly amounted to a break with major customs in one's community of birth. However, to the extent that individual congregations and the nascent church were constituted as fellowships of people sharing in common the same mother tongue, conversion did not in the end amount to a turning away from the space of the local, even if the configuration of the local was undergoing revision. If on the surface and from the missionary perspective, Westernization was the ultimate end desired for the converted African, it was like the much vaunted policy of Assimilation in the French colonies, a goal that could not be consistently pursued without altering the balance of power in the colonial church. Why, for example, deny leadership positions to African Christians as happened in many mission stations if African Christians and their Western mentors were exactly alike in faith and culture? Ultimately, it was in the interest of the missionaries to insist on the validity of at least some aspects of indigenous culture and to suggest that conversion to Christianity did not make the converts Western.

What the missionaries did, therefore, was to create new forms of the local, instead of abolishing the very concept of a local community. Thus, the privileging of chosen affiliations that we encounter in contemporary Charismatic churches does generate very different results from the requirements imposed upon African converts by early missionaries. These results became visible over time as the historic mission churches tended to become ethnic churches, dominated by speakers of one language even if they were not explicitly defined as such or divided into congregations organized along ethno-linguistic lines even in multi-ethnic urban settings. Bediako (1995: 50) describes the desire to produce a *volkskirche*, a localized and ethnic church, as an explicit goal of the German Basel missionaries who set up base in Akrompong in southern Ghana. Elsewhere in Ghana during the colonial period, Christian villages called *Kpodzi* established by German Bremen missionaries alongside 'pagan' villages in Ewe territory (Meyer, 1999: 8) functioned as alternative sites of the construction of the local for Christian converts, rather than as staging grounds for a disengagement from the space of the local. And in due course, according to Middleton (1983) and Meyer (1999: 120), membership of the historic mission churches in the Akwapim hills, as among the Ewe in southern Ghana became indistinguishable from citizenship in the immediate community.

Bediako (1995: 66–7) and even more so Sanneh (1993) attribute the accommodation that historic mission and 'spiritual' forms of Christianity eventually came to with indigenous culture to the practice of making vernacular languages the medium through which Christianity would be communicated. As Sanneh has argued, this may not have been the intention of many missionaries, but the very fact of centering Christian life around indigenous language Scriptures ultimately induced recognition of indigenous cultures. He writes: '[t]hat some missionaries wanted to dismantle the older indigenous cultural dispensation, to subvert the native genius, is without question, but employing mother tongues in their Scriptural translation is a tacit surrender to indigenous primacy, and complicates the arguments of Western cultural superiority' (Sanneh, 1993: 16–17).

A fourth characteristic of these movements using languages of wider communication is that they neither produce discourses of the vernacular nor do they make a significant investment in materials using languages that function solely as vernacular languages or mother tongues. Ghanaian and Nigerian pastors who found churches in countries like Ivory Coast will start out preaching in English and having sermons translated into French.[26] Later on, they may begin to preach directly in French, but virtually no effort is made to provide religious instruction in the appropriate vernaculars. Pastor Emily Buabasah likewise indicated that her church's missionary activity in a Krobo-speaking area of Ghana was carried out mostly in English with translation into Twi, the emergent lingua franca of Ghana.

Consistently, Charismatic pastors with whom I discussed in Accra spoke to me of the possibility of starting services in Twi and seemed concerned that people should hear the Christian message in a language they understood. However, none of those with whom I spoke placed the kind of premium on communication in the mother tongue that had been the hallmark of an earlier generation of Protestant missionaries.[27] In Italy, Germany, and Holland, according to Reverend Benjamin Anoh of the Christian Action Faith Ministries International, branches of the Ghanaian church continued to use mostly English rather than Italian, German, or Dutch though there was translation into these languages where possible. Obviously English was the language that was most widely understood by a congregation made up of mainly Ghanaian expatriates and in Anoh's opinion it was also understood by many Europeans. While Reverend Anoh's observations are probably accurate, they also reflected a certain attitude towards missionary work. In the first place, most of their missionary work in fact seems directed at a growing community of African immigrants, transplants and expatriates from the postcolonial world like themselves, though African Charismatics who have founded churches in the Western world occasionally depict their emigration as a missionary journey intended to evangelize Americans and Europeans.[28]

Furthermore, and in an almost complete reversal of the trends associated with earlier generations of Protestant missionaries who spent considerable amounts of time transcribing languages and translating the

Bible into diverse vernaculars, some contemporary African evangelical Christian groups with Charismatics in particular at the forefront, tended to assume that potential converts could be reached using languages that were not necessarily the mother tongues of the target audiences. The reasons for this change in orientation are not hard to discern. In some instances, these 'missionaries' are themselves immigrants in a new society catering mainly to other immigrants as is often the case with West African Charismatics living away from home.[29] In other instances, the missionaries are in a foreign country on a short-term contract of a year or two as transient embodiments of the expatriate lifestyle catering to the needs of individuals who aspire to become one day like the missionaries themselves, mobile subjects. And when such new-breed missionaries do make plans to stay abroad for longer periods of time, they rarely have the means or the administrative possibility of establishing the kinds of territorially-circumscribed and exclusive spheres of influence that were commonplace during the colonial period. In today's world, they are forced to compete with many other Christian and non-Christian groups for converts in the same place and must also keep in mind that their target populations are in contact with populations speaking other languages and constantly on the move within the nation-state itself or across national boundaries. Given the circumstances in which they now operate and the objectives they have set for themselves, these Charismatic churches do not envision language as a boundary, and for this reason, do not produce an explicit discourse on and activity around language as vernacular in the manner of many early Protestant missionaries.

By contrast, missionary groups that continue to work on translation and transcription tend to favor more isolated populations resident in areas where they may constitute the only Christian group present and thus find themselves in a position to delimit a territorially-circumscribed sphere of influence inhabited by a largely static population having minimal contact with populations speaking other languages. In other words, once you begin to use a language of wider communication in establishing a sodality, you also make the assumption that populations are possibly in flux and that exact congruence between particular vernaculars and particular territorial units cannot always be taken for granted. The motivations which justified earlier missionary interest in vernaculars are rendered moot where mobility becomes a virtue even for the convert, and individual churches and denominations no longer think of their membership in terms of discrete spheres of influence corresponding to territorial units to be distinguished from other territorial units under the control of other denominations inter alia by differences in the languages spoken by designated residents of the area.

Here, the success of the church is to be measured in its ability to attract members at significant intersections on the major trade and travel routes of the world: capital cities, regional capitals, port cities, market cities and so on. Much less effort is expended on obtaining a balanced representation of the church throughout a designated area. In some places, getting to church is itself a journey, a commute of several hours away from home and back home. Though there may be other churches located closer to home, members of West African Charismatic churches are often willing to undertake this journey: traveling is after all a major dimension of the spiritual vocation to which they have committed themselves. Even church membership is not stable and members are often just as ready to switch from one Charismatic church to another (Marshall-Fratani, 1998: 283) as they are to move from one country and region to another, unlike committed members of the historic mission churches who remain in the same denomination and where possible the same local church for life. To summarize, the reluctance of most West African Charismatic churches to invest in vernacular languages is more than evidence of cultural insensitivity: it, in fact, speaks to a certain re-evaluation of the relevance of rootedness and strongly localized attachments in the life of church members.

One should not, however, conclude that West African Charismatics consider European languages to be sacred languages, though they do tend to express preference for particular versions of the Bible. Quoting Andrew Walls, Bediako (1995: 109) draws special attention to the historic translatability of Christian doctrine. For Charismatics too, the Scriptures remain translatable, and perfectly accessible through translation, which is why it is possible to have authentic religious experiences using if need be a non-native language of wider communication. From the Charismatic point of view, translatability of Christian doctrine does not mean that you need to hear the Gospel in your mother tongue. It means that you can hear the Gospel in any language that you use on a frequent basis and you can have perfectly valid religious experiences using a language that is not a mother tongue. Wherever they carry out their missionary activities, Charismatics therefore use the language that is most widely understood by mobile subjects like themselves. And though they do make use of the services of a translator where possible and necessary, they make no sustained efforts to learn the individual languages associated only with one particular place. Instead, they will frequently propose to offer instruction, if need be, in one of the languages of wider communication which they speak. In other words, they prepare their converts to become like themselves mobile subjects.

Let me then seize this opportunity to underscore a point made earlier in Chapter 1. Most people speak one or a limited number of languages as their primary or home language; however, an ideological investment in the function of language as vernacular or mother tongue is not a given in human society. Such preoccupations emerge where there are some benefits to be gained by postulating a distinctiveness vested in language for communities associated with specific territorial units. In relatively wealthy states with growing immigrant populations, discourses of the vernacular will likely become one means among others for separating true indigenes who should enjoy privileged access to the resources of the state from diverse foreigners who are to be denied such access. In weak and impoverished states on the other hand, people will no doubt continue to speak their mother tongues, but will have little motivation to sponsor a discourse of the vernacular, which loses its *raison d'être* where association with a specific territorial unit is not expected to yield significant advantages. Where possible and feasible, inhabitants of such territories will establish as many new affiliations and learn as many languages as may be reasonably expected to improve their chances of attaining both material sufficiency and general security in the contemporary world.

Membership of a sodality with supposedly universal validity and reach is especially attractive when one has doubts about the efficacy of more localized memberships, and is a citizen of a failed state increasingly unable to deliver the promises of modernity. Cultural specificity remains important in such groups; however, it is a peculiarly delocalized and deterritorialized kind of cultural specificity. For West African Charismatics in particular, the cultural specificity of the ideal Christian community is embodied in its commitment to accurate translations of the Bible and correct interpretation, or in its fundamentalism, and not in the individual cultures that speakers of different mother tongues may bring to the group. And though I am not able to pursue this question in greater detail here, I think it is worth exploring what connections might exist between the emergence of such delocalized sodalities and the growing emphasis on fundamentalist theologies among those who seek to construct alternative and non-localized forms of cultural specificity constructed around the idea of commitment to accurate interpretation of a given written text.

Interactions with the West

One could read the positions and practices of West African Charismatic churches described thus far simply as evidence of a desire on the part of church members for assimilation into Western culture and for adoption of Western identity. There is little doubt today that some of the first converts to the form of Christianity introduced by Western missionaries to sub-Saharan Africa in the 19th and early 20th centuries may have sought precisely such an identification. As I have suggested in Chapter 1, the missionaries for their part became increasingly convinced over time and as nationalist sentiments took hold of African Christian congregations, that they did not in fact want African Christians to become Westernized in culture. On the contrary, they desired them to remain 'African,' that is culturally and therefore politically separate from Europeans living in Africa. The discourse on vernacular literacy produced by missionaries and bureaucrats in the former British colonies in West Africa had its origins in concerns about education, but also ultimately in this desire to maintain the line of separation between the colonized and the colonizers.

We have good reason to doubt, however, whether the exceptional growth of the Charismatic movement in West Africa represents a resurgence of the same trend witnessed among African Christian converts a century ago. For one thing, West African Charismatics living in the Western world, like many West Africans of other faiths, do not readily seek integration into Western cultural institutions. On the contrary, there is growing evidence to suggest that those West African Charismatics alongside other African immigrants who succeed in realizing the aspiration of emigrating to a location in the Western world are more likely today to join either churches and religious movements of African origin or other organizations comprising a high proportion of transnationals and other professional travelers. Olupona's (2001) recent study of African immigrant religious communities in the United States was prompted precisely by the realization that African immigrants to the United in the past few decades had been forming autonomous religious organizations rather than seeking integration into American religious bodies.[30]

Furthermore, while West African Charismatics abroad or at home are frequently sympathetic to the kinds of causes embraced by evangelical Christians in Europe and the United States, they are not uncritical supporters of Western policy in Africa and Western perceptions of Africans. Speaking for example about Western-dominated international institutions that need to be judged for the suffering they have inflicted on many, Emeka Nwankpa, the Nigerian evangelist, writes in his book, *Redeeming the Land*: 'I recommend without hesitation that one of the forces to be judged in the world is the International Monetary Fund. The IMF is a problem. It is an instrument of oppression. It ought not to be there' (1999: 50). In a similar vein, the Reverend Otabil Mensa, founder of the International Central Gospel Church based in Accra has argued in his books and sermons that Black people need to have pride in themselves, and to reject Western stereotypes about Blacks (Gifford, 1994: 249). West African Charismatics in the United States likewise speak openly about the difficulties of being Black and African in the United States (Olupona, 2001: 11). In fact, experiences of racism seem to provide at least one of many motivations for establishing autonomous spiritual entities in the US in particular. In short, West African Charismatics do not see themselves as completely identical with Europeans and Americans. They do recognize themselves as people with distinct origins and distinct experiences and who remain at some level strangers and foreigners in the societies where they now find themselves.

At the institutional level, Charismatic churches of West African origin in the Western world maintain crucial links and communication with similar-minded churches back at home and in some instances may facilitate the emigration of individual members from West Africa by providing testimonials and confirmation of the status of members (van Dijk, 1997: 150). In many cases, leaders of these churches abroad see it as their calling to protect members from being assimilated into the dominant Western culture, viewed not only as foreign, but also and ironically, as unchristian.[31] A deacon of the mainly West African Church of the Living God in Washington DC, interviewed in Olupona's study declared (2001: 162): 'We're better Christians in Africa. Most people come to the United States and think that it is a Christian nation, but instead they find pluralism and secularity . . .' A pastor of a different West African Charismatic church also in Washington DC stated that one of his objectives was to teach 'African social morals' (Olupona, 2001: 147) to members of his congregation. At yet another branch of the same church in Miami, the pastor spoke on the importance of teaching African mother tongues and cultures to the children of African immigrants in the United States (Olupona, 2001: 83).

But evidence of such interest in African mother tongues is not the same thing as saying that these West African Charismatics in the United States embrace discourses of the vernacular as defined earlier in this book. For one thing, they certainly do not envisage giving up English, the dominant language of the United States, in their professional lives. However, within the cultural politics of the United States, they seek to project themselves as one distinct group among many entitled to the same privileges and rights as other distinct groups. Proficiency in the African 'mother tongue' has its advantages for the immigrant community, but it is to be cultivated alongside proficiency in other languages used for other purposes. The intention, therefore, is not to institute a monolingual order where everyone speaks only their mother tongue. On the contrary, the ideal immigrant is a polyglot with connections to many places, and as versed in an African mother tongue as in other non-native languages. In this context then, the criticisms leveled against American society might be considered a reformulated expression of antipathy towards the local, directed in this case not so much at African ancestral ties as at other forms of corruption associated with a particular locality.

In West Africa itself, the function of these churches is unlike and yet parallel to the function of the well-known hometown associations than can be found in many African cities. If the function of the hometown association is to maintain connections with the 'hometown,' the function of the Charismatic church speaks to the need for connections that transcend both the hometown and the state, but only while one is still residing in a space that encompasses home in some way. Once abroad, the Charismatic church becomes a type of hometown association, comprising not so much people from the same place, as people on the same kind of journey and who hope to return 'home' at some point in the future, or to preserve memories of 'home.' The one type of sodality, the Charismatic church, does not necessarily supersede the other, the hometown association; and despite the antipathy of Charismatic churches in West Africa itself towards localized attachments, many people probably retain membership in both types of organizations. The fact is, survival in the present scheme of things requires both localized and more dispersed human networks, which is one of the major reasons why people have a continuing interest in non-native languages that are also languages of wider communication.

Thus, the hostility shown by West African Charismatic churches at home and abroad in respect of some expressions of local culture relates more so to the desire to create a framework for dealing with the reality of on-going migrations and interactions beyond the scope of the local than with a desire for assimilation into cultures still viewed as foreign. In this respect, Marshall-Fratani (1998: 294) attributes the success of Pentecostal movements in contemporary Nigeria to the 'community's ability ... to give regular people access to ... global repertoires' while van Dijk (1997: 137) calls attention in his study of Ghanaian Charismatic churches in Europe to the 'linkage between Christian fundamentalism/Pentecostalism and Ghanaian intercontinental labour migration ... '

It is important to point out, though, that Charismatics are not the sole West Africans who emigrate beyond their state of origin, and that all those who live for long or short periods abroad do not necessarily do so as an act of disengagement from localized cultures and communities. Cosmopolitans for example travel abroad in order to experience the strangeness of localized communities that are considered distinct from home. Missionaries too have historically provided justification for their work by differentiating between the spiritual needs of the localized space that they identify as home, and the localized space that they identify as the mission field. To the extent then that some of the other West Africans who travel widely and live abroad for some period of time make no conscious effort to dissociate themselves from associations constituted in their mother tongues as Charismatics often do, I am of the opinion that they in fact retain some sense of confidence in the space of the local as exemplified in a community sharing a common place of origin, a mother tongue and possibly a state. They are also more likely than members of the Charismatic churches to exhibit considerable commitment to the places identified as home by those with whom they share a mother tongue.[32]

However, the aspiration for access to globalized networks or emigration is widespread in urban Africa and this may explain part of the appeal that Charismatic churches have for young urban Africans in the contemporary period. By way of illustration, I return to a statement quoted earlier from Fredericksen's research in a Nairobi slum where one of her informants, an unemployed youth, declared: 'Me, I see myself somewhere in the US – somewhere like Michigan State' (1999: 49). Monga (2000: 205) notes the incidence of similar aspirations in contemporary Cameroon where the residents of the Denver neighborhood of Douala have apparently borrowed the name of their locality and their lifestyles from imaginations of Denver, Colorado, as featured in the famous soap opera, *Dynasty*. Simone (2001: 18) attributes these aspirations to what he calls the 'worlding' of African cities, observing that '[w]hen children across most African cities are asked about what they will do with their lives, the answer usually entails a life trajectory carried out far away from the place they consider "home."' As Simone explains it, this process of worlding entails a constant awareness of and readiness to interact with the world beyond the local. What residents of African cities seek then is not 'territorial encompassment or closure, but rather . . . a sense of open-endedness' (Simone, 2001: 25).

When in these circumstances we encounter coalitions of people using a language that they themselves recognize as not being a mother tongue, and which happens at the same time to facilitate the development of travel, trade, and religious networks spanning continents and states, we need to draw the appropriate conclusions and to acknowledge that these conclusions do not necessarily pertain to changes in national affiliation. A change in national affiliation will have considerable appeal where alternative infrastructures already exist to facilitate emigration of designated groups and where complete assimilation into a new nation is envisaged as a distinct possibility. When, however, the emigrants themselves are aware that cultural integration within the new nation is unlikely, and when emigration itself is fraught with all kinds of legal and other hazards, those who are dissatisfied with conditions in their present state may seek membership in a different kind of entity. The fact that they join sodalities using languages of wider communication certainly points to a disenchantment with conditions in the local community to which they belong by birth, but the alternative that they pursue is not always in the form of another national affiliation. For those who have already experienced or anticipate encountering difficulties in a multiplicity of localities, membership in a territorially-fixed sodality presents all kinds of limitations. Whether the dominant languages of wider communication in the sodalities of mobile people that they join instead are of non-African origin as with the languages used by most urban-based West African Charismatic churches, or indigenous lingua franca like Hausa and Dyula used in other types of sodalities also operating on a transnational scale, the incidence of these languages correlates in the first place with the need to establish networks that transcend the scope of the local, however the space of the local may be defined.

Conclusion

Those who seek proficiency in languages other than a mother tongue have a variety of motives for learning such non-native languages. Some acquire a new language as part of a process ultimately resulting in identification with native speakers of the learnt language. But this is only one of many possible motives, and as far as we can tell in contemporary Africa, this process now occurs most frequently with other indigenous African languages. Very few Africans, it would seem, learn French today in order to become culturally French or learn English in order to take on British or American or Australian identity.

Cosmopolitans, on the other hand, do not learn non-native languages with the intention of dissolving the boundary between their own society and societies previously considered foreign. On the contrary, cosmopolitans learn *foreign* languages. That is, they learn additional languages in order to mark the difference between their society and other societies. When particular languages are designated as foreign, it is a means not only of establishing sub-groupings within human community, it also serves to differentiate spaces to which we feel we legitimately belong from spaces to which we feel we do not belong, or foreign spaces. Hence the uproar when people inhabiting spaces we consider to be primary sites of belonging happen to speak languages which we find unintelligible or which we would describe as foreign languages. For many people, *foreign* languages have no place and should have no legal standing on home territory or in the space of the local.

In yet other instances, the acquisition of a non-native language may become one of the means by which members of one class differentiate themselves from others in their own society who speak the same mother tongue as they do. Diglossia remains a reality in contemporary Africa, though it is also true that mere knowledge of a European language in particular can no longer be considered a consistent marker of class status particularly in urban areas. Differing levels of proficiency probably play a greater role in this regard, especially since television and radio now provide more opportunities for those with limited or no formal education to acquire at least some proficiency in these and other non-native languages. In additional cases, such as those examined in Chapter 2, people who do not share the same mother tongue may begin using non-native languages in some activities as part of a project undertaken with the objective of reconfiguring and specifically expanding the space of the local.

It is clear then that not all languages foreign to a community function as languages of wider communication in the sense in which I defined the term earlier in this chapter.[33] Where those who have learnt a non-native language all share the same mother tongue, the non-native language does *not* necessarily serve them as a language of wider communication, except several other groups with other mother tongues have found it to their advantage to use the same non-native language as their second or third language. Those who have learnt any non-native language are certainly able to communicate with native speakers of the foreign language as opportunity may dictate, but not necessarily with any other groups of people who do not share their mother tongue if the language learnt does not become or is not already functioning as a language of wider communication. As I have indicated previously, a language plays a role in wider communication when it begins to enable individuals in a variety of places and or with a variety of mother tongues to congregate in one place, to communicate and to establish themselves as a community of shared purpose and convictions. Such languages of wider communication have a special appeal in many parts of the African continent where historically language communities have been relatively small in terms both of the number of speakers and of the territorial distribution of speakers of given languages.

If, furthermore a sodality comes into existence on the basis of such interaction in a language of wider communication, we have reason to assume that most members of the sodality have already traveled a short or considerable distance from the place that they themselves acknowledge as their primary place of belonging where they had no need to communicate using a language of wider communication. Thus the decision to communicate using a language of wider communication presumes the existence of potentially mobile individuals in contact with other mobile individuals. As a corollary, the determination to use a language specifically identified as a mother tongue frames the designated audience as a community at home that has not had significant need or opportunity to develop skills in other languages. When therefore, West African Charismatic churches consistently use languages of wider communication, they address members and potential converts as mobile people.

The attitudes and positions I have been considering in this chapter are in no way peculiar to West African Charismatics or even Christians. Nor am I suggesting any necessary correlation between language practices and theology *per se*. The point I am making is that the language practices of different sodalities do suggest a certain kind of orientation not only towards the nation as a possible entity, but also towards territorial units in general and specifically towards spaces of the local. The critical element that I wish to highlight here is not so much Charismatic theology, though the Charismatic church has served the purpose well in West Africa. My focus in this chapter relates in the first place to significant solidarities generated almost entirely through communication in non-native languages. We cannot assume that Charismatics as one type of sodality will necessarily use non-native languages of wider communication, but we can deduce that movements using languages that are for most members non-native languages of wider communication will likely adopt certain kinds of positions in respect of more localized allegiances. It is surely noteworthy that those who join these movements in West Africa do not generally mobilize their deeply held convictions, solely or mainly on behalf of nations, foreign and local, or in the service of any other kind of territorially-circumscribed entity. Instead they invest their loyalties in associations that self-consciously style themselves as international in membership and locations. Clearly, those who become active members of these kinds of sodalities using non-native languages of wider communication have allegiances that extend beyond the space of the local.

I also do not wish to give the impression that members of these sodalities of potentially mobile people are in any way more enlightened than those who prefer territorially-fixed sodalities. The difference between members of both types of associations is simply one of conviction and opportunity. Nor do I make any claim that the majority of the population anywhere in urban West Africa subscribes to Charismatic theology, though Charismatic Christianity is clearly a phenomenon of increasing significance in West Africa that might in some respects parallel the growth of millennial movements during the colonial period in many regions of sub-Saharan Africa. The point here is not to prove that this movement is representative or unrepresentative of some more 'natural' entity such as the nation or the ethno-linguistic unit. The fact is, it exists, it is representative of itself, it also represents one avenue among others for dealing with the growing insecurities surrounding local spaces in contemporary Africa. Those for whom expatriation is neither feasible nor desirable tend to react by pursuing a direction exactly counter to that chosen by the early African nationalists and Pan-Africanists, that is to say they undertake actions which result in a contraction of the space of the local and will direct their allegiances at ever smaller territorial units. Where it is not possible to shrink the space of the local any further, they may engage in acts of ethnic cleansing as a means of restoring presumed wholeness to a space of the local whose insecurity in their opinion, derives from the presence of designated strangers. Yet others still join the types of associations I have been discussing here as one possible response to the inadequacies of the space of the local. In any case, the number of strong believers in postcolonial African states as completely satisfactory spaces of the local seems to be on the decline.

For members of these sodalities, belonging to such associations is not about exclusive belonging to a place, for these are people with grave anxieties about place, whether it is the place where they were born or the place where they hope to move. Rather membership has to do with acquiring the means to move from place to place, from location to location as the circumstances may dictate. However, nomadism, wanderlust, itinerancy are not terms which apply here. This is not the domain of the cruise, the safari, or even the pilgrimage. Members of these sodalities do not journey for pleasure or transcendence alone. They flee insecure localities seeking the security once associated with the space of the local in other types of configurations and settings. Although West African Charismatics on occasion interact and collaborate with the state in a variety of ways,[34] the emergence of such movements probably signifies as Appadurai (1996: 169) has suggested, 'the steady erosion of the capabilities of the nation-state to monopolize loyalty' and a movement towards 'national forms that are largely divorced from territorial states.' We therefore need to be more alert to signs, manifested in language practices among other possibilities, that the nation and ethno-linguistic unit no longer offer the singular and preeminent model of community in which people desire to affirm their membership.

These signs, as I have argued throughout this book, point us both to changing imaginations of the local and to on-going disengagements from the space of the local. In some instances, perhaps the willingness to use non-native languages so extensively is indeed a departure from, if not a betrayal of the nation. But we have to remember that the idea of fixed and exclusive allegiances to a single nation-state is one with a fairly recent history. Languages identified as vernaculars will remain important in the ideological organization of human communities in those instances where people feel there are advantages to be secured by constructing 'nations' that they think of as localized entities and that have special connections to well-defined spaces or particular locations. If, however, for their own reasons, people decide to form communities that are not invested in the production of local subjects, it is likely that they will show minimal interest in promoting language as vernacular. Instead they will express their longing for non-localized sodalities by forming networks where communication occurs mostly in languages of wider communication, that is in non-native languages known to coalitions of individuals who do not share in common the same mother tongue and or who reside in a variety of dispersed territorial units.

In several instances then, a total language shift will not necessarily occur in favor of the more powerful language, the one with the larger number of speakers. Such shifts are especially unlikely in situations where privileged access to the resources of a particular location or designated territory is bolstered on the part of certain individuals by claims of indigeneity and cultural specificity exemplified in a number of markers, including the possession of a distinctive language. In these cases, the language of wider communication remains a non-native language, a second or third language expanding the repertoire of possible affiliations for its speakers. The truth of the matter is, people do not always learn additional languages simply because they consider their own mother tongues to be totally without value in the circumstances where they find themselves. Rather, in many contemporary situations, people learn additional languages as a way of gaining entry into affiliations with a wider territorial reach and in order to establish potentially profitable channels of communication that do not explicitly depend on shared membership of a place of origin and of a single territorially circumscribed unit. Such additional languages learnt are by definition non-native languages, they are also in this context languages of wider communication enabling interaction across recognized boundaries. As it becomes increasingly essential to establish such delocalized or multi-localized affiliations in order to further one's chances of survival, so too does it become more likely that a growing number born in the poorer societies of the contemporary world will learn additional languages without giving up their mother tongues. In the hopes of gaining wealth, security and personal fulfillment, they will, like many urban West Africans, make significant investment in activities carried out for the most part in non-native languages of wider communication.

Notes
1. Johann von Herder is of course widely recognized as one of the most influential proponents of the idea of an inevitable association between national identity and the mother tongue. Among his many famous pronouncements on the subject is the following: 'Denn *jedes* Volk ist Volk; es hat *seine* National Bildung wie seine Sprache' (cited in Anderson, 1991: 67–8) 'every people is a nation, endowed with its own national character and its own language' (my translation). See Edwards (1985) for a brief discussion of Herder's impact on nationalist movements.
2. Pennycook (1998: 193–200) supplies information on one interesting instance of

what he describes as 'colonial continuities' in the debates about the role of English in the educational system of Hong Kong during the 1980s. In cultural and literary studies too, the tendency still exists to interpret use of European languages in contemporary postcolonial settings specifically as capitulation to the structures of colonial rule. JanMohamed and Lloyd (1990: 2) argue from this perspective when they conclude that members of a marginalized or formerly colonized community who write in a dominant European language necessarily 'pay homage to Western intellectual and political hegemony.'
3. This corresponds to the general pattern envisaged by Laitin in his book, *Language Repertoires and State Construction in Africa*.
4. I start with the usual caveats: my reflections here are not those of a scholar of religion. I write here as an individual working with issues pertaining to language and literature. Several of the scholars I quote here have done extensive work on West African Charismatic churches and can be consulted for insights pertaining to religious studies. My intention is to draw conclusions relating to the way we discuss language and identity in literary and cultural studies.
5. See for example Marshall-Fratani (1998), van Dijk (1997), or Meyer (1998).
6. See Marshall-Fratani (1998: 284) and Peil and Opoku (1994: 211–12).
7. I have also visited Charismatic churches in Nigeria and Ivory Coast, and have attended Charismatic churches of West African origin in the United Kingdom and United States.
8. This perception was evident in interviews I conducted with Ben Boateng of the Challenge Bookstore in Accra, with Rev Dei Awuku of the African Christian Press, with Kofi Owusu of the Bible Society of Ghana, with Berimah Amoakohene of the Jesus Cares Center, with Geoffrey Gle of the Ghana Institute of Linguistics Literacy and Bible Translation, and with Professor Kwame Bediako of the Akrofi-Christaller Memorial Center among others.
9. I attended services at the following Charismatic churches in Sakumono: Christian Action Faith Ministries International, the Christ Family Foundation Chapel, the Springs of Life Chapel International. I also attended services at other non-Charismatic churches in Accra, mostly in historic mission churches of the Presbyterian and Methodist denominations.
10. Interview on August 23rd 2000. I think it is also important to point out that this preference for Twi has similarities with the present practice of using English in the Charismatic churches. Once again the emphasis is on using a language of wider communication rather than a mother tongue. In our discussion of sodalities in Africa, we should distinguish not only between those that use 'foreign' and 'local' languages, we should differentiate between those where the language of communication is a mother tongue for most members and those where the language in use is a language of wider communication. As a matter of fact, there are several Charismatic churches in Accra where Twi is the language of communication, but frequently it is not a mother tongue for all or the majority of the members. Rather it is a second or third language, a non-native language of wider communication.
11. Interview on August 21st 2000. And on each of the occasions when I did attend services at the Christ Family Foundation Chapel there were visitors present who identified themselves as non-Ghanaians. Incidentally, when I returned to the Christ Family Foundation Chapel in 2003, services were still held only in English.
12. I am quoting from the booklet: *Introducing Central University College*.
13. Interview on August 22nd 2000.

14. Smaller churches used two languages or whatever language seemed to be understood by the largest number of members.
15. The Yoruba in Accra are of course immigrants probably from Nigeria and or Benin. Since many of these immigrants have been in Ghana for several decades, it is likely that they understand at least one or more of the Ghanaian languages. The fact that the Baptist Convention in Ghana, which apparently started as a ministry to Nigerian immigrants in the then Gold Coast continues to offer services in the mother tongue of this community highlights the tendency of the historic mission churches to envision congregations as ethno-linguistic units.
16. Peil and Opoku (1994: 201) likewise noted the increasing use of qualifiers like 'World,' 'International' and 'Continental' among the churches they described as 'spiritual' churches in the Madina neighborhood of Accra. Gifford (1994: 257) and Rijk van Dijk (1997: 141) make the same observation specifically with respect to Charismatic churches in Ghana. According to van Dijk (1997: 142), some Charismatic churches show off flags from the countries where they have branches near the pulpit. Olupona reports a similar phenomenon for African Charismatic churches in the United States.
17. Marshall-Fratani (1999: 288) has observed similar trends with Charismatic churches in Nigeria while authors like Gifford (1994: 257) confirm Peil and Opoku's remarks in specific regard of the Charismatic churches in Ghana.
18. Quotation from the NIV Bible.
19. My translation. This book is written in French, and the blurb reads as follows in the original: 'Megnanou Bienvenu dispense des cours aux élèves missionairess de quelques école bibliques de Côte d'Ivoire, du Togo, et des cours par correspondance en France et en Belgique sur les "oeuvres de la sorecellerie, de l'occultisme et du fétichisme" . . .'
20. For example, in the *Daily Graphic* of August 21 2000, Joe Okyere reported that angry youth from an Accra neighborhood attacked worshippers at the Open Heaven Mission International Church for violating the ban on drumming.
21. John Awovor (2000a:1) wrote in *The Watchman*, an Evangelical/Pentecostal publication, '[f]or some time now our traditional rulers have decided to ignore our national constitution and impose arbitrary ban on drumming in their traditional areas at certain times of the year. Judging from the way and manner such bans are announced, it is clear that the real initiators of the ban are the priests of traditional religion in our midst . . . We know that the constitution of this country allows FREEDOM OF WORSHIP. Yet, Christians are NOT FREE to worship God the way they choose . . .'
22. See Awovar (2000b: 2) *The Watchman* 03/2000.
23. In this respect, they differ from the 'Spiritual' churches which have certainly achieved similar results but without any consciously undertaken program of cultural indigenization. Indeed members of the church would probably describe the characteristic practices of their church as African or indigenous. Rather, they might think of them as being more spiritual.
24. See Bediako (1995: 114–15) for information on Idowu's proposed reforms and Meyer (1999: 122–5) the discussion around reforms in the Evangelical Presbyterian Church.
25. It should be noted that in the particular case discussed by Meyer in a small Ewe town where most people apparently spoke the local language, the break-away Charismatic church continued to use the Ewe language. However, it showed signs of the growing detachment from localized ambitions that characterized

many Charismatic churches. For example, Meyer (1999: 116) notes that in 1985, the break-away church changed its name from Agbelengor to the Lord's Pentecostal Church suggesting, among other things, that it was no longer 'an 'ethnic' church but a national association.'

26. For example, the pastor of the Ivorian branch of the Winner's Chapel, a popular Charismatic church founded in Nigeria, the Reverend Joseph Ikegnukwu, preached in English at the Abidjan church (Pockpa, 2000). Sermons were then translated into French.
27. Indeed, a leading official in one of the Charismatic churches in Accra during his conversation with me, openly derided the work of a European couple, who, in his words, had wasted several years simply learning a local vernacular, when all the while they could have been 'preaching the gospel' using English or Twi and the services of a translator.
28. For example, van Dijk (1994: 155) reports the presence of Surinamese, Caribbean, North African and Iranian members at one of the Ghanaian churches he studied in Amsterdam. Livingspring, a Nigerian Charismatic church in Sacramento, similarly attracted a diverse pool of recent migrants to the United States from Africa, the Caribbean and Europe, even though Nigerians made up the majority of members. Jacob Olupona's study of African immigrant religious communities in the United States to which I refer later on confirms this trend over and over again. See Olupona (2001: 144) for one example: The Church of the Living God in Maryland.
29. For instance, several of the pastors of Charismatic churches in the United States and Europe decided on this line of work only after they had already settled abroad. They were immigrants first before they became Pastors.
30. Olupona's study examines Christian, Islamic, and Indigenous African religious communities established in seven major American cities over the past two decades. Some of the Christian movements do use African vernacular languages or mother tongues, and these are generally not the Charismatic churches.
31. However, the desire to avoid assimilation into American culture does not therefore signify a renewed commitment to the mother tongue community. Even abroad, members of the Charismatic churches remain distrustful of what they describe as 'tribalism.' And in my discussions with pastors of Charismatic churches in Sakumono, they were quite categorical in affirming that the church should never be equated with a tribal unit.
32. For example, Reverend Danquah of the Ghana Community Church in Atlanta, where services are held in Twi, actually encourages members of the church to return to Ghana (Olupona, 2001: 43–4). One is not likely to hear messages along these lines in a Charismatic church based in West Africa. Charismatics at home prefer to preach about the need to go forth and occupy new territories for God rather than on the need to make a permanent return to a place of origin.
33. Here again is the definition: The language of wider communication is one that enables the formation of sodalities whose members do not necessarily share in common the same mother tongue or primary site of belonging, and where therefore imaginations of the local are subject to reformulation. Because the language of wider communication is used by individuals who do not share the same mother tongue, it is frequently also familiar to at least some individuals in a multiplicity of sovereign territorial units where it may either enable members of particular sodalities to expand their conception of the space of the local or in

other instances to position themselves beyond the space and allegiances of the local.
34. Like the Sufi orders examined by Kane (1997: 58–60), leaders of Charismatic churches sometimes cooperate with the state and at other times distance themselves from the state. In any case, they do not view themselves as a solely national association whose primary commitment is to the cause of any one single state.

Conclusion

Having written so extensively about the possible uses of languages of wider communication in this book, I should point out in ending that this does not mean that I view with approval the kinds of policies of linguistic homogenization attempted at certain points in time by governments in such countries as Ethiopia and Sudan (Bulcha, 1997; Miller, 1986). Nor do I write from the perspective of one who sees the multilingualism of contemporary Africa as an ailment for which a cure must be sought. In short, I am not a partaker of the syndrome that a notable African linguist has described as 'the obsession with the one' (Bamgbose, 1994: 36), or the desire to make sense of Africa's cultural complexity by imposing oneness in the form of one national language, one uniform political system and in some extreme cases, even one religion.

To the contrary, I anticipate that widespread multilingualism will remain the rule in much of Africa and the developing world for many decades to come. Around the world today, monolingualism is the sole prerogative of citizens of wealthy states, who are not at the same time, recent immigrants or members of marginalized groups within the state, and of indigenes of communities in poorer societies living in relative isolation. For almost everyone else, multilingualism is and will remain a simple fact of life. In other words, an important percentage of the world's population lives in societies where several languages are spoken, and where each individual generally speaks a multiplicity of languages. That is to say that activities and communication in non-native languages will account for at least some proportion of the daily routine in many people's lives.

As long as the non-native language in question is not the mother tongue of an ethnic group that has exclusive access to positions of power within the community, there is likely to be minimal hostility directed at activities in and individuals speaking non-native languages. In the case of contemporary West Africa, with the formal end of colonial rule, texts and practices relying on European languages, in particular, do not commonly or systematically arouse animosity. It is clear, I think that, contemporary West Africans are often willing to engage with and respond to activities and practices in non-native languages, either because they have an expanded view of what it is that constitutes the local, or because they feel that the local, even in its expanded configuration, provides an inadequate framework within which to pursue all their interests and realize all their aspirations.

Individuals who have emigrated away from home, and from a community where they share the same mother tongue as the majority of residents, are likely to retain the highest degree of investment in discourses of the vernacular, whether or not they themselves actually use the vernacular in a significant way, and especially if they become members of a culturally subordinated immigrant community. By contrast, those who remain to some degree at home, or close to home, are likely to exhibit the greatest amount of openness towards activities in non-native languages, even though they continue to engage in practices requiring use of the vernacular. Such practices in non-native languages do not consistently run the risk of being apprehended as emblematic of foreign culture, provided they are subjected to specific processes of localization, as often happens when local innovators of new cultural trends must compete on the same market with identical products imported from abroad. In other words, a willingness to engage in practices relying on non-native languages rarely amounts to a repudiation of the politics of cultural specificity and identification with the local. And even in the solidarities with a dispersed membership where communication occurs in non-native languages, the politics of a delocalized cultural specificity retains its appeal.

Thanks to the possibilities offered by new technology for recording in audio, video and compact disc format, performances in vernacular languages spoken by either small or large language groups, are able to generate significant audiences within and beyond national boundaries, especially when they are packaged in a form with which audiences are able to engage, without having to rely exclusively on verbal cues. Indigenous African languages will be heard within the context of creative performance on the national and international stage, even if they are not always read. As I have argued strongly throughout this book, the political and economic dynamics of publishing in particular, are not quite as favorable to the proliferation of written literatures in the majority of languages spoken on the African continent today, even if literacy programs were instituted in many of these languages. Those who are committed to strengthening creative writing in indigenous African languages should give consideration to the possibility of focusing their efforts on a selected number of languages within individual states and sub-regions. There is no doubt that literacy programs will achieve the highest rate of success when carried out in the languages which people actually speak. But that is not to say that published literatures are feasible in every language for which a literacy program has been developed. More than in any other area, when it comes to the publishing of creative literature, discourses of the vernacular are apt to lead us astray if our intention is to secure visibility and prominence for creative writing in indigenous languages within a multilingual state.

My intention in this book has been to move scholars in cultural and literary studies away from speaking of communication in and through the vernacular as the all-sufficient superstructure within which postcolonial subjects organize their non-professional lives. The truth is that, without repudiating identities based on shared mother tongue, postcolonial subjects have also and increasingly been affirming belonging to, and seeking involvement with sodalities where membership is not based on shared mother tongue. People, who for the sake of survival, are either obliged to or desire to move, from the rural country to the city, from one postcolonial periphery to another postcolonial periphery, and from the former colony to the former metropolis, are likely to seek additional memberships in sodalities forged on the basis of shared aspirations rather than that of shared origins.

As I have suggested in the second chapter of this book, the identities which emerge in connection with such sodalities are realized, first and foremost, through communication networks where dialog and interaction occurs in selected languages over matters of common interest. Without this field of verbal interaction in mostly non-native languages, Blackness and Africanness among other self-assigned identities now claimed by millions of people on opposite ends of the African continent today, could hardly have come into existence. The same principle holds true for the new identities that are currently being elaborated in postcolonial societies around the world. In the coming years, in my opinion, the impetus to use non-native languages of wider communication will emanate not so much from an interest in building the nation as from an investment in reinforcing transnational affiliations. One can safely assume then, that Africans, like many other postcolonial subjects, will continue for the foreseeable future, to draw upon languages of wider communication that are at the same time non-native languages for the majority of their associates, in their efforts at constructing both delocalized solidarities and expanded imaginations of the local.

Bibliography

Interviews
Amoakohene, B. (7 August 2000) *Interview with M. Adejunmobi,* Accra.
Amoi, A. (14 September, 2000) *Interview with M. Adejunmobi,* Abidjan.
Anoh, B. (8 August, 2000) *Interview with M. Adejunmobi,* Accra.
Antoh, J. (22 August, 2000) *Interview with M. Adejunmobi,* Accra.
Bediako, K. (17 August 2000) *Interview with M. Adejunmobi,* Akropong.
Boateng, B. (9 August 2000) *Interview with M. Adejunmobi,* Accra.
Bognini, J. (4 September, 2000) *Interview with M. Adejunmobi,* Abidjan.
Boguifo, M. (13 September 2000) *Interview with M. Adejunmobi,* Abidjan.
Buabasah, E. (21 August 2000) *Interview with M. Adejunmobi,* Accra.
Dei-Awuku, Rev. (14 August 2000). *Interview with M. Adejunmobi,* Accra.
Ekuban, J. (23 August, 2000) *Interview with M. Adejunmobi,* Accra.
Gle, G. (7 August 2000) *Interview with M. Adejunmobi,* Accra.
Koulibaly, I.B. (11 September 2000) *Interview with M. Adejunmobi,* Abidjan.
Langdon, A. (18 August, 2000) *Interview with M. Adejunmobi,* Accra.
Larbi, K. (22 August 2000) *Interview with M. Adejunmobi,* Accra.
Owusu, K. (17 August 2000) *Interview with M. Adejunmobi,* Accra.

Compact Discs
Lagbaja! (2001) *WebeforeMe.* New York: IndigeDisc.
Ransome-Kuti, F. (1995) *Vol. 1 & 2.* N. Bergen, NJ: MIL Multimedia.

Selected Videography
Bamiloye, M. (Director) (1997) *The Blood Covenant.* Ile-Ife: Mount Zion Faith Ministries International.
Bamiloye, M. (Director) (1993) *Perilous Times.* Ile-Ife: Mount Zion Faith Ministries International.
Collins, S. (Producer) (1998) *Scores to Settle.* Onitsha: Great Movies and Ossy Affason Production.
Ejiro, C. (Director) (1996) *Onome ... Another Love.* Lagos: Consolidated Fortunes.
Ejiro, Z. (Director) (1997) *Domitilla.* Lagos: Zeb Ejiro Production.
Igwe, A. (Director) (1995) *Rattlesnake.* Lagos: Moving Movies Ltd.
Kelani, T. (Director) (1994) *Ti Oluwa ni ile* (Part 2). Lagos: Mainframe Film and Television Productions.
Nnawuba, L. S. (Producer) (1997) *Blind Trust.* Lagos: Infinity Films.
Nnebue, K. (Producer) (1993) *Living in Bondage.* Lagos: Nek Video Links.

Onukwufor, C. (Director) (1994) *Glamour Girls*. Lagos: Nek Video Links.
Soaga, K. (Director) (1997) *Lagos na Wah*. Lagos: Topway Productions.

Selected Adoras Novels

Dernasse, C. (2000) *Premiers frissons*. Abidjan: Nouvelles éditions ivoiriennes.
Hill, C. (1998) *Parfums d'Assinie*. Abidjan: Nouvelles éditions ivoiriennes.
Kazi, B. (2000) *Nuit fatale*. Abidjan: Nouvelles éditions ivoiriennes.
Koné, F. (1998) *Cache-cache d'amour*. Abidjan: Nouvelles éditions ivoiriennes.
Koné, F. (1999) *Folie d'une Nuit*. Abidjan: Nouvelles éditions ivoiriennes.
Pemberton-Nash, G. (2000) *Les liens sacrés d'amour*. Abidjan: Nouvelles éditions ivoiriennes.
Stone, E. (1998) *Aurore*. Abidjan: Nouvelles éditions ivoiriennes.
Williams, B. (1998) *Sugar Daddy*. Abidjan: Nouvelles éditions ivoiriennes.
Williams, B. (1999) *Tu seras mon épouse*. Abidjan: Nouvelles éditions ivoiriennes.

Secondary References

Abdulaziz, M. and Osinde, K. (1997) Sheng and Engsh: Development of mixed codes among the urban youth in Kenya. *International Journal of the Sociology of Language* (125), 43–63.
Achebe, C. (1964) *Arrow of God*. London: Heinemann.
Achebe, C. (1975) *Morning Yet on Creation Day*. London: Heinemann.
Achebe, C. (1990) New songs of ourselves. *New Statesman and Society* (9 February 1990), 30–2.
Achebe, C. (2000) *Home and Exile*. New York: Oxford University Press.
Adéèkó, A. (1998) *Proverbs, Textuality and Nativism in African Literature*. Gainesville: University Press of Florida.
Adejunmobi, M. (1994) African language writing and writers: A case study of Jean-Joseph Rabearivelo and Ny Avana in Madagascar. *African Languages and Cultures* 7 (1), 1–18.
Adejunmobi, M. (1996) *JJ Rabearivelo, Literature and Lingua Franca in Colonial Madagascar*. New York: Peter Lang.
Adejunmobi, M. (1998) Translation and postcolonial identity: African writing and European languages. *The Translator, Studies in Intercultural Communication* 4 (2), 163–81.
Adejunmobi, M. (1999) Routes: Language and the identity of African literature. *Journal of Modern African Studies* 37 (4), 581–96.
Adekoya, A. (1997) *Sept étapes pour recevoir la délivrance*. Abidjan: Editions World Wide Jesus Crusade.
Adeleye-Fayemi, B. (1997) Either one or the other: Images of women on Nigerian Television. In K. Barber (ed.) *Readings in African Popular Culture* (pp. 125–31). Bloomington: Indiana University Press; Oxford: James Currey.
Adesanya, A. (2000) From film to video. In J. Haynes (ed.) *Nigerian Video Films* (pp. 37–50). Athens: Ohio University Press.
Adiaffi, J. M. (1980) *La carte d'identité*. Paris: CEDA.
Aggarwal, K. (1999) *Amadou Hampâté Bâ et l'africanisme: de la recherche anthropologique à l'exercise de la fonction auctoriale*. Paris: L'Harmattan.
Aig-Imoukhuede, M. (1961) On being a West African writer. *Ibadan* (12), 11–12.
Ajayi, A. (1961) Nineteenth century origins of Nigerian nationalism. *Journal of the Historical Society of Nigeria* 2 (2), 196–210.

Ajayi, A. (1963) The development of secondary grammar school education in Nigeria. *Journal of the Historical Society of Nigeria* 2 (4), 517–35.
Ajayi, A. (1965) *Christian Missions in Nigeria 1841–1891, The Making of a New Elite*. Evanston: Northwestern University Press.
Akwaboah, F. (1994) *Bewitched*. London: Christian Hope Ministry.
Altbach, P. (1999) The dilemmas of publishing in African languages: A comparative perspective. In P. Altbach and D. Teferra (eds) *Publishing in African Languages: Challenges and Prospects* (pp. 1–10). Oxford: Bellagio Publishing Network.
Aluko, T.M. (1949) Case for fiction. *West African Review* (November), 1237–9.
Amadiume, I. (1987) *Male Daughters, Female Husbands: Gender and Sex in an African Society*. London: Zed Books.
Amselle, J.L. (1998) *Mestizo Logics: Anthropology of Identity in Africa and Elsewhere*. Stanford: Stanford University Press.
Anderson, B. (1991) *Imagined Communities, Reflections on the Origin and Spread of Nationalism*. Revised edition. London: Verso.
Ansre, G. (1971) Language standardisation in sub-Saharan Africa. *Current Trends in Linguistics* (7), 680–698.
Anyidoho, K. (1992) Language and development strategy in Pan-African experience. *Research in African Literatures* 23 (1), 45–63.
Appadurai, A. (1988) Putting hierarchy in its place. *Cultural Anthropology* (3), 36–49.
Appadurai, A. (1996) *Modernity at Large, Cultural Dimensions of Globalization*. Minneapolis: University of Minnesota Press.
Appiah, A. (1992) *In My Father's House, Africa in The Philosophy of Culture*. New York: Oxford University Press.
Armah, A.K. (1976) Larsony: Or fiction as criticism of fiction. *Asemka* (4), 1–14.
Asamoah-Gyadu, J. (1998) The Pentecostal/Charismatic experience in Ghana. *Journal of African Christian Thought* 1 (2), 51–7.
Asante-Darko, N. and Van Der Geest, S. (1983) Male chauvinism: Men and women in Ghanaian Highlife songs. In Christine Oppong (ed.) *Male and Female in West Africa* (pp. 242–65). London: George Allen and Unwin.
Ashcroft, B., Griffiths G. and Tiffin, H. (eds) (1995) *The Post-Colonial Studies Reader*. London and New York: Routledge, 1995.
Awolowo, O. (1947) *Path to Nigerian Freedom*. London: Faber.
Awoniyi, T. (1975) *Yoruba Language in Education 1846–1974, A Historical Survey*. Ibadan: Ibadan: University Press.
Awonoor, K. (1973–4) Tradition and continuity in African literature. *Dalhousie Review* (53), 665–71.
Awovor, J. (2000a) Ban on drumming, implications for national security. *The Watchman*. (02/2000), 1, 6.
Awovor, J. (2000b) Ban on drumming? *The Watchman*. (03/2000), 2.
Ayandele, E.A. (1966) *The Missionary Impact on Modern Nigeria 1842–1914*. London: Longmans.
Ayandele, E.A. (1974) *The Educated Elite in The Nigerian Society*. Ibadan: Ibadan University Press.
Azikiwe, B.N. (1934) How shall we educate the African? *Journal of the African Society*. (33), 143–51.
Bâ, H. (1973) *L'étrange destin de Wangrin*. Paris: Union générale d'éditions.
Balogun, O. (1998) Africa's video alternative. *The Unesco Courrier* (November), 40–2.
Bamgbose, A. (1974) *The Novels of D.O. Fagunwa*. Benin City: Ethiope Publishing Corporation.

Bamgbose, A. (ed.) (1976) *Mother Tongue Education: The West African Experience*. London: Hodder and Stoughton.

Bamgbose, A. (1991) *Language and the Nation: The Language Question in Sub-Saharan Africa*. Edinburgh: Edinburgh University Press.

Bamgbose, A. (1994) Pride and prejudice in multilingualism and development. In R. Fardon and G. Furniss (eds) *African Languages, Development and the State* (pp 33–43). London and New York: Routledge.

Bamgbose, A. (1995) English in the Nigerian environment. In A. Bamgbose, A. Banjo and A. Thomas (eds) *New Englishes, A West African Perspective* (pp. 9–26). Ibadan: British Council.

Bamgbose, A. (2000) *Language and Exclusion, The Consequences of Language Policies in Africa*. Münster: Lit Verlag.

Barber, K. (1982) Popular reactions to the Petro-Naira. *The Journal of Modern African Studies* 20 (3), 431–50.

Barber, K. (1986) Radical conservatism in Yoruba popular theater. In E. Breitinger and R. Sander (eds) *Drama and Theatre in Africa* (pp. 5–32). Bayreuth: Bayreuth University Press.

Barber, K. (1987a) Popular arts in Africa. *African Studies Review* 30 (3), 1–78.

Barber, K. (1987b) Response. *African Studies Review*. 30 (3), 105–11.

Barber, K. (1995) African-language literature and postcolonial criticism. *Research in African Literatures* 26 (4), 3–30.

Barber, K. (1997a) Introduction. In K. Barber (ed.) *Readings in African Popular Culture* (pp. 1–12). Oxford: James Currey; Bloomington: Indiana University Press.

Barber, K. (1997b) Preliminary notes on audiences in Africa. *Africa* 67 (3), 347–62.

Barber, K. (2000) *The Generation of Plays: Yorùbá Popular Life in Theater*. Bloomington & Indianapolis: Indiana University Press.

Baron, D. (1990) *The English-Only Question, An Official Language for Americans?* New Haven: Yale University Press.

Bayart, J.F. (1993) *The State in Africa: The Politics of the Belly*. London: Longman.

Bediako, K. (1995) *Christianity in Africa, The Renewal of a Non-Western Religion*. Edinburgh University Press.

Ben-Amos, P. (1977) Pidgin languages and tourist art. *Studies in the Anthropology of Visual Communication* (4), 128–39.

Berghe, P. van den (1968) Language and nationalism in South Africa. In J. Fishman, C. Ferguson and J. D. Gupta (eds) *Language Problems of Developing Nations* (pp. 215–24). New York: John Wiley & Sons Inc.

Bernsten, J. and Myers-Scotton, C. (1993) English loans in Shona: Consequences for linguistic systems. *International Journal of the Sociology of Language* (100/101), 125–48.

Bersselaar, D. van den. (1997) Creating 'Union Ibo': Missionaries and the Igbo language. *Africa* 67 (2), 273–95.

Bezoro, E. (1932) *La soeur inconnue*. Paris: Eugène Figuière.

Bgoya, W. (1996) Publishing in Africa: culture and development. In P. Altbach and S. Hassan (eds) *The Muse of Modernity: Essays on Culture and Development in Africa* (pp. 151–79). Trenton: Africa World Press.

Bishop, R. (1988) *African Literature, African Critics: The Forming of Critical Standards, 1947–1966*. Westport, CT: Greenwood Press.

Blyden, E. (1887) *Christianity, Islam, and the Negro Race*. 1887. Reprint. Edinburgh: Edinburgh University Press.

Bodunde, C. (ed.) (2001) *African Languages Literature in the Political Context of the 1990s*. Bayreuth: Bayreuth University.

Bokamba, E. (1982) The Africanization of English. In B. Kachru (ed.) *The Other Tongue: English Across Cultures* (pp. 77–98). Urbana: University of Illinois Press.

Bourdieu, P. (1991) *Language and Symbolic Power*. Cambridge: Harvard University Press.

Brennan, T. (1997) *At Home in the World, Cosmopolitanism Now*. Cambridge: Harvard University Press.

Brenzinger, M., Heine, B. and Sommer, G. (1991) Language death in Africa. In R. Robins and E. Uhlenbeck (eds) *Endangered Languages* (pp. 19–44). Oxford: Berg Publishers Ltd.

Brown, D. (1992) Language and social history in South Africa: A task still to be undertaken. In R. Herbst (ed.) *Language and Society in Africa, The Theory and Practice of Sociolinguistics* (pp. 71–92). Johannesburg: Witswatersrand University Press.

Bulcha, Mekuria (1997) The politics of linguistic homogenization in Ethiopia and the conflict over the status of 'Afaan Oromoo'. *African Affairs* 96 (384), 325–52.

Cévaër, F. (1993) Edition et sédition: nouvelle génération d'écrivains africains et institutions françaises. *Présence francophone* (43), 182–95.

Chakava, H. (1988) A decade of publishing in Kenya: 1977–1987. One man's involvement. *The African Book Publishing Record* (14), 234–41.

Chukwuemeka, B.I. (1969) The problem of language in African literature. *African Literature Today* (3), 15–26.

Cole, P. (1975) *Modern and Traditional Elites in the Politics of Lagos*. Cambridge: Cambridge University Press.

Cope, T. (ed.) (1968) *Izibongo: Zulu Praise Poems*. Oxford: Clarendon Press.

Crawford, J. (2000) *At War with Diversity, US Language Policy in an Age of Anxiety*. Clevedon: Multilingual Matters.

Crummell, A. (1862) *The Future of Africa*. New York: Charles Scribner.

Dadié, B. (1971) *Climbié*. Trans. Karen Chapman. London: Heinemann.

Dakubu, M.E. Kropp. (1997) *Korle Meets the Sea, A Sociolinguistic History of Accra*. New York: Oxford University Press.

Das Gupta, J. and Gumperz, J. (1968) Language, communication and control in North India. In J. Fishman, C. Ferguson and J. Das Gupta (eds) *Language Problems of Developing Nations* (pp. 151–66). New York: John Wiley & Sons Inc.

Deleuze, G. and Guattari, F. (1986) *Kafka, Toward a Minor Literature*. Minneapolis: University of Minnesota Press.

Diallo, B. (1985) *Force-bonté*. Dakar: NEA, ACCT.

Dickey, S. (1995) Consuming utopia: Film watching in Tamil Nadu. In C. Breckenridge (ed.) *Consuming Modernity, Public Culture in a South Asian World* (pp. 131–56). Minneapolis: University of Minnesota Press.

Dimendaal, G. (1989) On language death in Eastern Africa. In N. Dorian (ed.) *Investigating Obsolescence. Studies in Language Contraction and Death* (pp. 13–21) Cambridge: Cambridge University Press.

Diop, B. (1961) *Les contes d'Amadou Koumba*. Paris: Présence africaine.

Diop, D. (1956) Contribution au débat sur la poésie nationale. *Présence africaine* (6), 113–15.

Diop, O.S. (1938) *Contes et légendes africaines d'Afrique noire*. Paris: Nouvelles éditions latines.

Dodson, D. (1973) The role of the publisher in Onitsha market literature. *Research in African Literatures* 4 (2), 172–87.
Dougall, J. (1938) The development of the education of the African in relation to Western contact. *Africa* 9 (3), 312–25.
Dunn, J. and Robertson, A.F. (1974) *Dependence and Opportunity: Political Change in Ahafo*. Cambridge: Cambridge University Press.
Durán, L. (2000) Sweet music. *BBC Focus on Africa* (January–March), 54–5.
Eastman, C. (1984) Language, ethnic identity and change. In J. Edwards (ed.) *Linguistic Minorities, Policies and Pluralism* (pp. 259–76). London: Academic Press.
Echeruo, M. (1977) *Victorian Lagos, Aspects of the Nineteenth Century Lagos Life*. London: Macmillan Educational Limited.
Edwards, J. (1985) *Language, Society and Identity*. Oxford: Basil Blackwell.
Edwards, J. (2001) Languages and language learning in the face of world English. *Profession 2001*, 109–20.
Ejiro, Z. (1998) We are the leaders. *Nigerian Videos*. 4 (3), 18–9.
Ekwensi, C. (1950) Outlook for African writers. *West African Review* (January), 19.
Ekwensi, C. (1956) The dilemma of the African writer. *West African Review* (27), 701–4, 708.
Ekwuazi, H. (2000) The Igbo video film: A glimpse into the cult of the individual. In J. Haynes (ed.) *Nigerian Video Films* (pp. 131–47). Athens, Ohio University Press.
Elugbe, B. and Omamor, A. (1991) *Nigerian Pidgin, Background and Prospects*. Ibadan: Heinemann Educational Books, Nigeria.
Emenyonu, E. (1972) African literature: What does it take to be its critic? *African Literature Today* (5), 1–11.
Emenyonu, E. (1978) *The Rise of the Igbo Novel*. Oxford: Oxford University Press.
Erlmann, V. (1991) *African Stars: Studies in Black South African Performance*. Chicago: University of Chicago Press.
Erlmann, V. (1999) *Music, Modernity and the Global Imagination*. New York: Oxford University Press.
Fabian, J. (1983) *Time and Other*. New York: Columbia University Press.
Fabian, J. (1986) *Language and Colonial Power: The Appropriation of Swahili in the former Belgian Congo 1880–1938*. Cambridge: Cambridge University Press.
Fagunwa, D. (1950) *Ogbójú Ode Nínú Igbó Irúnmalè*. London: Thomas Nelson.
Fajana, A. (1982) *Education in Nigeria 1842–1939: An Historical Analysis*. Lagos: Longman Nigeria.
Fardon, R. and Furniss, G. (1994) Introduction: frontiers and boundaries. In R. Fardon and G. Furniss (eds) *African Languages, Development and the State* (pp. 1–24). London: Routledge.
Featherstone, M. (1993) Global and local cultures. In J. Bird *et al.* (eds) *Mapping the Futures: Local Cultures, Global Change* (pp. 169–87) London: Routledge.
Fishman, J. (1989) *Language and Ethnicity in Minority Sociolinguistic Perspective*. Clevedon: Multilingual Matters.
Fiske, J. (1989) *Understanding Popular Culture*. London, Routledge.
Flint, J. (1969) Nigeria: The colonial experience from 1880 to 1914. In L.H. Gann and P. Duigan (eds) *Colonialism in Africa 1870–1960*, Vol. 1 (pp. 220–60). Cambridge: Cambridge University Press.
Foucault, M. (1972) The discourse on language. In *The Archaeology of Knowledge*. London: Tavistock.

Fredericksen, B.F. (1999) 'We need that life.' Global narratives and local aspirations among youth in a Nairobi slum. In N.N. Sørensen (ed.) *Narrating Mobility, Boundaries and Belonging* (pp. 49–64) Copenhagen: Centre for Development Research.

Fredericksen, B.F. (2000) Transnational and Pan-African Black Popular Culture. Presentation at the University of California, Davis, (9 March).

Furniss, G. (1995) *Ideology in Practice, Hausa Poetry as Exposition of Values and Viewpoints*. Cologne: Rüdiger Köppe Verlag.

Furniss, G. (1996) *Poetry, Prose and Popular Culture in Hausa*. Edinburgh: Edinburgh University Press; Washington DC: Smithsonian Institution Press.

Furniss, G. (1998) Hausa creative writing in the 1930s: An exploration in postcolonial Theory. *Research in African Literatures* (29) 1, 87–102.

Gates, H.L. (1990) Authority, (white) power, and the (black) critic; It's all Greek to me. In A. JanMohamed and D. Lloyd (eds) *The Nature of Minority Discourse* (pp. 72–101). New York: Oxford University Press.

Gecau, K. (1972) Do African languages divide the nation? *African Perspectives*, (2), 15–18.

Gellner, E. (1983) *Nations and Nationalism*. Ithaca: Cornell University Press.

George, O. (2003) *Relocating Agency, Modernity and African Letters*. New York: State University of New York Press.

Gérard, A. (1971) *Four African Literatures, Xhosa, Sotho, Zulu, Amharic*. Berkeley: University of California Press.

Gérard, A. (1981) *African Language Literatures*. Washington DC: Three Continents Press.

Gérard, A. (1990) *Contexts of African Literature*. Amsterdam: Rodopi.

Gifford, P. (1987) 'Africa shall be saved'. An appraisal of Reinhard Bonnke's Pan-African crusade. *Journal of Religion in Africa* 17 (1), 63–91.

Gifford, P. (1994) Ghana's Charismatic churches. *Journal of Religion in Africa* 24 (3), 241–65.

Gikandi, S. (1991) The epistemology of translation: Ngugi, Matigari, and the politics of language. *Research in African Literatures* 22 (4), 163–7.

Gikandi, S. (1996) *Maps of Englishness, Writing Identity in the Culture of Colonialism*. New York: Columbia University Press.

Githiora, C. (2002) 'Sheng: peer language, Swahili dialect or emerging Creole?' *Journal African Cultural Studies* 15 (2), 159–81.

Goodwin, K. (1982) *Understanding African Poetry, A Study of Ten Poets*. London: Heinemann.

Gorman, T.P. (1974) The development of language policy in Kenya with particular reference to the educational system. In W. Whiteley (ed.) *Language in Kenya* (pp. 397–453). Nairobi: Oxford University Press.

Griswold, W. (2000) *Bearing Witness: Readers, Writers, and The Novel in Nigeria*. Princeton: Princeton University Press.

Griswold, W. and Bastian, M. (1987) Continuities and reconstructions in cross-cultural literary transmission. The case of the Nigerian romance novel. *Poetics* (16), 327–51.

Hair, P.E. (1967) *The Early Study of Nigerian Languages: Essays and Bibliographies*. London: Cambridge University Press.

Hamilton, R. (1991) Lusophone literature in Africa: Language and literature in Portuguese-writing Africa. *Callaloo* 14 (2), 313–23.

Hannerz, U. (1987) The world in creolisation. *Africa* 57 (4), 546–59.

Hannerz, U. (1990) Cosmopolitans and locals in world culture. In M. Featherstone (ed.) *Global Culture: Nationalism, Globalization and Modernity* (pp. 237–51). London: Sage Publications.

Harries, P. (1988) The roots of ethnicity: Discourse and the politics of language construction in south-east Africa. *African Affairs* (87), 25–52.

Hartmann, G. (1997) *The Fateful Question of Culture*. New York: Columbia University Press.

Haynes, J. (1997) Nigerian cinema: Structural adjustments. In J. Haynes (ed.) *Cinema and Social Change in West Africa* (pp. 1–15). Jos: Nigerian Film Corporation.

Haynes, J. and Okome, O. (2000) Evolving popular media: Nigerian video films. In J. Haynes *Nigerian Video Films* (pp. 51–88). Athens: Ohio University Press.

Hill, A. (1988) *In Pursuit of Publishing*. London: John Murray.

Hobsbawm, E. (1994) *Nations and Nationalism since 1870*. Cambridge: Cambridge University Press.

Hountondji, P. (1977) *Sur la philosophie africaine, critique de l'ethnophilosophie*. Paris: François Maspero.

Hussey. E.R. (1932) The Languages of literature in Africa. *Africa* 5 (2), 169–75.

Ibagere, E. (2001) An acting dynasty. *BBC Focus on Africa*, (April–June), 56–7.

Innes, C.L. (1996) 'Forging the conscience of their race': Nationalist writers. In B. King (ed.) *New National and Postcolonial Literatures* (pp. 120–39). Oxford: Clarendon.

Introducing Central University College. Accra: Central University College.

Irele, A. (1981) *The African Experience in Literature and Ideology*. London: Heinemann.

Irele, A. (2000) Second language literatures, An African perspective. *Anglophonia/Caliban* (7), 7–22.

Isola, A. (1992) The African writer's tongue. *Research in African Literatures* 23 (1), 17–26.

Izevbaye, D. (1997) Elesin's homecoming: The translation of 'The King's Horseman'. *Research in African Literatures* (28) 2, 154–70.

James, A. (1990) *In Their Own Voices: African Women Writers Talk*. London: James Currey Ltd.

JanMohamed, A. and Lloyd, D. (1990) Toward a theory of minority discourse: What is to be done? In A. JanMohamed and D. Lloyd (eds) *The Nature and Context of Minority Discourse* (pp. 1–16) New York: Oxford University Press.

Jeyifo, B. (1990) The nature of things: Arrested decolonization and critical theory. *Research in African Literatures* 21 (1), 33–48.

Johnson, D. (2000) Culture and art in Hausa video films. In J. Haynes (ed.) *Nigerian Video Films* (pp. 200–8). Athens: Ohio University Press.

Jones, E. (1957) The potentialities of Krio as a literary language. *Sierra Leone Studies* (9), 40–8.

Jones-Quartey, K.A.B. (1949) Our language and literature problem. *Africana* 1 (3), 23–4.

Julien, E. (1999) Visible woman; or, a semester among the Great Books. *Profession 99*, 225–35.

Kachru, B. (1986) *The Alchemy of English: The Spread, Functions and Models of Non-native Englishes*. Oxford: Pergamon Press.

Kane, O. (1997) Muslim missionaries and African states. In S.H. Rudolph and J. Piscatori (eds) *Transnational Religion and Fading States* (pp. 47–62). Boulder, Colorado: Westview Press.

Katz, C. (1994) Playing the field: Questions of fieldwork in geography. *Professional Geographer* 46 (1), 67–72.
Kingsley, M. (1897) *Travels in West Africa, Congo français, Corisco and Cameroons.* London, New York: Macmillan.
Klein, D. (2000) *Yoruba Bata: Politics of a Pop Tradition in Erin-Osun and Overseas.* PhD thesis, University of California, Santa Cruz.
Klíma, V., Rù ièka, K. and Zima, P. (1976) *Black Africa, Literature and Language.* Prague: Academia.
Koné, A. (1992) Le romancier africain devant la langue d'écriture: problèmes des relations entre la langue et l'identité. *Francofonia* (22), 75–88.
Koulibaly, I.B. (1991) *Ah! Les hommes... Tous des menteurs!* Lomé: Editions Haho.
Koulibaly, I.B. (1995a) *Ah! Les femmes...* Lomé: Editions Haho.
Koulibaly, I.B. (1995b) *Encore les femmes... Toujours les femmes.* Lomé: Editions Haho.
Koulibaly, I.B. (1996) *Mon mari est un chauffeur de taxi.* Abidjan: Editions Passerelle.
Koulibaly, I.B. (1999a) *Que Dieu protège les femmes.* Abidjan: Editions Passerelle.
Koulibaly, I.B. (1999b) Interview avec Fibla Koné *Amina* (354), 69.
Kourouma, A. (1970) *Les Soleils des indépendances.* Paris: Editions du Seuil.
Kourouma, A. (2000) *Allah n'est pas obligé.* Paris: Seuil.
Kunene, M. (1992) Problems in African literature. *Research in African Literatures* 23 (1), 27–44.
Kuria, M. (2001) Transcending boundaries: Comedy in the streets of Nairobi. In C. Bodunde (ed.) *African Languages Literature in the Political Context of the 1990s* (pp. 91–102). Bayreuth: Bayreuth African Studies.
Laitin, D. (1992) *Language Repertoires and State Construction in Africa.* Cambridge: Cambridge University Press.
Landau, J. (1996) Language and ethnopolitics in the Ex-Soviet Muslim Republics. In. Y. Suleiman (ed.) *Language and Identity in the Middle East and North Africa* (pp. 133–52). Richmond, Surrey: Curzon Press.
Larbi, K.E. (2000) Triumphs and challenges of Ghanaian Pentecostalism, 21st Century agenda. *Centre for Pentecostal & Charismatic Studies* 1 (2).
Larkin, B. (1997) Indian films and Nigerian lovers: Media and the creation of parallel modernities. *Africa* 67 (3), 406–40.
Larkin, B. (2000) Hausa dramas and the rise of video culture in Nigeria. In J. Haynes (ed.) *Nigerian Video Films* (pp. 209–41). Athens: Ohio University Press.
Larson, C. (1972) *The Emergence of African Fiction.* Bloomington: Indiana University Press.
Laughton, W. (1938) The teaching of African languages in schools: A note on the position in Kenya. *Africa* 9 (8), 221–25.
Launay, Robert (1997) Spirit media: The electronic media and Islam among the Dyula of Northern Côte d'Ivoire. *Africa* 67 (3), 441–52.
Law, R. (1976) Early Yoruba historiography. *History in Africa* (3), 69–89.
Law, R. (1996) Local amateur scholarship in the construction of Yoruba ethnicity 1880–1914. In L. de la Gorgendière, K. King and S. Vaughn (eds) *Ethnicity in Africa: Roots, Meanings and Implications* (pp. 55–90). Edinburgh: Centre of African Studies, University of Edinburgh.
Lawuyi, O. (1997) The political economy of video marketing in Ogbomoso, Nigeria. *Africa* 67 (3), 476–90.
Leenhardt, M. (1930) Dowry systems among primitive peoples. *International Review of Missions* 19 (74), 220–30.
Letters to the Editor (1998) *Nigerian Videos* 4 (1), 6.

Letters to the Editor (1998) *Nigerian Videos* 4 (3), 12.
Lindfors, B. (1982) *Early Nigerian Literature*. New York: Africana Publishing Company.
Lipschutz, R. (1992) Reconstructing world politics: The emergence of global civil society. *Millennium: Journal of International Studies* 2 (1), 389–420.
Liyong, T.L. (1993) On translating the 'untranslated': Chapter 14 of Wer pa Lawino by Okot p'Bitek. *Research in African Literatures* 24 (3), 87–92.
Lucas, B. (1927) The educational value of initiation rites. *International Review of Missions*.
Lugard, F. (1928) The International Institute of African Languages and Cultures. *Africa* 1 (1), 1–12.
Lugard, F. (1965) *The Dual Mandate in Tropical Africa*. London: Frank Cass.
Mahood, M.M. (1977) *The Colonial Encounter: A Reading of Six Novels*. Totowa: Rowman.
Manessy, G. (1994) *Le français en Afrique noire*. Paris: L'Harmattan.
Mann, K. (1985) *Marrying Well. Marriage, Status and Social Change among the Educated Elite in Colonial Lagos*. Cambridge: Cambridge University Press.
Manuel, P. (1993) *Cassette Culture, Popular Music and Technology in North India*. Chicago: University of Chicago Press.
Marshall-Fratani, R. (1998) Mediating the global and local in Nigerian Pentecostalism. *Journal of Religion in Africa* 28 (3), 278–315.
Massey, D. (1993) Power-geometry and a progressive sense of place. In J. Bird *et al.* (eds) *Mapping the Futures: Local Cultures, Global Change* (pp. 59–69). London: Routledge.
May, C. and Stapleton C. (1987) *African All-Stars, The Pop Music of a Continent*. London: Quartet Books.
Mazrui, A. (1975) *The Political Sociology of the English Language. An African Perspective*. The Hague: Mouton.
Mazrui, A. and Mazrui, A. (1998) *The Power of Babel: Language and Governance in the African Experience*. Oxford: James Currey Ltd.
McCluskie, K and Innes, L. (1988) Women and African literature. *Wasafiri* (8), 3–7.
McLaughlin, F. (1995) Haalpulaar identity as a response to Wolofization. *African Languages and Cultures* 8 (2), 153–68.
McLaughlin, F. (2001) Dakar Wolof and the configuration of an urban identity. *Journal of African Cultural Studies* 14 (2), 153–72.
Megnanou, B. (2000) *Un ex-sorcier devient évangéliste*.
Meinhof, C. (1928) Sprache und Volkstum. *Africa* 1 (1), 23–9.
Memmi, A. (1965) *The Colonizer and the Colonized*. New York: Orion Press.
Meyer, B. (1998) 'Making a complete break with the past': Memory and postcolonial modernity in Ghanaian Pentecostalist discourse. *Journal of Religion in Africa* 28 (3), 316–49.
Meyer, B. (1999) *Translating the Devil. Religion and Modernity among the Ewe of Ghana*. Trenton, NJ: Africa World Press.
Michelman, F. (1995) French and British colonial language policies: A comparative view of their impact on African literature. *Research in African Literatures* (26) 9, 216–25.
Middleton, J. (1983) One hundred and fifty years of Christianity in a Ghanaian town *Africa* 53 (3), 2–19.
Miller, C. (1986) Langues et intégration nationale au Soudan. *Politique africaine* (23), 29–41.

Mlama, P.M. (1990) Creating in the mother tongue: The challenges to the African writer today. *Research in African Literatures* 21 (4), 5–14.

Monga, Y.D. (2000) Dollars and lipstick: The United States through the eyes of African women. *Africa* 70 (2) 192–208.

Moore, G. (2002) The transcription center in the sixties: Navigating in narrow seas. *Research in African Literatures* 33 (3), 167–81.

Mosco, V. and Kaye, L. (2000) Questioning the concept of the audience. In I. Hagen and J. Wasco (eds) *Consuming Audiences? Production and Reception in Media Research* (pp. 31–46). Creskill, NJ: Hampton Press.

Mphahlele, E. (1963) Letter. *Transition* (11), 7–9.

Mulokozi, M. (1999) Publishing in Kiswahili: A writer's perspective. In P. Altbach and D. Teferra (eds) *Publishing in African Languages: Challenges and Prospects* (pp. 11–41). Oxford: Bellagio Publishing Network.

Mumford, B. (1929) Education and the social adjustment of the primitive peoples of Africa to European culture. *Africa* 2 (2), 138–59.

Murdoch, G. (2000) Peculiar commodities: Audiences at large in the world of goods. In I. Hagen and J. Wasco (eds) *Consuming Audiences? Production and Reception in Media Research* (pp. 47–70). Creskill, NJ: Hampton Press.

Myers-Scotton, C. (1990) Elite closure as boundary maintenance: The case of Africa. In B. Weinstein (ed.) *Language Policy and Political Development* (pp. 25–41). Norwood, NY: Ablex.

Newell, S. (1996) From the brink of oblivion: The anxious masculinism of Nigerian market literatures. *Research in African Literatures* 27 (3), 50–67.

Newell, S. (1997) Anatomy of masculine power: Three perspectives on marriage and gender in Nigerian non-fiction. In S. Newell (ed.) *Writing African Women: Gender, Popular Culture and Literature in West Africa* (pp. 170–90). London: Zed Books.

Newell, S. (2000) *Ghanaian Popular Fiction: Thrilling Discoveries in Conjugal Life and Other Tales*. Athens: Ohio University Press; Oxford: James Currey.

Ngugi wa Thiong'o (1980) *Caitaani Mũtharabainĩ*. Nairobi: Heinemann.

Ngugi wa Thiong'o (1981a) *Decolonising the Mind, The Politics of Language in African Literature*. London: James Currey; Nairobi: EAPH; Portsmouth: Heinemann.

Ngugi wa Thiong'o (1981b) *Matigari Ma Njirũũngi*. Nairobi: Heinemann.

Ngugi wa Thiong'o (1989) *Matigari*. Trans. Wangũi wa Goro. Oxford: Heinemann.

Ngugi wa Thiong'o (1993) *Moving the Centre, The Struggle for Cultural Freedoms*. London: James Currey.

N'Koumo, H. (2000) Biton Koulibaly, il collectionne les femmes. *Ivoir'Soir*, (3320), 1.

Ntangaare, M. (2001) Democracy and the proletariat's dream in Byron Kawadwa's The Song of Wankoko. In C. Bodunde (ed.) *African Languages Literature in the Political Context of the 1990s* (pp. 63–89). Bayreuth: Bayreuth African Studies.

Nwana, P. (1963) *Omenuko*. London: Longman.

Nwankpa, E. (1999) *Redeeming the Land, Interceding for the Nations*. Achimota: African Christian Press.

Nwankwo, V. (1999) Publishing in local languages in Nigeria. A publisher's perspective. In P. Altbach and D. Teferra (eds) *Publishing in African Languages: Challenges and Prospects* (pp. 110–28). Oxford: Bellagio Publishing Network.

Nwoga, D. (1973–4) The limitations of universal critical criteria. *Dalhousie Review* (53), 608–30.

Nzekwu, O. (1961) *Wand of Noble Wood*. London: Hutchinson.

Obiechina, E. (1973) *An African Popular Literature: A Study of Onitsha Market Pamphlets*. Cambridge: Cambridge University Press.
Obbo, C. (1980) *African Women: Their Struggle for Economic Independence*. London: Zed.
O'Brien, D.C. (1998) The shadow-politics of Wolofisation. *The Journal of Modern African Studies* 36 (1), 25–46.
Obumselu, B. (1966) The background of modern African literature. *Ibadan* (22), 46–59.
Ogundipe-Leslie, M. (1987) African women, culture and another development. *Présence Africaine* 141 (1), 123–39.
Ojo, M. A. (1998) The contextual significance of the Charismatic movements in independent Nigeria. *Africa* 58 (2), 175–92.
Okara, G. (1963) African speech ... English words. *Transition* (10), 15–6.
Okara, G. (1964) *The Voice*. London: André Deutsch.
Okome, O. (2000) Onome: ethnicity, class, gender. In J. Haynes (ed.) *Nigerian Video Films* (pp. 148–64). Athens: Ohio University Press.
Okonkwo, J. (1976) African literature and its language of expression. *African Quarterly* 15 (4), 56–66
Okpewho, I. (1978) African fiction: Language revisited. *Journal of African Studies* 5(4), 414–26.
Okwu, E. (1966) A language of expression for Nigerian literature. *Nigeria Magazine* (91), 313–15.
Okyere, J. (2000) Teshie youth besiege church to enforce ban on drumming. *Daily Graphic* (21 August), 16.
Olatunji, O. (1993) *Beyond the Spoken Word: An African Language Literature Experience*. Ibadan: University of Ibadan Press.
Olupona, J. (2001) *African Immigrant Religious Communities: Identity Formation in America's Pluralistic Society*. Report to the Ford Foundation (mimeo).
Omu, F. (1978) *Press and Politics in Nigeria 1880–1937*. London: Longman.
Onovoh, P. (1998) *Afrikaner erzählen ihr Leben, Sammlungen afrikanischer Autobiographien als Ereignis der späten dreißiger Jahre*. Bayreuth: Bayreuth African Studies.
Osofisan, F. (1999) Theater and the rites of post-Negritude remembering. *Research in African Literatures* 30 (1), 1–11.
Osundare, N. (1993) *African Literature and the Crisis of Post-Structuralist Theorising*. Ibadan: Options Book and Information Service.
Owomoyela, O. (1992) Language, identity and social construction in African literature. *Research in African Literatures* 23 (1), 83–94.
Owusu, M. (1978) Ethnography of Africa: The usefulness of the useless. *American Anthropologist* 80 (1), 310–34.
Owusu-Ansah, K. and B. (1997) *Power in All-Night Prayer*. Accra: Great Line Presentations.
Oyelaran, O. (1982) Yoruba as a medium of instruction. In A. Afolayan (ed.) *Yoruba Language and Literature* (pp. 300–12). Ife: University of Ife Press.
Oyewumi, O. (1997) *The Invention of Women, Making an African Sense of Western Gender Discourses*. Minneapolis: University of Minnesota Press.
Oyono, F (1970) *Une vie de boy*. Paris: Presses Pocket.
Paden, J. (1968) Language problems of national integration in Nigeria: The special case of Hausa. In J. Fishman. C. Ferguson and J. D. Gupta (eds) *Language Problems of Developing Nations* (pp. 199–213). New York: John Wiley & Sons Inc.

P'Bitek, O. (1966) *Song of Lawino*. Nairobi: East African Publishing Company.
P'Bitek, O. (1969) *Wer pa Lawino*. Nairobi: East African Publishing House.
Peil, M. and Opoku, K.A. (1994) The development and practice of religion in an Accra suburb. *Journal of Religion in Africa* 24 (3), 198–227.
Peires, J. (1979) The Lovedale press: Literature for the Bantu revisited. *History in Africa* (6), 155–75.
Perham, M. (1960) *Lugard, The Years of Authority, 1898–1945*. London: Collins.
Perlstein, M (1943). L'enseignement en Afrique équatoriale française. *Africa* 14 (3), 130–5.
Pennycook, A. (1994) *The Cultural Politics of English as an International Language*. London: Longman.
Pennycook, A. (1998) *English and the Discourses of Colonialism*. London: Routledge.
Perry, J. (1999) Comparative perspectives on language planning in Iran and Tajikistan. In Y. Suleiman (ed.) *Language and Ethnicity in the Middle East and North Africa* (pp. 154–74). Richmond, Surrey: Curzon Press.
Pockpa, M.A. (2000) Ici, on prospère: Eglise WOFBI. *Ivoir'soir* (12 September), 9.
Poku, O.K. (1948) We must develop and preserve our vernaculars. *West African Review* (19), 900–1.
Priebe, R. (1978) Popular writing in Ghana. *Research in African Literatures* 9 (3), 395–425.
Quayson, A. (1997) *Strategic Transformations in Nigerian Writing*. Oxford: James Currey; Bloomington & Indianapolis: Indiana University Press.
Quenum, M. (1946) *Légendes africaines: Côte d'Ivoire, Soudan, Dahomey*. Rochefort: A. Thoyon Thèze.
Rabearivelo, J. J. (1987). *L'interférence*. Paris: Hatier.
Radway, J. (1984) *Reading the Romance, Women, Patriarchy and Popular Literature*. Chapel Hill: University of North Carolina Press.
Rajan, R.S. (1992) Fixing English: Nation, language, subject. In R.S. Rajan (ed.) *The Lie of the Land, English Literary Studies in India* (pp. 11–9). Delhi: Oxford University Press.
Rakotoson, M. (1994) La littérature francophone à Madagascar. *Sepia, revue culturelle et Pédagogique francophone* (15), 10–12.
Rapport, N. and Dawson, A. (1998) Home and movement: A polemic. In N. Rapport and A. Dawson (eds) *Migrants of Identity, Perceptions of Home in a World of Movement* (pp. 19–38). London: Berg.
Rathgeber, E. (1992) African book publishing: lessons from the 1980s. In P. Altbach (ed.) *Publishing and Development in the Third World* (pp. 77–99). London: Zell Publishers.
Rattray, S. (1928) Anthropology and Christian missions, Their mutual bearing on the problems of colonial administration. *Africa* 1 (1), 99–106.
Ricard, A. (1987) *Naissance du roman africain: Félix Couchoro 1900–1968*. Paris: Présence africaine.
Ricard, A. (2000) *Ebrahim Hussein: Swahili Theatre and Individualism*. Trans. Naomi Morgan. Dar es Salaam: Mkuki Na Nyota Publishers.
Romance African style (1998) *The Unesco Courrier* (November), 42.
Rudolph, S.H. (1997) Introduction: Religion, states, and transnational civil society. In S.H. Rudolph and J. Piscatori (eds) *Transnational Religion and Fading States* (pp. 1–24). Boulder, CO: Westview Press.
Samba, J. (1952) The tribal or trade language. *The Bible Translator* 3 (2), 49–50.

Sanneh, L. (1993) *Encountering the West, Christianity and the Global Cultural Process: The African Dimension*. Maryknoll, NY: Orbis Books.

Saro-Wiwa, K. (1985) *Sozaboy, A Novel in Rotten English*. Port Harcourt: Saros International.

Saro-Wiwa, K. (1992) The language of African literature: A writer's testimony. *Research in African Literatures* 23 (1), 153–7.

Schipper, M. (1987) Mother Africa on a pedestal: The male heritage in African literature and criticism. *African Literature Today* (15), 35–54.

Schmidt, W. (1930) The use of the vernacular in education in Africa. *Africa* 3 (2), 137–49.

Senghor, L. (1973) *Poèmes*. Paris: Editions du Seuil.

Seton-Watson, H. (1977) *Nations and States: An Enquiry into the Origins of Nations and the Politics of Nationalism*. Boulder: Westview Press.

Simone, A. (2001) On the worlding of African cities. *African Studies Review* 44 (2), 15–41.

Simpson, D. (1986) *The Politics of American English 1776–1859*. New York: Oxford University Press.

Smith, E. (1926) *The Christian Mission in Africa*. London: The International Missionary Council.

Smith, E. (1934) A story of the Institute. A survey of seven years. *Africa* 7 (1), 1–27.

Smith, P. and Kunene, D. (eds) (2002) *Tongue and Mother Tongue*. Trenton and Asmara: Africa World Press, Inc.

Smythe, H. and M. (1960) *The New Nigerian Elite*. Stanford: Stanford University Press.

Sollors. W. (ed.) (1998). *Multilingual America, Transnationalism, Ethnicity, and the Languages of American Literature*. New York: New York University Press.

Sorensen, J. (2000) *The Grammar of Empire in Eighteenth-Century British Writing*. Cambridge: Cambridge University Press.

Soyinka, W. (1965) *The Interpreters*. London: Anchré Deutsch.

Soyinka, W. (1975) *Death and the King's Horseman*. London: Eyre Methuen.

Soyinka, W. (1988) Language as boundary. In *Art, Dialogue and Outrage* (pp. 132–45). Ibadan: New Horn Press.

Stratton, F. (1994) *Contemporary African Literature and the Politics of Gender*. London: Routledge.

Strevens, P. (1992) English as an international language: Directions in the 1990s. In B. Kachru (ed.) *The Other Tongue, English across Cultures* (pp. 27–47). Chicago: University of Illinois Press.

Swietochowski, T. (1991) The politics of a literary language and the rise of national identity in Russian Azerbaijan before 1920. *Ethnic and Racial Studies* 14 (1), 55–63.

Swigart, L. (1994) Cultural creolisation and language use in post-colonial Africa: The case of Senegal. *Africa* 64 (2), 175–88.

The Executive Council (1928) Textbooks for African Schools: A Preliminary Memorandum. *Africa* 1 (1), 13–21.

The Holy Bible New International Version. (1984) Grand Rapids, Michigan: Zondervan Publishing House.

Toungara, J.M. (1997) Changing the meaning of marriage: Women and family law in Côte d'Ivoire. In G. Mikell (ed.) *African Feminism, The Politics of Survival in Sub-Saharan Africa* (pp. 53–76). Philadelphia: University of Pennsylvania Press.

Tuan, Y.F. (1977) *Space and Place: The Perspective of Experience*. Minneapolis: University of Minnesota Press.

Tutuola, A. (1952). *The Palm-Wine Drinkard*. London: Faber.
Van Dijk, R.A. (1997) From camp to encompassment: Discourses of transubjectivity in the Ghanaian Pentecostal Diaspora. *Journal of Religion in Africa* 27 (2), 135–59.
Vauguy, A. (2000) M. Guy Lamblin (DG des NEI): L'année 1999 nous a été favorable *Notre Voie*, (19 January).
Veal, M. (2000) *Fela: The Life and Times of an African Musical Icon*. Philadelphia: Temple University Press.
Venuti, L. (1995) *The Translator's Invisibility, A History of Translation*. London: Routledge.
Venuti, L. (1998) *The Scandals of Translation: Towards an Ethics of Difference*. London: Routledge.
Vernacular Text Book Committees and Translation Bureaux in Nigeria. (1931) *Oversea Education* (3), 30–3.
Viswanathan, G. (1989) *Masks of Conquest: Literary Study and British Rule in India*. London: Faber and Faber.
Wali, O. (1963) The dead end of African literature. *Transition*, (10), 13–5.
Ward, I. (1941) The provision of vernacular literature for Africa. *Oversea Education* 12 (4), 162–73.
Wästberg, P. (ed.) (1968) *The Writer in Modern Africa*. New York: Africana Publishing Corporation.
Waterman, C. (1990) *Jùjú, A Social History and Ethnography of an African Popular Music*. Chicago: University of Chicago Press.
Wauthier, C. (1979) *The Literature and Thought of Modern Africa*. Washington DC: Three Continents Press.
Webb, V. and Kriel, M. (2000) Afrikaans and Afrikaner nationalism. In N. Kamwangamalu (ed.) *Language and Ethnicity in the New South Africa* (pp. 19–49). Berlin and New York: Mouton de Gruyter.
Webster's Third New International Dictionary of the English Language Unabridged. (1971). 3rd edn. Springfield: G. & C. Merriam Co.
Westermann. D. (1926) The value of the African's past. *International Review of Missions* 15 (59), 418–37.
Westermann. D. (1929) The linguistic situation and vernacular literature in British West Africa. *Africa* 2 (4), 337–51.
Westermann. D. (1931) The missionary as an anthropological field-worker. *Africa* 4 (2) 164–77.
Westermann. D. (1934) *The African Today*. London: Oxford University Press.
Westermann. D. (1937) The work of the International Institute of African Languages and Cultures. *International Review of Missions* 27 (104), 493–99.
Westley, D. (1992) Choice of language and African literature: A bibliographic essay. *Research in African literatures* 23 (1), 159–71.
Whiteley, W. (1956) The changing position of Swahili in East Africa. *Africa* 26 (4), 345–53.
Whitsitt, N. (2003) Islamic-Hausa feminism meets northern Nigerian romance: the Cautious rebellion of Bilkisu Funtuwa. *African Studies Review* (46) 1, 137–53.
Williams, P. and Chrisman, L. (eds) (1994) *Colonial Discourse and Post-ColonialTheory*. New York: Columbia University Press.
Williamson, K. (1993) Development of minority languages: Publishing problems and prospects. In S. Bello and A. Augi (eds) *Culture and the Book Industry in Nigeria* (pp. 203–39). Lagos: National Council for Arts and Culture.

Wren, R. (1991) *Those Magical Years, The Making of Nigerian Literature at Ibadan: 1948–1966*. Washington DC: Three Continents Press.
Wright, G. (1991) *The Politics of Design in French Colonial Urbanism*. Chicago: The University of Chicago Press.
Wrong, M. (1934) *Africa and the Making of Books: Being A Survey of Africa's Need of Literature*. London: International Committee on Christian Literature for Africa.
Young, C. (1938) The 'native' newspaper. *Africa* 9 (1), 63–72.
Zabus, C. (1991) *The African Palimpsest: Indigenization of Language in the West African Europhone Novel*. Amsterdam: Rodopi.
Zachernuk P. (1991) The Lagos elite and the idea of progress. In T. Falola (ed.) *Yoruba Historiography* (pp. 147–65). Madison: University of Wisconsin Press.
Zachernuk, P. (2000) *Colonial Subjects, An African Intelligentsia and Atlantic Ideas*. Charlottesville: University Press of Virginia.
Zell, Hans (1980) The problems of publishing in African languages. *West Africa* (3282), 1071–73.

Index

Achebe, C. 12, 20-22, 37, 82, 96
Adiaffi, J. 1
African literature 57, 62, 68, 89, 94
– IALC competitions 6-7, 63
Afrikaans 2, 43-44
Alsacien 68
Akan 24, 58-59
Ajayi, J.F.A. 9, 23
Anderson, B. 22, 45, 94, 98, 154, 167
Amharic 49-50, 69, 98
Ansre, G. 60
Apartheid 17, 29, 30, 40, 43
Appadurai, A. 93, 115, 119, 170, 184, 197
Arabic 21, 66, 116, 118, 168
Armah, A.K. 63, 99
Asmara
– Against All Odds Conference 71
Assimilation 15-16
Awolowo, O. 14
Awoniyi, T. 5, 41
Azikiwe, N. 14

Bamgbose, A. 27, 46-47, 59, 125
Barber, K. 46-47, 109, 118, 127-130
Bible
– translation 60, 176, 186-188
Black identity 81, 153, 159, 169, 190, 205
Blyden, E. 55
Bokamba, E. 125
Breton 68

Central University College 177
Christian Action Faith Ministries 172, 175, 181, 184, 186
Christianity
– Charismatic 170-194, 196
– Evangelical 18, 174, 177
– Pentecostal 18, 111, 114-115, 174, 177, 183

– spiritual churches 175
Code-switching 78, 99, 102, 125
Colonialism 4-10, 166
– British 15-16, 77
– French 16, 18, 42, 44, 77
Creole vii, 7-8
Crumell, A. 55, 97

Dadié, B. 1, 4, 13, 142
Dakubu, M.K. 43-44, 110, 128
Dialects
– Akan 24, 58-59, 97
– Igbo 50
– Yoruba 60
Diglossia 194
Dyula 49, 90, 102, 116, 118-119, 194

Education
– colonial policy 4-10, 45
– instruction in mother tongue 4, 39-40, 43, 45, 191
– missionary involvement 5-9, 11, 42, 58
– native education 9-10, 13-14
– schoolroom experiences 1-2
– teaching English 10-12, 20, 22-24, 40-41, 45
Efik 40, 46
Elugbe, B. 78, 99, 123
English
– and African Nationalism 22-24, 44, 55, 88
– as global language 167-8
– teaching of 10-12, 20, 22-24, 40-41, 45
English-Only movement 2, 17
Ewe 66, 178, 185, 200

Fabian, J. 8, 23, 26, 58, 60
Fagunwa, D. 12, 27, 41, 47, 60, 95, 150
Fanti 24, 58-59, 97, 178

222

Index

Fela 131-134, 152-153, 160
Fishman, J. 2
Furniss, G. 24-25, 27-28, 161

Ga 43, 81, 128, 178-179, 182-183
Gaelic 68
Gérard, A. 24, 27, 29, 42, 46, 64, 98, 100
Ghana 58-59, 104, 174, 179
Gikuyu 39, 41, 44-45, 74, 76, 81

Hausa 25, 27, 39, 44, 50, 90, 104, 116, 145, 150, 161, 168, 194
Heinemann Educational Books 12, 70, 82, 95
Herder, J. 87, 164, 198
Hindi 116, 128
Hussein, E. 64, 97
Hussey, E. 8

Igbo 12, 22, 41, 50, 104-106, 109, 111, 120
Immigration 129, 172, 180, 183-184, 187, 191-193, 200-201, 204
– African immigrants and Western culture 190
– Africans in Europe 119, 186
– Africans in the United States 173, 181, 190-191
Indirect rule 13-16, 42
Indonesia 21, 32, 43
International Institute of African Languages and Cultures 6, 63
Ivory Coast 57, 84, 95, 116, 181
– romance narratives in 137

Juju music 107, 110-110, 127

Kachru, B. 168, 171
Kampala
– Conference of African Writers 71, 82
Kikongo 8
Kiswahili 8, 21, 39, 45, 49, 58, 64, 66, 88, 91, 168
Koulibaly, I.B. 139, 142-144, 147, 150, 159, 161
Kourouma, A. 72, 78, 84, 142
Krio 90

Lagos Colony 9, 55-56

Laitin, D. 199
Languages of wider communication
– definition 166, 201
Language policy 38
– in Africa 21, 49, 168-9, 203
Latin 67
Liberia 55
Lingala 8, 49, 91, 117, 119, 129
Lingua franca 7, 19, 21, 29-30, 32-35, 38, 67, 102, 120, 168-169
Lugard, F. 6-7, 10, 13-16, 42
Luo 76

Mandinka 102
Malinke 78, 84-87
Mazrui, A. 88, 96
Meinhof, C. 7
Mphahlele, E. 66, 99
Missionary education 5, 8, 11-12
Missionaries 182-183
– Belgian missionaries 58
– British Wesleyans 58
– C.M.S. 5, 12, 41-42, 50, 60
– German Basel missionaries 58, 185
– German Bremen missionaries 185
– Swiss missionaries 59
Mlama, P. 64, 97
Mofolo, T. 27
Mother tongue education 17, 39, 43, 98
Mozambique 52, 59, 96
Multilingualism 20, 23, 32-33, 38, 43-44, 50-51, 98, 117
Mumford, B. 7, 9, 11, 13
Music
– Afrobeat 131-133, 152-153, 157, 160
– Gospel 119
– Highlife 159
– Juju 107, 110-111, 127-128
– Soukouss 117, 119, 129, 159
– drumming 182-183, 200
Musicians
– Baaba Maal 117
– Fela 131-133, 152-153, 160
– Salif Keita 117
– Angélique Kidjo 117, 128
– Youssou N'Dour 128, 139
Myers-Scotton, C. 125

Negritude 26

Ngugi 29, 41, 71, 73, 81, 87-88, 96, 118
Nigeria 30, 35, 102, 151, 174
Nwana, P. 41
Nyerere, J. 21

Olatunji, O. 47
Omamor, A. 78, 99, 123
Onitsha market literature 47, 102, 108-110, 126-127, 145-146, 150
Oromo 44, 98
Owusu, M. 83-84, 100

Pan-Africanism 61, 66-67, 88-89, 119, 196
Pennycook, A. 45, 121, 198
B'Pitek, O. 73, 76, 132
Pidgin vii, 8, 49, 78, 90-91, 99, 123, 129, 131, 134, 163
Publishing
– in European languages 47, 49-50
– in indigenous languages 28-31, 49-50, 99, 204-205
– missionary influence 27-28, 47
Pulaar 102, 117

Rabemananjara, J. 71, 79
Romance narratives
– Adoras 137-141, 161
– Harlequin 137
– Soyayya 116, 145-150, 161-162
Ronga 52, 59, 96

Sanneh, L. 42, 98, 100, 185
Saro-Wiwa, K 78
Senghor, L. 70, 81
Serer 102, 124
Sierra Leone 60, 159

Soyayya 116, 145-146, 148, 161-162
Soyinka, W. 12, 26, 46, 67, 77, 122, 130

Tansi, S.L. 1
Tanzania 21, 38, 45, 49, 64
Translation 25, 46, 72-76, 99
Tsonga 59
Twi 49, 90, 97, 172, 176, 178, 186, 199, 201
– Akwapim Twi 24, 58-59
– Asante Twi 24, 58-59

Vernacular
– and Church use 178, 184-185
– discourses 2, 4, 19-20, 90, 168, 186, 189, 191
– major discourses 4, 15-18, 23
– minor discourses 19
– vernacular literacy 3, 5-9, 13-14, 39-40, 43, 45-46, 191
Vischer, H. 13, 42

Wali, O. 71, 79, 81, 98, 118
Westermann, D. 6-7, 9, 13-15, 39
Williamson, K. 46
Wolof 49, 92, 124

Yoruba 91
– dialects 60
– films 102, 111, 120
– nationalism 60, 111, 115
– teaching 5, 12, 60
– writing 27-28, 41, 45, 95, 100

Zabus, C. 42, 72, 78, 123
Zachernuk, P. 2, 38-39
Zulu literature 73-75, 80-81, 97

For Product Safety Concerns and Information please contact our EU Authorised Representative:

Easy Access System Europe

Mustamäe tee 50

10621 Tallinn

Estonia

gpsr.requests@easproject.com

www.ingramcontent.com/pod-product-compliance
Lightning Source LLC
Chambersburg PA
CBHW052036300426
44117CB00012B/1853